THE ADVENTURE GUIDE
TO
JAMAICA

THE ADVENTURE GUIDE TO JAMAICA

Steve Cohen

HUNTER PUBLISHING, INC.
Edison, N.J.

Hunter Publishing, Inc.
300 Raritan Center Parkway
Edison NJ 08818
(201) 225 1900

ISBN 1-55650-064-5

Printed in Singapore through Palace Press

Photo Credits
Steve Cohen: 18, 24, 36, 73, 87, 89, 92, 94, 178, 180, 205, 217, 223.
Jamaica Tourist Board: viii, 10, 16, 21, 28, 34, 38, 44, 51, 54, 55, 58, 62, 66, 77, 83, 98, 106, 112, 115, 120, 122, 124, 128, 131, 137, 140, 144, 150, 153, 158, 160, 169, 171, 179, 183, 188, 192, 197, 202, 213, 231, 238, 247, 252.

Published in the UK by:
Moorland Publishing Co. Ltd.
Moor Farm Road, Airfield Estate
Ashbourne, Derbyshire DE6 1HD
England

ISBN 086190-244-0

CONTENTS

"I smile all the time. Everyone smiles back and then stares politely at my ignorance. Slowly they change my mind."—Kevin Kelly, *The Essential Whole Earth Catalog.*

PART I

INTRODUCTION TO ADVENTURE

There is more to Jamaica than meets the eye of most beach potatoes.

Many visitors to Jamaica see only the top-ticket tourist resorts. You can fly here, be driven in an airport limo directly to a guarded and walled hotel, and never get to see more than a fleeting glimpse of Jamaica's people at work, at play and in their homes. All the special places for the best in local customs, foods, hospitality and adventurous things to do would be obscured by formalities, lavish service, lots of food, plenty to drink and a hefty tab, all catering to indulgent expectations. Add Jamaican sunshine reflecting off the clear sea, the heavy, salty air, still and steamy, and you just baking on the rack of a beach chair—well, the life of a beach potato does have its sublime moments in Jamaica. No problem, mon, if you are content with that day in, day out.

If, on the other hand, you are looking for action and chance, from a full-blown adventure trip, to maybe adding just a little Jamaican pepper to a routine baked potato, you need only venture outside the gates and walk right into the conflicting mainstreams of Jamaican living. Outside, you cannot count on being served "cocktails at 4," but then you will not be going through the motions of a vacation by rote, either. Everywhere, except the super-controlled resorts, is a colorful, Third World, brimming all the time with new extremes in beauty and ugliness, wealth and poverty, adventure and misadventure, in short, real life, its beating heart setting the rhythm for a healthy alternative form of tourism.

If you open your eyes and mind, your honest approach to differences and similarities with new people in a new environment bridges great distances. You can always be learning something new by allowing yourself to be acted upon by forces the less adventurous might prefer to stand apart from and judge. The adventure in this sort of travel brings out elements of the unknown hidden within each one of us, informing character out of someplace unsuspected and unreachable within daily routines, as if by magic.

Adventure in its broadest sense encompasses more than sport and palpable danger. A traveler who expands on the context of choices already known, the copious foods, air-conditioned suite, tennis or golf, invites challenges in coping with the new. Insight can strike on a tricky river-canoeing course or a hiking trail, when you taste a new fruit or start a friendship with someone who lives very differently than you.

The challenge helps sharpen our focus on the moment. It clarifies our needs. Truths shine in that clarity. In the fleeting reflection we can glimpse ourselves. To the adventurous, discovery is what travel is all about.

There's challenge in knowing the Jamaican people, from their King's English to their scandalous patois, from their volcanic anger and haggling arguments to their hospitality. By stepping into their history, land and culture you can make any Jamaican visit a lot more fun than an ordinary vacation. The adventure of taking a chance on Jamaica and yourself can be your ticket to an unforgettable time and place.

Whether you choose to spend some of your trip in a cushy resort, or none at all, this book will guide you through the guardhouse gates and open the door to the real Jamaica.

What you find on the other side is up to you.

"So take JAH Sun, and JAH Moon
And JAH Rain, and JAH Stars
And forever yes erase your fantasy, yeah."
—Bob Marley, *Stiff Necked Fools.*

CHAPTER ONE

PEOPLE, HISTORY & LANGUAGE

Columbus "discovered" Jamaica. Prior to 1494 Jamaicans were exclusively Arawak Indians, aborigines who favored living in coastal villages. They called their island "Xaymaca," land of wood and water, and they fished for seafood, grew maize, sweet potatoes, guavas and cashews. They paddled out in dugout canoes to meet the Spanish ships.

Arawaks kept no written history, but one of the things the Spanish noticed about them was a custom of tying wooden boards to a baby's head to make the skull flat and hard enough to serve as a primitive crash helmet, presumably offering a measure of protection from elemental dangers, including man-eating Carib Indians from nearby islands, who sometimes made forays against their less aggressive neighbors.

Hard-headed Arawaks attacked Columbus's ships with primitive weapons from their canoes, but Spanish dogs and guns were more effective, wounding and killing several Indians that very first day. The following morning, the humbled Jamaicans carried food and trade offerings in friendship to the visitors and thereafter exchanged produce and supplies for Spanish trade items, in good faith and with Stone Age honesty.

From that point on the Europeans took every possible advantage of the Indians.

Over the next 150 years colonies and vast plantations were established by Spanish land grants carving up segments of Jamaica for developments that destroyed Arawak farm lands and homes. The trusting Arawaks were induced into becoming workers. Eventually formalities were dispensed with and they became slaves. Many died from overwork. Resistors were killed. Later, choosing stubborn pride over slavery, mass suicides were reported. Mothers killed their children to prevent them from falling into Spanish hands. Add to this European-introduced diseases, and by the time the Spanish were booted out by the English in 1655, the Arawaks were no more. These earliest Jamaicans simply became extinct, poof.

Spanish settlers transplanted citrus crops, bananas, sugar, cotton, cocoa and tobacco. They brought horses, goats, chickens, pigs and cattle to Jamaica, settled Spanish Town and lived the hot and politically isolated lifestyle of far-away colonists. Left largely on their own, too far away for Spain to butt into local affairs with regularity, they became self-directed and practically self-governing. Adapting perhaps a little too well to the island precept that heat and hurry do not mix, the raggedly organized Spanish easily lost control of the island to an invading armada carrying 8,000 British troops that sailed into what would become Kingston Harbor in May, 1655.

Black African slaves were first landed in Jamaica in 1517, by the Spanish, to supplement the dwindling ranks of Arawaks. When the British arrived, Spaniards scattered into the hills, hastily freeing blacks, who made for the safety of the rugged mountains. These were the earliest Maroons, the first group of independent-minded black Jamaicans, whose ranks were expanded in successive years by other runaways following the same path. Maroons eventually settled areas of the untillable and virtually impenetrable Cockpit Country, where unwanted and wildly overgrown limestone pits and haystack-shaped mountains provided protection from capture. The Windward Maroons settled later in the rainy John Crow Mountains, on the far side of the Blue Mountains, near the east coast.

Spain and England fought over Jamaica until 1670's Treaty

of Madrid gave control to the British. Around this time a brisk business in piracy gave Jamaica a deservedly spicy reputation for adventure that persists to some extent today.

Buccaneers, as they were known, were mainly French, English and Dutch outcasts, including indentured workers, called bondsmen, who had run off from their contracts, escaped criminals, political refugees and other disgruntled and self-reliant societal cast-offs. These were people twice removed from nationalistic attachments, once from a mother country. and again from one or another Caribbean outpost. Many settled in remote villages, finding a sense of loose unity in their mutual estrangements.

Around 1630, when Spain tried to starve an isolated village on Hispaniola, in today's Haiti, the outcasts turned outlaw, seeking retribution in acts of piracy against Spanish vessels, then settlements, first using only small boats and canoes, later attacking from captured Spanish ships.

It was the buccaneers' hatred of the Spanish that led them to settle in Jamaica's Port Royal. The British port could service their ships and the settlement was a friendly place to trade stolen Spanish loot. As far as the English and their holdings in Jamaica were concerned, so long as the buccaneers were wearing down the Spanish, authorities were willing to look the other way regarding piracy. Besides, although the pirates were a rough lot, giving Port Royal a reputation as the most wicked city in the Caribbean, business was good. Port Royal boomed and Jamaica prospered until 1664, when Sir Thomas Modyford, the British-appointed Governor of Jamaica, decided to clean up the city. He kicked the buccaneers out. They returned to a previous stronghold on the island of Tortuga, off the coast of Hispaniola.

Back in Jamaica, reality intruded on the Governor's short-lived reverie. Modyford got wind of a Dutch plan to attack Jamaica, and short of manpower for defense, was compelled to reenlist the aid of the buccaneers, under the leadership of Henry Morgan. Official commissions were given to the pirates, legally sanctioning them to pillage and plunder Spanish properties, as well as other real or imagined threats to Jamaica.

Repatriated booty was usually split among the pirates according to an honor code, only now a share would be put aside for politicians in Jamaica who okayed their exploits.

Eventually, the King, in England, caught on to this Jamaican shell game and demanded a stop to the authorized piracy. Buccaneers again dispersed from Port Royal, planting farms, opening pubs or shops, weaving into the fabric of Jamaican culture, briefly. By 1670 Spanish attacks were increasing again.

Morgan and his followers were enticed out of retirement by yet another commission. The pirate leader was given the title and power that went with being called "Admiral and Commander-in-Chief of all the ships of war belonging to this harbor."

Panama City, Panama was the Spanish crown's flagship city in the New World, site of its furthest development in architecture and culture, soon to be site of its greatest defeat. Morgan and his men marched through an "impenetrable" Central American swamp to take the city by surprise. In the celebrations that followed, coupled with looting and violence, the city was accidentally burned to the ground.

Morgan returned to Port Royal a hero. Government commendations were awarded to the entire fleet in 1671, the only little catch being that the Treaty of Madrid had been signed in July, 1670, settling British-Spanish hostilities before the attack on Panama. Evidence suggested that Modyford knew of the treaty before Morgan's fleet sailed through Bluefield's Bay. If so, he would have been able to recall the fleet and prevent the destruction of Panama City. Despite knowledge that peace had been attained, he let the plan unfold, also knowing the loss of Panama City would permanently loosen Spain's hold on the Caribbean.

Spain was irate. To save face, Modyford was sent to jail in London. Morgan was called there a year later, ostensibly to explain his part in the broken treaty. Instead, the pirate became a celebrity, while Modyford was wined and dined in prison until the fuss abated. Later, both men were exonerated. Morgan was knighted and became Lieutenant-Governor of Jamaica. Modyford returned to Jamaica and was buried in the Cathedral in Spanish Town beneath a tombstone calling him "The Soule and Life of All Jamaica, Who first made it what it now is."

The buccaneers' victory in Panama eliminated the need for buccaneering. Pirates were again strongly encouraged to disperse. Many did not. Morgan, in his job as Governor, sent numerous diehards to prison. Others were hung. Port Royal, however, continued as the main trading center for the island, as well as its primary slave port, a busy community of 8,000 when it was leveled by an earthquake and destroyed by ensuing fires on June 7, 1692. All the ships in the harbor sank in the storm. The earthquake killed 25% of the city's population and caused enough damage to make the government relocate the settlement across the harbor in what would become known as Kingston.

Throughout the 18th century the British established a profitable slave trade, to supply growing sugar plantations which made a lot of money in Jamaica and the rest of the Caribbean. Any person of means was said to be as "wealthy as a West Indian planter." Such was the reputation of the sugar growers.

The Maroons, freed by the Spanish years earlier, lived outside Jamaican law by means of guerilla warfare. From hiding spots in the Cockpits, they would attack British troops sent to capture them, then quickly surprise the formally-trained military pursuers from another unpredictable location.

The British initiated a peace treaty that was signed in 1739, 100 years before slavery was outlawed in Jamaica. In return for land in the Cockpits and freedom to govern themselves, the Maroons agreed that they would stop fighting the British and accept no more runaway slaves into their ranks. They would be available to help the government resist foreign or local attacks and would actually help recapture other runaway slaves.

Jamaican heroes emerged in the ensuing year, leaders of slave rebellions. Tacky's Rebellion was led by a one-time African tribal chief. His statue stands today in Port Maria where his short-lived revolt began in 1760. Sam Sharpe led an 1831 slave revolt and was hanged in a downtown Montego Bay city square that came to be named after him. You find his statue on the spot today. Paul Bogle led ex-slaves near Morant Bay. Another statue downtown. National heroes, all.

The sugar trade had come to dominate the island's economy after earlier attempts at growing tobacco and cocoa had proven less profitable. Sugar business squeezed out small farmers in favor of huge landholders who could control virtual slave armies required to farm the labor intensive sugar crop, tend the fields, run the mills and processing factories.

Jamaica was to become the world's largest sugar producer, thanks to an equable environment and slave labor.

Bondsman were also tried on the plantations. Some of these men were criminals sentenced to ten years or more of contract labor, others the plainly desperate, willing to sign their services and rights away for years in exchange for the promise of eventual freedom.

Plantation overseers found the black Africans more suited to the hot tropical climate and work demands. More slaves poured in, with whites filling more responsible positions in management or skilled trades. Coromantees, from Africa's Gold Coast, Eboes and Mandingoes, foreigners to each other, not even sharing a native tongue, all became Jamaicans, right alongside retired pirates, Spanish expatriates, British planters, bonded criminals, Maroon rebels and the merely adventurous, seekers of life in a new world.

Sam Sharpe's rebellion led to the end of slavery in 1839. Once free, ex-slaves refused to work on the plantations for wages. Sugar production declined and life remained hard. Bogle's Rebellion, in 1865, brought continuing inequities to light and resulted in hundreds of deaths, losses eventually leading to additional reforms under a Crown Colony system, centering power in the hands of British governors.

Kingston became the capital in 1872. Ambitious changes started to shape up, government agencies were formed to administer public works, education and social services. Diversified agriculture took prominence over single-minded sugar production. Bananas joined sugar, molasses, rum, pimento and coffee as major export crops. Plantains, nutmeg, cloves, yams and cinnamon supplied secondary crops. Meanwhile, hurricanes, earthquakes and fires plagued the island, devastating Kingston time and again. The city was always rebuilt, fields replanted.

A labor movement came to prominence only in the late 1930's when political parties were established, finally, after 350 years of misrepresentation, setting up the infrastructure for independence. Alexander Bustamante and Norman Manley helped write a new constitution in 1944, giving adult Jamaicans the vote and ending the Crown Colony period. In the heady time prior to independence, fringe groups also attracted followings.

A Jamaican named Marcus Garvey was far from being a charismatic leader when he promoted a series of black unity ideas, beginning in 1914 with the Universal Negro Improvement Association in Kingston. From his Jamaican base Garvey sought to establish schools, colleges and universities for blacks, an equitable social standing and a black homeland in Africa.

Finding little support for his theories in Jamaica, Garvey moved to America in 1916, started a newspaper and a worldwide campaign to promote black achievement. Few blacks listened but frightened authorities did. Nervous foreign investors held valuable properties in the volatile communities in Cuba, Trinidad and Jamaica that Garvey preached to.

Big money helped put the publisher in jail in 1922, for two-and-a-half years, on questionable mail fraud charges. On his return to Jamaica in 1927, and on through the 30's, Garvey's blend of black nationalism melted together with growing lower class anger regarding widespread unemployment and a sense of racial rejection by the white world dooming islanders to hopeless poverty. Frustrated sentiment picked up for crowning a black King in Africa.

When Haile Selassie was named King of Ethiopia in 1930, poor Jamaicans, who had already rejected the white world and its Christian totems, had the necessary evidence to start a new religion they called Rastafarianism.

Rastas today eat no meat, preferring "Ital" (vital and natural) vegetarian foods, and smoking pot as a religious sacrament. Men wear their hair long in uncut, uncombed mountainous curls called dreadlocks, the helmets that make them look fierce although they are, by belief and practice, the opposite, gentle and kindly. True rastas shun the values of the world of "Babylon," their term for a culture destroying itself with material excesses and racial inequality.

The ideal of living in the country, growing one's own and leaving Babylon to the forces of degeneration, is lived up to by only a small number of rastas, many of whom are young urban dwellers living in the belly of the beast. The rastas were pretty gung-ho for the spirit of a 1970's socialist government, (led by Michael Manley, son of the 30's and 40's political crusader), strutting their Lion and Judah, mighty God "Jah," radical lost tribe of Israel stance, blowing smoke rings in the face of hypocritical authority.

Through the 80's, a conservative government's direction was mandated by the failure of the socialists to improve people's lives, forcing many of the rastas underground. Rastas exist,

Rastafarian

still on the outs with the mainstream, still cherishing peace and love over money, only less visibly so than in past years. Oddly, in Jamaica today you see fewer honest-to-goodness rastas, but many dreadlocked young men, especially among the hustlers and hasslers trying to sell ganja or beg some consideration. The shame is that true rasta belief is found in the heart, not merely as decoration for the head.

Enough histories of Jamaica have been written so that you do not have to rely on this scanty one. History is glanced at here only to shed light on adventure. Knowing Jamaicans' mixed backgrounds can help you form a closer understanding of these people. In a crowded little island such as Jamaica, your success with the people you meet can make or break the adventure awaiting you.

Jamaicans come from many different races, places, social levels, economic circumstances. They are people of the Third World, the developing world, mixing in a steamy tropical cauldron spiced by political cronyism and power plays, charged memories of slavery and racism, religious faith and flexible allegiances, slow-cooked for close-to 400 years to create a modern country awash in poverty, as politically uncertain as ever, independent less than 30 years and still ripe with the potentials of youthful energy.

Jamaica has always been developing, not developed, at least in terms of its people feeling satisfied with themselves.

Independent since 1962, Jamaica has come far in a short time, creating new administrations for justice, police and a Jamaican Defense Force that serves to protect the island in place of a standing army. Since the mid 60's, banking regulations are all new, as are structures for corporate development. Expansion of world markets for bauxite and Jamaican agriculture was considered necessary, international machinery put into place, hopes up, plans in gear, all enthusiasm for a time.

Population continued to swell. Medical care, particularly birth control measures, barely existed. Jamaicans exiting to Florida to cut cane, or to Brooklyn or England, to escape chronic unemployment in a packed pressure-cooker economy, continue today to be a steam outlet.

It was this building pressure that swept Michael Manley, son of constitution-forging Norman, into power in 1972, riding a wave of reform, sloganeering that it was "time for a change."

With his victory, moves were made to nationalize foreign investments, including the major Reynolds aluminum works. The government tightened its grip on commercial banking. "Democratic socialism," turned previous post-independence positions upside-down, not coming out directly for communism, but not coming out against it, either.

The far-fetched plans came tumbling down around the increase in world oil prices in the mid-60's. Agricultural and industrial costs skyrocketed and profits dwindled. More workers were laid off. Foreign exchange began to disappear when investors found an unfavorable climate for risk-taking and tourists found shortages in basic services, food and transportation.

Many more than cane cutters emigrated to the US and Canada. The educated and skilled, along with others who could afford it, joined them.

The 1980 election turned things around once again. Pledging economic reforms and realignment with the west, a new impetus was given to private industry to rebuild the damaged framework of Jamaican culture. There have been improvements. Air Jamaica runs, perhaps not always on time, but close to it. Quite a few rural areas now have electrical power. In fact, new hydrodevelopments are under consideration for at least one of Jamaica's unspoiled river adventure sites, to make "progressive" use of the secluded and beautiful YS Falls, north of Black River in south central Jamaica.

As for the Jamaicans, things are still tough. Some believe things are working again, some do not, and everyone agrees nothing is easy. Professionals, employed service personnel and the self-employed all bemoan the state of inflation. Services bring small profit. Wages are low.

The British left behind a sense of formal etiquette and this politeness has survived. You can still find very proper Jamaicans addressing each other and visitors with terms of respect, always saying Mr. Brown or Miss Sweet, never using a first name, saying yes too frequently and wearing white gloves. Others beg for spare change. Beneath the surface of these extremes dwells a fierce nationalism that unites Jamaicans both rich and poor. It is represented in the "patois" Jamaicans speak among themselves, an underground language that can be understood by visitors only if the native speakers want it understood.

Jamaicans all understand it, though.

The patois started with the slaves, creating a new language from their many African dialects, combining it with inflections of Spanish, English and French. It is not much different today, a corner of life Jamaicans can call their own, the rights to an impulsive, confrontational language.

A majority of Jamaicans would likely prefer a small squatter's garden on a distant unwanted hillside to paying rent, just to have a little for their own. They can get feisty about it, too, haggling, turning it into a fight, then a game and back again, trying to make you believe it does not matter, only it matters, almost as much as the right to argue about it.

Polite, argumentative, playful, sinful, funny, angry, Jamaicans' emotional natures are manifested in a verbal sense of imagery, irony and the absurd that have survived their history. Leavened slowly by the weighty certainty of time, along with an environment guaranteed to wear an injudicious man down, you meet today's "no problem" Jamaican.

"Plenty of problems all the way around," says a waiter at Montego Bay's Sign Great House, a once popular tourism property, 50 acres of bougainvillaea draped privacy, tennis courts and warm Jamaican hospitality located 6 quiet miles from the country's biggest, noisiest, and most heavily hustled tourist center. Newly rebuilt (with American money), staffed and set to go, Sign offers a sense of old Jamaica in the midst of new Jamaica. Cattle graze and moo among coconut palms and bananas out your window, and there are no hustlers anywhere. No problem? Just one. No guests anywhere.

Jamaicans have always had forces working against them and this continues.

You need to work with them for your visit to be a success.

You can get around cooperating with Jamaicans by staying at a do-nothing-for-yourself resort. Paid servants saying yes have a strong tradition here.

Most Jamaicans want you to have whatever you desire. They need your money. And they would still like to trust your friendship, even though foreigners have not always earned respect here.

That may be the subliminal essence of Jamaican pride, the strength of endurance, the power of survivors. Hope for the best. Be prepared to rebuild from scratch. The nitty-gritty: From slave rebellions to emancipation, sanctioned piracy to independence, Jamaica has always sort of been up for grabs, looking for a messiah.

Part of a Jamaican adventure is that, yes, they are looking for you.

"Every night... need certain amount of money, so when you don't workin' in a day it hard. Every night you need dinner to buy. I 'gyarden.' Everyday. Sell goods everyday. Have to spend money everyday."—Leonard "Baps" Cole, age 53, pioneer Blue Mountain hiking guide.

CHAPTER TWO

THE OTHER JAMAICA

There may as well be two Jamaicas, one that sedentary tourists experience, the other for adventurous travelers interested in seeking out real Jamaican life. Independent, free-thinking travelers with energy for exploring the island's lyrical and seductive rhythms, bounteous scenery, seminal reggae, diverse produce and distinct personalities can find the genuine tropical beauty of this island.

Geographically, what you find here are 4411 square miles of Caribbean liveliness that many believe to be the most beautiful of all the East and West Indies. You can hardly miss finding legendary white sand beaches, secluded coves, waterfalls and harbors fringed by jungle overgrowth at every turn. Coconut palm and banana plantations slope up from the sea, rising to a lush interior that ranges from hilly to mountainous. The highest point, and one no adventure in Jamaica is complete without a visit to, is Blue Mountain Peak at 7402 feet. On clear dawns, when the blue mists rise high above the sea, Cuba is visible from up there, a thin land line ninety miles away across the emerald expanse of the shimmering Caribbean.

Profuse plant life, medicinal herbs and foods growing in Jamaica enhance the physical beauty of the country with the richness of function. It looks as if there is enough food to go around, if there were some good way for it to get around.

The back country

Transportation exists. Communication is at least fair in even the more remote parts of the island. Money is what fails to reach into all strata of society. No problem, mon, when everyone controls a little piece of land, a goat and a garden. Something else, though, when more than 900,000 live in urban Kingston and must deal with chronic unemployment, inadequate housing and inflation. Less grass for grazing goats in concrete Kingston. That is one reason why Jamaicans go hungry.

Bananas appear to be the most prolific of Jamaican crops. These are grown mainly for export and even in the remote Blue Mountains wiry mountain men quietly tote banana shoots on their heads.

On the steepest slopes far above Kingston large-scale agriculture is impossible. Small-holdings mimic the last century. Successful men ride to work on a mule. Most walk many miles to steep trails between home and the spot they cultivate. All swing machetes. Some of the women do, too. Those farm baskets you see on the women's heads? These usually weigh around forty-five pounds. Squatters mainly, they come from nearby villages to work sloping plots that no one else would want. They clear the rocky soil, work their legs and lungs into robust good health and count on good rain to bring in the harvest.

Hikers and climbers enjoy the same terrain. Foot trails skirt neatly terraced gardens defining subsistence farmsteads. Bananas, yams, carrots, thyme, scallions, maybe some coffee and a small plot of "sinse," yes ganja, "hola herb," marijuana, and just another part of the greenery here, are found in most patches.

Closer in, far down from the hills, where there are many more tin-roof cottages and bigger and bigger villages, goats, chickens, pigs and cattle scuttle around twisting, pot-holed roads. Nearby, count on dogs in no hurry, ducks, children. People of all ages, without enough work to go around, man the streets.

When a visitor appears roadside entrepreneurs pop up out of nowhere offering sugar cane, Pepsi, Red Stripe beer, white rum. Someone will probably try to sell you a wooden bird, a bamboo drum, a mango or a smoke.

The mangos grow wild and are generally free for the picking. You might have to pay 10 cents Jamaican if you buy one, less than 2 cents US at the exchange rate of nearly $5.50 JA to $1 US.

"Avocado pears," what Americans call an avocado, are frequently available for free. Swaying coconut palms are also abundant, although you might have to pay $1 JA for a meal-size coconut.

There are more than 3,000 varieties of flowering plants in Jamaica.

Few fruits and vegetables are native. Having been brought here by early sailors or birds, all kinds of sweet and succulent things grow on the island. Ethiopian, or star apples, taste similar to a pomegranate. Try Jamaican chocolate beans. Sweet cassava gets pounded into a flour, then shaped and fried into a filling sort of pancake called a "bammy." Soursop is a strange

flaky-textured fruit said to be good for steadying nerves. It tastes like creamy citrus and comes apart in layers, like broiled fish, when you bite into it. Breadfruit was brought here by the infamous Captain Bligh, whose crew on the Bounty mutinied against him. Jamaican Blue Mountain coffee is regarded by connoisseurs as the best in the world. Cashews grow inland from the southwest coast. Cane fields fill the broad southern valleys between the mountains and the sea. You can find marijuana everywhere.

Ganja, introduced during the nineteenth century by indentured Indian workers brought here to work the cane fields, is the island's biggest cash crop, a fact scarcely denied by even the highest ranking government officials. Since the drug is illegal, dealers are the jumpiest of all the street vendors, though not by much. A little discrete ganja blowing is no problem, mon. The penalty for possession of a small amount would likely be a fine, if it got beyond a token bribe on the spot.

Dealers find you.

Island business typically operates at the languid and casual "soon come" pace that hangs over these tropics like a pretty veil of wet flowers. In Negril, Montego Bay or Ocho Rios, illegal offers can come fast, a mumbled word, a quick look or gesture. A sale is a precious commodity here. We are talking poor, as in government-supplied figures admitting 26% unemployment.

Women seem more independent than men. Fewer rely on strangers. Female vendors work from established stalls more than roving free lance. Perhaps they have to in order to tend to children, cook and traditionally hold Jamaica together. Illegitimate births are routine. Families commonly do not stay together. Women raise the children. One of the bravest and most clever Jamaican National Heroes was a Maroon woman named "Nanny." Legend has it that she used to capture British soldiers and boil them in a big pot. Strong Jamaican women keep busy, making them less visible in the glaring daytime of the shuffle and scratch to survive economy.

Nights are different, just as hot, but dark, for liaisons and

---

Blue Mountains

casting problems out of the light of day. Entranced disco dancers sway and duck in an unlit bunker on Treasure Beach. A bare bulb hangs high over an energetic domino game in a bar in downtown Montego Bay. You walk an invisible rasta mountainside trail, without a flashlight, and the trees closing out the stars.

The north coast glitters like the beacon of tourism that it is. Montego Bay to Ocho Rios is awash with ritzy-ditzy hotels and condos sporting high in-season rates and promoting tourism under bright lights. What you get is what you see, a tidy, clean and predictable little package, up there with what you would expect on Miami Beach or Paradise Island: "THE TROPICAL RESORT VACATION OF YOUR DREAMS"–you know, the one with the Pina Colada that comes with the free buffet breakfast. Each drink is served at pool side in a hollowed coconut shell by a shiny black waiter in a starched white shirt.

Outside the resort compounds are small towns and villages, each with a special character, people walking past whitewashed town halls, sadly understaffed medical clinics, big and small churches, schoolyards brimming with uniformed children. Villagers wash clothes and bathe at streetside community water taps. Some prefer the relative privacy of a riverbed. Three out of four households are without indoor plumbing, half without electricity. Many who have lights cannot afford to use them.

Modern architecture tends toward the utilitarian. In the country or the ghetto you see bamboo or wood pallet-framed walls supporting wood scraps or pasteboard tacked together beneath a corrugated tin roof. Cinder block and concrete are more the middle-class city-style. Rougher parts of west Kingston resemble bombed-out Beirut. Vacant lots sprout brick piles, clotted street markets spilling out of the rubble. Shopping centers behind contemporary facades are for the middle-class living behind barred windows, but even the best hotels eschew windowpanes. Too hot. Slatted bamboo louvers or open-air are sensible, but not without steel window-bars, below 3500 feet, in more populous areas.

Washing clothes in the river

There has been a successful street-cleaning campaign that has noticeably spiffed-up Montego Bay and Kingston. Spots that once were knee-deep in refuse have been transformed into streets. Government contracts are at stake, and jobs. This one is being well-done, reliably, like the rain mountain farmers count on. Possessive Jamaicans still throw litter on the ground, only now someone picks it up.

The cities house governments, the highest evolution of Jamaican culture as represented in arts, sciences and contradictions.

You fly into Kingston or Montego Bay, one the capital city, the other an unselfconscious tourist town. Instantly you become a target for cab drivers and would-be tour guides as you step through Jamaican customs. Ordinary Jamaicans, in these cities and smaller ones, such as Ocho Rios or Spanish Town, live competitively, far from idyllic mountainsides. A swarm of Kingston newspaper vendors, none older than eight or nine, have more than selling papers in mind when they surround a car filled with tourists at a stop light. If by chance or design one can grab a wallet or flee with the change from a large bill, the challenge will often be engaged. Certain Jamaican sports call for caution in newcomers. Jamaica is 97% black. Tourists are easy to spot. Most Jamaicans think you have a lot of money. Compared to them, earning $3 JA per hour at hard stoop labor cutting cane, or $16 US weekly for a country-wide average, you do.

Tourism is officially the biggest industry on the island. Jamaica is a major world producer of bauxite for aluminum, but low market prices have forced cutbacks in mining. Hundreds of people lost jobs in the industry slowdown. Bananas are still big business and all the coffee that can be produced finds a ready market. These businesses touch relatively few Jamaicans. Hustling is open to all. Jamaicans love to verbally joust with each other; selling goods or services to a visitor is a logical extension of business as usual.

Good judgement is always in order. Most Jamaicans are polite, but out of nearly 2.5 million, some are scoundrels. You ask for directions or to take a photo and an opportunistic Jamaican asks for money in return. Reach Falls is a little-known beauty spot at the bottom of a short trail, off the east coast, south of Port Antonio. There is no charge to swim or hike along the riverbed. There are, however, self-appointed attendants working there, who usher you to the falls. They are friendly enough, answering your questions, suggesting a walk with you over slippery rocks to a better vantage point, but it is just this help-giving, whether you want it or not, that chafes. Something from you is always expected in return for services, real or imagined, even if you have persistently repeated "no, thanks." This can feel intimidating if you are miles from the nearest town at Reach Falls and are unused to Jamaican ways.

"Jes' leave somet'ing for I, for I troubles," your newest Jamaican friend says softly. "One love, bredren. Jes' a likkle."

Welcome to Jamaica.

It works out if you know what to expect. There may be moments when you have to outlast an especially pushy salesman or woman. Say no when you mean it, then say it again several more times. Remember, your small tip of $2 Jamaican is less than 40 cents US. Your American dollar is worth nearly six Jamaican.

Bartering is always acceptable, prices are always negotiable. What begins as a bare hustle may turn into a chance for communication and cultural exchange. Stopping short of saying no, you enter into the verbal rounds by default. No charge for conversation. Speaking with Jamaicans is how you learn the ropes and see how their humor and politeness can survive great hardships with energy left over to dream.

As valuable as tourism is for foreign exchange the economy of the country would be worse off without the marijuana trade. The United States, major supplier of tourists, foreign aid and big money markets for Jamaican herb, has a government that knows this.

Mutual Jamaican and American interests weave a tricky sidestep around the burning issue of marijuana. For the record, both sides condemn drug traffic. Publicized busts make small copy in Kingston's Daily Gleaner, a drop in the bucket, usually nothing more than a symbolic gesture, postcard greet-

Dread with spliff in Maroon Country

ing to appease big lenders of government millions in Washington. Top, top dollars are made selling Jamaican pot, and plenty of pocket change on the street.

Many Jamaicans walk around with a small quantity of ganja rolled in a torn scrap of newspaper or a brown paper bag. Friends frequently exchange small quantities for a taste of island-wide variety. A visitor can smoke his lungs raw, in days, or hours, if that is what he wishes. Pocket change.

Higher finance is involved in supplying major quantities outside Jamaica. This is the trade that filters back into the culture and supplies needed cash that comes from nowhere else.

A conservative Jamaican government has become in recent years the closest ally of the United States in the Caribbean. Solid anti-communist credentials go far in making a neighborly US government look the other way, for now.

US interests flexed their muscle a few years back when typical Jamaican political enthusiasm turned violent around election time in 1980. US-Jamaican relations had turned sour over the course of the sitting Manley government. Michael Manley's socialist-populist programs hoped to guarantee minimum wages to build hospitals, local clinics and low-cost housing. Foreign investment and ownership were discouraged. Establishing relations with Cuba iced Manley's decline. US Foreign Aid backed out. Then, when several police cars were burned and shots were fired in rough areas of Kingston where tourists are as common as snow, all of a sudden Jamaica was reported to be dangerously unsafe for tourism.

What the bad press failed to mention was that volatile politics have always been part of the Jamaican style, nothing out of the ordinary; always ready to consider a change, vocal, expressive opposition characterizes it historically.

The negative publicity was so effective in placing fear in the minds of potential and past North American visitors that years later and with an entirely new, pro-US government firmly in power, the first question always asked about traveling in Jamaica is this: "Is it safe?"

It may never have been unsafe. It may have been psychologically uncomfortable here for Americans with money. It can feel that way today if you walk around the streets flaunting gobs of expensive jewelry, or if you let the hustling get under your skin, the poverty and want get to you.

Tourism has been up recently, the first big upswing since the late 70's. Some of the scared money is finally coming back.

Down, a little dangerous, excitable and sometimes scary, Jamaica remains challenging, moody and looking for a good time.

The US government seems to look at the drug business as a trade-off for staunch anti-communist sentiment, and worth the $125 million in aid it costs yearly. Assuming the US could put out the ganja, obviously bad conditions in Jamaica would turn worse. Politics would get hot, fast. Boom, you have another government turnaround, a power transfer and good American dollars down the Caribbean drain again.

Life for most Jamaicans is hard enough. Government debt to the tune of 60% of export earnings means no money for new jobs, and terrible wages anyway. Inflation corrupts any sense of getting ahead. Take away the underground economy, which produces primary sources of income, and the shaky community of interest ceases on the spot. Jamaicans, for all their troubles, believe in their stake in the country. 87% voted in 1980. US interests dictate that, as long as that right line holds and makes a show against drugs, the ganja will continue to flower.

A lot of Jamaicans do not smoke pot, only grow it. Some do not sell it at all. Many have nothing to do with it.

Illegal ganja trade is not enough to support a country. The population keeps growing. Opposition will always exist here, if only for argument's sake. Areas of west Kingston are likely to remain off limits to smart visitors for a long time. Do not cross a Jamaican picket line. Hire on as an election eve pamphleteer at your own risk.

Money from outside the country, as in tourism-generated dollars, is always welcome. If you want an easy trip in a beautiful place you can buy a packaged week on the north coast and watch Jamaicans hustle to carry your golf clubs at one of the pretty resorts.

For adventure, remember that life in paradise has never been easy for Jamaicans. By all means watch your step while you strut to the reggae, and take compassion along. It will increase your chances for experiencing the other Jamaica and maybe learning a thing or two.

Nothing ventured, nothing gained.

"... the fairest island that eyes have beheld; mountainous and the land seems to touch the sky... all full of valleys and fields and plains."—Christopher Columbus, 1494.

CHAPTER THREE

GEOGRAPHY, BOTANY & CLIMATE

Volcanic-formed mountains, fertile plains fed by major and tributary rivers, mineral springs, rain forests, wetland swamps and a scalloped coastline varying from rocky cliff outcrops to luxuriant white sand beachfronts all combine to give Jamaica the most diverse and possibly the most beautiful geography in the Caribbean. The contour of the land and the seasonal conditions of climate influence island life daily, as well as the options for adventure available to any visitor here.

Kingston, Jamaica's capital, is the largest, southernmost English speaking city in the Northern Hemisphere. Jamaica is the largest English speaking country in the West Indies, which are divided into two island groups, the Greater Antilles and the Lesser Antilles. The Lesser Antilles are made up of Anguilla, Antigua, Barbados, Dominica, Grenada, Guadeloupe, Martinique, Montserrat, Nevis, St. Kitts, St. Lucia, St. Vincent, Tobago and Trinidad. The four largest islands comprise the Greater Antilles. These are Cuba, Hispaniola (Haiti and the Dominican Republic), Puerto Rico and Jamaica.

All these islands are bounded by the Caribbean Sea.

Jamaica is 90 miles south of Cuba, 100 miles west of Haiti. It is 1 1/2 hours by jet from Miami, a distance of nearly 700 miles. The island contains 4411 square miles of varied terrain, measuring 146 miles east to west, from Morant Point to Negril, with its greatest width running 51 miles north to south, from St. Ann's Bay to Portland Point. The narrowest width is only 22 1/2 miles from Annotto Bay on the north coast to Kingston.

Jamaica's warm climate and fertility have attracted people for centuries. Today it is a popular tourist destination for approximately one million people each year, many of whom come primarily because of the fine beaches. Most of the major tourist developments cluster on the beachfronts, particularly along the north coast, from Montego Bay to Ocho Rios. Despite a road circumference of 460 miles, and actually many more miles of irregular coastline, it is mainly the pretty surf and sand of the north coast beach resorts that most visitors see. The Caribbean stays cooperatively languid almost all the time and the island's position at 18 degrees north of the equator keeps those gentle shores appealing warm all year round.

Seasons are hard to differentiate. It is always warm and humid, usually hot. Moderating trade winds blowing in from the sea, that Jamaicans call the "Doctor Breeze," cool the temperature down a little during the day. A night wind sweeping down off the mountains is called an "Undertaker's Breeze." The names come from a Jamaican talent for hyperbole and fascination with verbal imagery. When you are used to 80–90 degree temperatures day and night, a cooling day wind keeps you healthy. Those rare, chilly 70 degree nights are cold enough for catching your death of cold.

Approximately half of Jamaica lies above 1000 feet. A mountainous backbone running the length of the country gives the island its special character as much more than just another beach resort. The entire West Indies chain is apparently the top of a submerged volcanic mountain range, one that may have, at one time eons ago, loomed above the sea in one giant land mass connected to Central America and the South American continent in Venezuela.

Ridges and valleys dominate the terrain of the island. The central range of the Blue Mountains, northeast of Kingston, connects with the John Crow Mountains farther east to form the tallest mountains on the island. These range up to 7402 feet at Blue Mountain Peak, a mystical, deeply forested and nearly mythic Jamaican power spot, known country-wide as "The Peak." It is usually shrouded in clouds of watery blue mist, giving the mountain and the range their names. Other mountains trail off from the Blues westward. These pass through the rare Karst limestone topography of the cratered, cave-filled, steep-sided Cockpits, into the Dolphin Head mountains outside of Montego Bay, the largest city on the west coast, second largest city on the island, after Kingston.

Smaller ridgelines and valleys branch from north to south off the central east-west mountain spine. Rivers drop out of the mountains, forming fertile basins close to the sea where you find coconut palms, mangoes, limes, and 3000 varieties of flowering plants, including 800 indigenous varieties. Count among these over 500 types of ferns and 200 species of wild orchids.

The air in Jamaica smells sweet, always damp, incredibly alive, from its mountain peaks supporting tropical montane and miniature elfin forests, to hot southern plains growing native prickly pear cactus outside cultivated acres of sugar cane. Thick trunk-like vines that would please a swinging Tarzan knot their way in hanging trails down enormous 350-year old silk cotton trees, the same as ones carved by Arawaks into dugout canoes that held as many as fifty paddlers.

The pimento tree, that produces allspice, the lignum vitae, a dense hardwood that sprouts the purple national flower, the mahoe, the national tree, bullet wood and ebony are among the woods found here. Many varieties of bamboo, used for construction, grow all over the island. When a stand sways in the night wind, the wooden creaking and hollow click-clacks become a percussive backbeat. Add the serenade of whistling tree frogs and cicadas, and it sounds like every sing-song dialect and reggae riff put together in a virtuoso natural Jamaican symphony.

You can still see some rare mahogany in the remote swamps, although this prized furniture-making wood has been extensively logged into virtual extinction from the landscape. Other stands of valuable woods in wetlands and mountains have faced the same fate. Due to the country's small size and the world's seemingly voracious appetite for a dwindling supply of tropical hardwoods, some environmentalists predict that Jamaica's lush and scenic forests will continue to shrink through the end of this century, and possibly disappear completely unless adequate conservation and reclamation steps are taken.

Because of the rugged lay of the land, highland mountainsides and isolated valleys manage to provide poor Jamaicans with land they can call their own. No one else wants the remote properties. They are too steep, too rocky or too inaccessible for commercial agriculture or development.

Hard working independent mountainfolk continue a long tradition of sustenance farming. A personal piece of land is the place where a proud Jamaican earns self-respect. Even the most difficult terrain is worked for coffee, cocoa and vegetables, for essential food needs, and in good years, to sell or barter.

Marijuana cultivation has been widely added to the standard roster of crops. It can be found growing from seedlings to flowering tops virtually all over the island. Economic necessity dictates that many Jamaicans who do not smoke it grow it for sale.

Mountains are visible from almost anywhere on the island. Of these, the Blue Mountains are the highest and most massive, running for 44 miles through about two-thirds of the length of Jamaica. Aside from Blue Mountain Peak at 7402 feet, other substantial peaks include Mossman's Peak, in St. Thomas parish, near Blue Mountain, at 6700 feet, Sugar Loaf Peak in neighboring Portland parish, at 7,000 feet, Sir John's Peak, in St. Andrew, at 6330 feet, Catherine's Peak, also in St. Andrew, at 5,056 feet. Main transportation routes through the mountains climb through high passes at Hardwar Gap, at 4,000 feet, and the Newcastle Training Camp, of the Jamaican Defense Force, at 3,702 feet. Farms and villages are scattered throughout these lightly populated areas, and a network of rocky footpaths used by residents can provide challenges for hikers unaccustomed to the steep terrain.

You can still feel a primitive, nearly prehistoric sense of distance from the mainstream in the cool, higher mountains. Farmers favor machetes. The highlands lack electricity and there are few cars or trucks. The well-to-do ride a mule or horse. Many barefoot people walk everywhere, most with heavy baskets or bundles on their heads. Apparently they get their lean, limber and strong shapes from ducking, weaving and swaying, under load, up and down endless hills, for generations. Up in the clouds it is hard to believe that the rarefied emptiness and coolness of Blue Mountain Peak sits only ten miles away from downtown Kingston and its swelling population of more than 900,000, situated far below on a steamy coastal plain.

The unusual forests that cover the mountain highlands and much of the country owe their existence partly to the heavy rainfall that drenches Jamaica. The Blue and the John Crow Mountains receive the most rain.

Rainfall, slope, soil conditions and altitude that make commercial cultivation of most crops impossible provide nearly perfect conditions for growing what many experts consider to be the finest coffee in the world, Jamaican Blue Mountain. So prized are these beans that grow only between 2500–5000 feet that approximately 90% of the crop is purchased by Japanese investors who turn a nifty profit in trendy Oriental coffee shops where people are paying $7, or more, for a cup of the famous brew.

American buyers can find Blue Mountain coffee for $25–$40 per pound in gourmet shops, placing these beans among the world's most expensive coffees, but is it the tastiest? Fortunately, prices are much better in Jamaica. If you know where to go for beans, you can sample Blue Mountain for yourself, at the source. If you like it, bring home pounds from the grower and save a bundle. More on this in a later chapter.

Jamaica's mountains are also the source of many of its 120 rivers. Riverheads spring from underground or begin as mere trickles in the higher elevations, winding down through the hills and valleys, branching off into slower-moving southerly

flows and quicker northerly ones, all coursing toward the sea. Of these waterways, twelve major year-round rivers and a variety of smaller seasonal ones offer adventurous opportunities for navigation, either by poled bamboo rafts or inflatable canoes.

Sport has come only recently to the rivers. They have long provided water for drinking and washing clothes, necessary irrigation in drier southerly regions, free power for hydroelectric generators and homes for such delicacies as famed hot-peppered "shrimps." These are the delectable little crustaceans Jamaicans call "swimps," and which are sold by roadside vendors in the town of Middlequarters, north of the Black River, the island's longest.

The rivers carry rich soil deposits out of the hills to spread over lowland plains. Clay soils that drain poorly in the west, south and extreme southeastern portions of the island contribute to the formation of swamps, such as the Black River Morass, which is Jamaica's largest crocodile refuge. The Great Morass lies just inland from Negril on the west coast. Morant Morass surrounds Morant Point, the island's easternmost point.

The rivers are short on this small island, and were previously believed to be largely unnavigable due to the speed picked up from the quick, steep drops out of the mountains. It is only since the early 1980's, with the advent of new inflatable rubber boat technology, that canoeists have attempted passages on certain known and unknown stretches. Navigable white water has been reported in several locations.

Jamaica and New Guinea are thought to be the only tropical locations in the world offering river canoeing. Because of the relative newness of the sport, it is still possible to discover previously untraveled areas, providing the canoeist with the exciting opportunity for a first descent. Many enthusiasts enjoy "canuding," as well, a comfortable option for even the shy paddler on remote waterway stretches. The water is warm all year-round, the rivers mainly private, the day all your own, so why not?

Blue Mountains

Hikers near Y.S. Falls

Dramatic waterfalls can be reached in several little-known and rarely visited locations. A remote beauty spot is located on the Y.S. River, at the end of a thorny two-mile hike. Scenic Reach Falls, near the east coast is easier to get to, a close runner-up for beauty.

Well-known waterfalls have been developed as major tourist attractions at Dunn's River, near Ocho Rios, and at Somerset Falls outside Port Antonio.

Unfortunately for lovers of natural environments, hydroelectrical developments are being considered for the Y.S. Falls and are already pumping power out of the nearby Roaring River and others. Without coal or petroleum reserves, Jamaica is trapped at the mercy of high world energy prices. Rural hydropower stations are the only way to light up a poor country. Population growth and industrial development will continue. The isolated beauty of these spots is already threatened.

Underground rivers line the Cockpit Country. The ground is mainly fossilized limestone residue from the days when Jamaica was submerged, a rugged, never-settled Karst landscape (named for the region in Yugoslavia where this type of terrain was first quantified) characterized by rocky, sharp-sided hollows, "cockpits," alternating with conical-shaped hills as tall as 1000 feet high.

The soft, porous limestone is eroded by water, creating caves along major underground fault lines. Where the rooftops of these caves have collapsed, you find the open-topped cockpits, which have a similar shape to the pens for fighting cocks. Since water cannot accumulate on the surface of the limestone, it drains through cracks into underground passages, forming rivers and streams. The washed away mineral content of the limestone eventually finds its way to the sea, contributing to the coastal reefs that ring the island.

Although some of the rivers appear aboveground for short distances, they characteristically disappear into sinkholes when they meet the limestone cap, only to reappear miles away. The Quashie River, for example, splashes over a series of small waterfalls near Albert Town, disappears into a cave, then reappears at Dornock Head, ten miles away, where it turns into the Rio Bueno river.

Dornock Head, on the northern border of the Cockpits, is one of the more accessible areas in the lightly traveled region, situated only five miles south of Discovery Bay, with a good road between. Warning: Because water drains through the Cockpits, drinking water is scarce and frequently unavailable. Carry water with you if you plan to spend time in the Cockpit Country.

Underground waters have carved out numerous caves which pock the limestone, some large and inviting, up to two miles long, and half-a-mile wide. Local guides, usually unemployed young men found outside any bar or shop, can help you here. You will not find tour guides handing out maps to these caves, many of which are more or less unexplored, except by local kids fooling around. They will be glad to help you and to get a chance to earn a few dollars.

Underground water sources also feed numerous mineral springs, some radioactive and running hot out of the ground. These are said to have therapeutic value. The most well-known springs are located at Milk River, in Clarendon, and at Bath, in St. Thomas. Spas have been built around each of these natural phenomena, with accommodations available, as well as therapy programs for sufferers from muscular aches and pains, arthritis, sciatica and a host of other illnesses. These will be covered in detail in a later chapter.

The harbors and bays of Jamaica buttress the land and the sea. Kingston Harbor is the largest and most important port for shipping, followed by Port Antonio on the north coast, a once thriving banana and produce-shipping center, now catering mainly to small pleasure craft and cruise ships. Ocho Rios is now mainly another cruise ship destination. Sugar ports are on the south coast. Little coves and bays hug the coastal perimeter.

Small islands, called cays, lie just offshore at Port Royal, as well as farther away from Morant Point and Portland Point. The uninhabited Port Royal cays are a short boat ride from the historic town that gave them their name, and a prime destina-

The Blue Lagoon, Port Antonio

tion for sun lovers, beachcombers, swimmers, snorkeling enthusiasts and fishermen and women.

Jamaica's position near the equator keeps the island hot most of the year. Temperatures in the mountains do get cooler than the lowlands, frequently in the 50's and 60's in the Blue Mountains and colder than that at Blue Mountain Peak before dawn.

The coolest time of year is November through March. Year round, the temperature varies only a few degrees, although the angle of the sun in summertime makes it feel hotter in July than December, more so than the temperature differential would indicate.

The mountainous ridgeline across the island blocks the trade winds, forcing breezes to climb up the north side of the island, then descend to the south. The rising action causes the winds to cool at higher altitudes, with a corresponding drop in pressure. Condensation follows, building vapor-laden rain clouds. The greatest amount of average yearly rainfall tends to occur on the high northern mountain slopes, at the peak of the climb. The wettest parts of the country are found on the north faces of the Blue Mountains and east of there, in Portland parish, on the north facing upper reaches of the John Crow Mountains.

Rainy seasons occur in May and October, when it may rain daily, although not constantly. Sporadic daily downpours are commonly surrounded by periods of clear sky. More rainfall is likely in the summer than other times of year. The rainfall determines the water level of the rivers, which change frequently. River runners take note. These levels change daily, sometimes faster. Expeditions are best informed by someone on the spot to report which rivers, or stretches, are currently runnable and which are not.

Jamaica finds itself in the path of hurricanes with some historical consistency. Through recorded history the island has repeatedly been hit and damaged by storms. Jamaicans come out and pick up the pieces every time, rebuilding their cities and their bamboo huts, retrenching roads and gardens, starting all over again, if necessary. Maybe that is a reason why no one seems to be in a hurry down here. Life is too short and tenuous. Survival is rough in the best of times. Disaster is as close as the wind turned suddenly nasty. Hurricane season lasts from June through October.

The climate, geography and botany of Jamaica create one of the most diverse natural environments in the Caribbean tropics. Part of any adventure here is to take advantage of the variety of settings you can find away from tourist beaches. The following chapters will introduce you to the whole island and spectrum of forms that adventure can take here.

"River canoeing and hiking, along with sun, sand, sea, great wild tropical caves, mineral spas, birding, water sports galore, wilderness backpacking, fishing, horseback riding, bicycle touring, the backdrop of a fascinating culture and of course, the beat of reggae—all within one to five hours drive."—Peter Bentley, President, Jamaica Alternative Tourism Camping and Hiking Association.

PART II

ADVENTURES GUIDE

Jamaica can challenge you on its swift rivers or steep climbs, provide you with great beaches for baking or sport, expose you to a steaming Caribbean culture and dare you to partake in it. Jamaica can tease you, filling your dreams with the beauty of its lush valleys, woods, waters and mountaintops, as well as its people.

It can rock you with reggae or to sleep under stars in a rope hammock hung from bamboo trees. It can roll you big spliffs, then feed your munchies sweet mango.

Adventure can be sport, hiking, horseback riding, skinnydipping in a clear mountain pool with river flowers blooming, frogs singing. You can scuba dive, snorkel and find great swimming all over Jamaica. Try boating in a dugout canoe or a runabout, a river canoe, bamboo raft, glass bottom or sailboat. Hold on to the back of a mule to get to Blue Mountain Peak. Watch birds, butterflies or bats in a cave.

Adventure can take the form of cultural explorations, visiting "tourist" sites most guidebooks leave out, tracking the roots of reggae or Jamaican arts, sampling roadside offerings of local foods or dining in small restaurants frequented only by

Jamaicans, or in a Jamaican home. A trip to a Jamaican market to haggle over the price of yams on market day can be an adventure. Sipping white rum or roots wine under a mammoth cotton tree with a dreadlocked rasta probably qualifies for many of us. Staying in a small guest house, a private home or camping out can fill the bill. Driving on Jamaican roads, riding a train or a crowded mini-bus down a hill will definitely provide thrills.

If you come to Jamaica looking for something out of the ordinary to do on or in the water, on land, in the air or underground in caves, the following pages will serve as an introduction to your individual adventure.

"Up a cane river to wash my dread
Upon a rock I rest my head."—
Bob Marley, *Trench Town*.

CHAPTER FOUR

SWIMMING, SNORKELING, SCUBA DIVING & SKINNYDIPPING

You never get very far away from water in Jamaica. The island is practically ringed by good beaches for swimming. Snorkeling is often possible within one hundred yards of the shoreline, in clear and calm water where you can see more than fifty varieties of corals, sea urchins, sponges, starfish, angelfish, tangs, batfish and peacock flounders. Scuba diving is available through numerous certified operators. Spearfishing is allowed on most reefs.

A constantly changing river network pours down from the mountains. Tropical downpours send waterfalls crashing into jungle swimming holes. You can float in a legendary "Blue Hole," called bottomless, but actually a limestone sinkhole holding water from deep underground springs. Lie perfectly still in a motionless cove or splash under a waterfall. Snorkel near the beach or a mile off shore. Backflip off a rock. Dive from a 50 foot cliff, then complete your tan on a clothing op-

Dunn's River Falls

tional beach. Getting into the water is a time-honored way to stay cool just about everywhere in hot Jamaica.

MONTEGO BAY

Montego Bay's Sangster International Airport is the gateway to Jamaica for most foreign visitors. Jamaica's second largest city is geared-up as its most tourist-conscious town. The veneer of all the hotels and attractions reflects a corny vision of Jamaica, highlighted by limbo contests in the sand and "native shows" featuring Calypso music, which is not even Jamaican, but from Trinidad. What you scratch at under the surface of that are merely the lives of 75,000 Jamaicans who call Mo-Bay home. City-style adventures can be found here, nightlife, discos, a beach-spud-by-day, party-animal-by-night style town.

There are more rugged and scenic sites you can find on the island, but the local beaches do give you a chance to dip into the currents of the culture and get your feet wet. Personal favorite spots include *Cornwall Beach*, on Gloucester Avenue, in the heart of downtown, and *Damali Beach*, at Ironshore, five minutes north of town, out past the airport.

Cornwall Beach—There is a small admission charge here ($1–$2 JA), as with all of Montego Bay's beaches, that entitles you to swim, sunbathe and use a changing room. This little public beach is located close to the popular and larger Doctor's Cave Beach in the heart of the main tourist strip, a great place to start from, get a fix on where you have just landed, mix a little with higglers and hustlers, scope out your fellow tourists, then be on your way, out of town, on the road to adventure, wherever it may lead you.

Ambitious sales people swim up to beachgoers, hawking black coral jewelry, shell necklaces, tickets to a beach party, drugs and so forth. It is a very public beach, so particular discretion is advised.

It is common knowledge that many visitors are at least partly attracted to Jamaica because of its reputation for easy access to good pot. You will be offered marijuana on the beach, cocaine, too, if you look the slightest bit interested. This is illegal in Jamaica. More details on this later. For now, bide your time and learn first how it is done in Jamaica.

Herb soon come after arrival, no problem, if that is what you want.

There is a Jamaica Tourist Board office at the beach, making this a convenient place to stop soon after you get here, grab some maps and brochures, double check your reservations, then when your business is done, go for a swim in the clean water.

The beach is covered in soft sugar sand, deep enough for your feet to sink in covering your toes. You can swim and relax in the barely cool sea. Watch out for the hot sun. Light skin burns fast. Sunscreen, a hat and an umbrella can be useful sunblockers.

Scuba diving gear, snorkeling masks and flippers can be rented on the beach, from *Culture Resources*, operated by Don Mowatt, a certified dive operator. You can explore Cornwall's underwater park featuring close-in coral formations. After a swim, a bonus is the bird Watchers Bar, an outdoor cold drink oasis, built around a giant almond tree.

Damali Beach—is privately owned and operated by Parchi Parchment and Audley Arnold, who can answer most of your questions about Montego Bay, help you with tour bookings locally and island-wide, and accommodate you here, camping on the beach, or nearby, in the Sunshine Villas (complete apartments with private swimming pools, a cook, maid and gardener-driver).

Aside from a large curve of rarely busy beach, there are cabanas at Damali, a good, inexpensive open air seafood restaurant and bar under a high thatch roof, along with a jerk pork stand outside in the parking lot. You can select a camping space right on the beach, within yards of the water, or back off in a protected inner courtyard.

There are coral beds offshore. It is an easy swim, or walk, of around a quarter-mile in the shallow water to reach the reef, or you can be ferried out there in a glass bottom boat operated by a knowledgeable twenty-year veteran of the local waters named Jeff. He charges $10 US per hour, per person, or $15 for two hours. Swimmers need to watch out for power boats towing skiers or parasailers. It may be hard for drivers of these fast boats to see you.

Certified scuba operator George Cunningham works out of Damali, and there is also a parasailing concession. A small cut at one end of the beach is popular with nude swimmers.

Seawind Beach Resort is located at Montego Freeport, a few miles south of the crafts market. The large high-rise hotel and condo development has a well-known nude beach. It is not the most secluded in Jamaica. Lots of lookers reported. *Discovery Bay Diving Co.*, run by Jim Pair, operates a scuba diving concession at the resort.

All the dive operators listed here under Montego Bay and in the rest of this chapter meet Jamaican certification standards, which include employing at least one internationally certified dive instructor, using certified dive guides trained in first-aid, meeting air standards for compressors, testing tanks at specified intervals and carrying insurance. Check with individual operators for tank rentals, instructions and air supplies. Some of the scuba operators rent underwater cameras and video equipment.

Poseidon Nemrod, at the Chalet Caribe Hotel, is in Reading, south of Montego Bay, on Spring Gardens Ridge. Operator, Theo Smit. A lot of people think this is the best scuba area near Mo-Bay. You can dive off the end of the jetty, without a boat ride, unless you want to go farther out. The reef starts only twenty yards from the jetty, and corals and fish are visible in six to one hundred twenty feet of water within a quarter mile of the beach. Caves and canyons are found in a drop-off only a hundred and fifty yards offshore. Black coral, pillar coral and sponges can be seen. The resort caters mainly to divers with numerous package rates available, including a specified number of dives. Day and night dives are offered, along with equipment rentals, cameras and video equipment.

Sea Crabs is at the Chatham Beach Hotel, on Kent Ave., Montego Bay. Operator, Shakka Dalley.

Sea World is at the Cariblue Beach Hotel, Roy Watkins, operator.

Island Watersports, 122 Gloucester Ave., Donald Linville, operator.

Scuba Jamaica is at the Half Moon Hotel, Rose Hall, Patrick Reichter, operator. This site is 10 miles east of Montego Bay, much less crowded than the city, at a big, ritzy hotel.

Free Spirits operates at Sandals Resort Beach Club, on Kent Ave., Steve McClure, operator. Another fancy hotel concession.

Tojo Watersports is at the plush Trelawny Beach Hotel, Falmouth, 23 miles east of Montego Bay.

Royal Caribbean, at the Royal Caribbean Hotel on Mahoe Bay, is about 6 miles east of Mo-Bay. Operator Dean Cooper.

Rose Hall, at the Wyndham Rose Hall Beach & Country Club, is 10 miles east of Montego Bay. Robert Stewart, operator.

RUNAWAY BAY, ST. ANN'S BAY, OCHO RIOS

Columbus landed somewhere along this north coast stretch. Today it is less noted for the adventure of discoveries than for tourist resorts. Nevertheless, you can find good swimming, snorkeling and certified dive operations.

A lot of people love this area, particularly Ocho Rios, for all the activities centered there. Others find it overly commercial. If you enjoy busy beaches with lots of people and plenty to do, including windsurfing, jet-skiing, waterskiing and deep sea fishing, all going on at once, amid a larger carnival atmosphere of buyers and sellers, hustlers with heavy raps, higglers haggling, deals to be made, then "Ochee" could be your place.

The certified dive operators in the general area are:

Island Dive Shop, located on Columbus Beach in Priory, 2 miles west of St. Ann's Bay, Edgar Rose, operator. This a quiet spot outside of the resort area. The shop specializes in scuba instruction and the reefs nearby are a virtual marine lab of diverse corals and fish. Also good hiking inland.

Sea & Dive Ja. Ltd. is at the Arawak Inn in Mamee Bay, operator, Mike Drakulich. Mike also operates a concession by the same name at the Shaw Park Hotel, just west of Ocho Rios. Mamee Bay is quiet and private; Shaw Park is in a much busier tourist area.

Sundivers Ja. Ltd. is at the Club Caribbean in Runaway Bay, operated by Craig Larson.

Watersports Enterprises, at the Americana Hotel, is on famous Mallard's Beach in Ocho Rios, operator Ernie Smatt.

Nigel's Dive Shop is at the Sans Souci Hotel, Ocho Rios, Nigel Andrade, operator. This hotel has a private mineral spa, reported to have healing properties.

Reid's Watersports is a concession at the Runaway Bay Hotel, Runaway Bay, King Reid, operator.

The reefs off-shore from Ocho Rios and east to Salt Gut Bay, near Oracabessa, contain a wide structural variety of unusually thick corals. The residue of centuries of mineral deposits washing out of the porous limestone hills and settling in shallow, protected waters makes this stretch desirable for snorkeling, diving and glass bottom boating. East from Ocho Rios to White River Cay at Frankfort Point, there is a scenic double reef, with good protection for scuba divers.

For other watersports besides diving:

Eden II, a couples only, all-inclusive resort in Ocho Rios, advertises a nude beach, but you have to pay around $1800 a week, per couple, to use it. *Couples* is another expensive resort, also for couples only, with a teensie off-shore island for nude sun bathers. The resort has a shuttle boat back and forth to the islet with its open bar (drink all you like, it is also all-inclusive), hammocks, mats and beach chairs for baking beach potatoes. The water surrounding the island is filled with sharp rocks, making for hazardous swimming.

The most heavily used beaches in and around Ocho Rios are *Turtle Beach*, *Mallard's Beach*, *Shaw Park Beach*, and *Dunn's River Beach*.

Dunn's River Falls is the famous waterfall you see in all the PR photos with people holding hands forming a human chain to walk up natural limestone steps from the sea to the top of a tiered waterfall. It is a very beautiful and heavily commercialized spot. Chock-a-block craft shops sell wooden carvings, foods, t-shirts and all the rest. There are many other waterfalls in Jamaica, at least equally as scenic, definitely less tampered with, and with fewer people around.

Swimming in the *White River* is excellent. The recommended best place is called "Irie Beach". It is a secluded spot at the end of a dirt road from *Bonham Spring*, about 1 1/2 miles east, then 1 mile south of Ocho Rios.

There is adventure of sorts found in the streets of Ocho Rios and along its beaches in keeping yourself from being stopped every ten feet by someone trying to sell you something. The town is possibly the most heavily packed in all of Jamaica with tourist shops and stalls, as well as roving freelance salespeople. Veteran Jamaica travelers insist that once you acquire a tan the sellers leave you alone, figuring if you have been around long enough to catch the sun then you already have what you need or know where to get it. The trick is getting through those first few days here. There are a lot of hustlers, so take care.

CASTLE GARDEN, PORT MARIA, STRAWBERRY FIELDS

East of Ocho Rios and west of Port Maria, *Castle Garden* is a blink-and-you-miss-it size tiny fishing village and a good north coast spot if you are looking for seclusion, as well as snapper, grunts, blacks, red fish (Jamaicans call them "Conga Tony"—you will have to ask why for yourself), doctor or jack fish. Local fishing boats, mostly dugout canoes, usually have room for a passenger or two. You can hire a boatman to take you fishing or you can buy fresh sea food, or a cooked fresh fish dinner along the beach.

Sea Lawn Coral Beach, in Castle Garden, is a small, very Jamaican spot operated by Mike Higgins. Mike has grassy or sandy tent spaces along the beach for campers, and his wife serves meals of fresh lobster or other fresh catch in their home. Mike can guide you to some of the best snorkeling on the north coast off the Hurricane Allen coral reef, directly across from Blowing Point. Good coastal hiking nearby.

The tourist developments thin out by the time you reach *Port Maria*, a relatively large town with few hotels, thus few tourists. It does have neat old churches and other old buildings situated around a large cove with pretty, undeveloped beaches. Padre Island, also known as Cabarita Island, is seven acres of sand and palms in the harbor. It is a one-mile swim from the beach. Good snorkeling. Lobsters.

Strawberry Fields was one of the most popular counterculture locations in the 60's and 70's, offering cheap camping and seclusion amid stunning coastal beauty, a choice place and time to get high and be left alone, wander beachside cliff trails, act frivolously, stargaze off a dark coast at night, swim all day, negotiate for your supper with a dugout canoe lobsterman, then haggle with his wife over a price to cook it for you.

You can still have local people prepare fresh seafood for you at reasonable prices. The campsites are inexpensive, around $5 US, and today there are several rental cottages. The coast is just as gorgeous as it ever was.

The clientele these days is largely Jamaican. You have to travel west from Annotto Bay for five unpaved miles off the main road to get here. Much of the stretch is undeveloped beachfront, good looking, too, until you catch sight of Strawberry Fields, situated in a small horseshoe cove.

Scrubby shade trees grow out of short sand cliffs, tracing a rim of transparent blue water. It is almost always calm enough for children to play in the shallows, and there is good snorkeling at the mouth of the cove. Coastal cliffs line the sea north of here and hikers can find little streams with waterfalls tumbling onto deserted beaches. It is absolutely idyllic for quiet coast lovers, peaceful, and with good access to the busy north coast.

HOPE BAY, PORT ANTONIO & THE EAST COAST

Rio Sol Mar is the name of a guest house just west of Hope Bay. Paula Espeut runs a tidy operation situated at the confluence of the Swift River and the sea. She rents out two rooms in her home, as well as two antique-filled apartments, with kitchens. The buildings are situated close to the noisy main road and within sight of a unique cast iron bridge, but the choice of salt or freshwater beaches is enticing. Ruby James cooks and runs the place when Mrs. Espeut is gone.

You will find few tourists around here. The expansive beachfront has not been developed. Along the river and the sea coast Jamaican women trailing small children seem to be umbilically connected to endless miles of colorful wash. After they scrub clothes in the river, they must carry the heavy baskets of wet clothes to the sand and rock jetty between the river and the sea. The ladies drying wash on the beach usually will not want you to take photos of them in less than Sunday best, but they enjoy chatting while they spread the wet clothes in the sun. This is a fine place for meeting unpretentious Jamaicans who live outside of the tourist economy.

Rio Sol Mar welcomes naturists. Sea coast nudity can be a good conversation opener, or you can walk a short distance up the river to find a private place to swim. A typical afternoon here: Skinnydip in the river. Walk down to the beach at sunset to buy fresh Conga Tony from a fisherman. Ask Ruby to cook it and serve you as you sit, *sans* clothing, or dressed, on an antique veranda within sight of the Caribbean through breeze-swaying palms.

Somerset Falls, about a mile west of Hope Bay is one of those other waterfalls where you will not find the same big crowds as at Dunn's River. You will find a bar and jerk pork stand, as well as a raftsman who will carry you on his bamboo craft to the base of the falls, unless you prefer to swim. The Daniels river is deep, dark green and cool in the fertile shade of an overhanging rain forest canopy where it always feels as if it is raining. This is a convenient roadside stop, good for a quick dip or Tarzan-style diving off large rocks. Check the parking lot first for tour buses if you are looking for complete privacy here.

Port Antonio was once the prosperous center of the island's fruit-shipping trade. Its docks see more pleasure craft now than banana boats. This is a good area for water sports, also hiking, and access to the east coast and the Blue Mountains. The Portland terrain is lush, with the heaviest island rainfall, and rugged enough to keep Port Antonio inconvenient to reach so that despite its prolific beauty and charm, the area continues to discourage mass development. There are top resorts here, the gourmet Trident, or the Marbella Club at Dragon Bay, but these are smaller properties, no high-rises, nor crowds of tourists.

Port Antonio still shows traces of country calm and a small-town sense of place. Everyone recommends the same good restaurants. There is a cliquish, almost artsy feel to it, making it seem like a hideaway in a hard-to-reach banana port, sandwiched between the sea and the rainy mountains. It is not a city and not the sticks, but a small-city retreat where a calm

Port Antonio

version of urban Jamaican life takes place, yet with many things for visitors to do.

Navy Island, 993-2667, lies about a quarter-mile offshore, between the East and West Harbors, a great swim. There is also a 24-hour boat/ferry—free for guests,$10 JA for non-guests—across from the Esso station on West Street. This is the island that was once owned by Errol Flynn. Today, the sixty-five acre property is occupied by The Admiralty Club Resort, Yacht Club and Marina, which has a nude beach, and bamboo-decorated cottages with retractable walls and mosquito netting over the beds. As the name states, this place has a clubby, yachtie ambience, a sense of exclusivity befitting a vacationing Admiral, haughty with a hint of naughty *and* overpriced. It is skillfully done, though, in an impeccable setting, if you like that sort of thing.

Huntress Marina, on West St., 993-3318, across from Navy Island, is the in-town center for water sports. A democratic variety of charter services operate here, for fishing excursions, glass bottom boat tours, or snorkeling, and there is a scuba center next to the pier. The sailing yacht "Artemis" is available for half-day or full-day charters. The "Coral Baby," 993-3086, and "Soon Come," are charter boats available with tackle, bait, ice and all equipment.

Farther to the east, past town, are good private beaches with public access. *Frenchman's Cove* was once an ultra-expensive, exclusive resort, with private, staffed bungalows and charter seaplane airfare from Mo-Bay or Kingston included in your tariff. It is more budget-minded today, looking for a family trade, (children under 10 stay and eat for free). The private cove and beach bar are still classy. Good snorkeling. Top-notch scenic setting.

The *San San* area is known primarily for its big villas. You rent a house, with cook, maid and driver. Good deals are available on the villas in off season. There is a protected beach with an admission charge for non-members of the San San Association.

Frenchman's Cove

The Blue Hole, also known as the Blue Lagoon, is just east of San San. This is among Jamaica's best-known attractions, a reputedly bottomless body of water. It is classically pretty, surrounded by mango trees and close-in jungle growth. The spring-fed salt water lagoon is one of the larger bodies on the island that is filled with mesmerizing emerald water. In the right dreamy mood it is easy to see why they call it bottomless. It is also disturbingly easy to see how a beautiful spot is rapidly becoming obscured by gift stands, restaurants and concessions. Granted, you can get decent jerk pork here, but it is a shame when expanding commerce competes unfavorably with the natural activity that brought you here. As soon as you step out of your car you are surrounded by young men dangling strings of beads from their arms, someone asks if you want to waterski, someone else offers a scuba trip. Jump in the water. Swimming is free.

Blue Lagoon Watersports is operated by Seldon McLean, and some people think he can show you the best snorkeling the island has to offer, on the reef at the mouth of the lagoon, not in the blue hole, where it is too dark. You can arrange to scuba dive, waterski or rent a windsurfer at the Blue Hole for around $100 JA per hour.

The Marbella Club at Dragon Bay, just west of Boston Beach is a luxury hotel with a pretty beach. Raymond Allen, beach manager, rents equipment for snorkeling, windsurfing, sailfishing and paddleboating. There is a charge for non-hotel guests using the beach.

Fairy Hill Beach in *Winnifred* is maintained by the Portland parish council. There are changing rooms and showers. Admission to the secluded white sand beach is free.

Boston Bay, *Long Bay* and *Innes Bay* curve around the east coast of the island. The farther you move south and along the coast toward Kingston, the fewer people, particularly other tourists, you will encounter. A lot of visitors drive around to Kingston on this road, but few stop.

The terrain changes in through here, growing more lush. The inland region gets the island's heaviest rainfall, backing off the rainforest-covered John Crow Mountains as they trail down to the sea. After Boston Beach the coast road people are not always friendly toward fast-moving, photo-snapping tourists. Go slow, if you can. Talk to locals. Ask first before taking photos. The east coast scenery is beautiful and under-appreciated.

Boston Beach, ten miles east of Port Antonio, is best known for its outdoor jerk pork stands. "Jerking" is the spicy, slow barbecue cooking method that originated in the Portland hills with the Windward Maroons. They hunted wild pigs near here. You can smell the meat cooking on green pimento stick roasting racks as you drive on the main road. If you get here early enough in the morning, the slow fires just heating up, look around you at what will be cooking that day. Notice slabs of pork, heads and hooves laid out on display in several open-air butcher shops. Later, you will know what you are eating when you can sample Jamaica's best jerk pork cooking while you sit within ten feet of the crashing sea.

If they are not sold out by the time you arrive, you can sample jerk chicken or fish. The pork, however, is the mainstay. It tastes smoky, and leaves the inside of your mouth seared from the spice heat.

If you like the tender pork, after your eyes stop watering and your blood simmers back to a low boil, you may be interested to know that you can buy bottles of this absolutely legal, yet clearly mind-altering concoction, the Boston Beach pepper sauce marinade. It is made out of crushed country pepper, little round or crenelated red and yellow ones, nothing else. A straight taste of the hot sauce might make you wonder why pot, which is milder, is illegal. Superlatives fail. The stuff is hot. It makes Tabasco sauce taste like tomato juice. With minuscule doses your nose drips. The hot sauce, really more like a relish, takes on characteristics of a short duration hallucinogen in overdose. Take home a quart, which would probably last a small family for years, and divvy it up in little bottles for piquant gifts. Great for Bloody Marys.

Boston Beach often has the biggest waves on the island. Young men rent surfboards and give lessons. Come out at sunrise. Start your day watching the sun come up over the sea beyond the east coast of the island. Smell the start of the cooking fires in the early morning. Work up an appetite surfing or

Boston Beach jerk pork stand

go for a swim. Around 10:30-11 AM the first of the jerk pork, chicken and fish is ready to eat.

Long Bay is the site of a proposed recreation area, for now just a scenic and undeveloped beach you can have to yourself. There is a strong undertow.

Manchioneal is an unfriendly fishing village on the coast road. You can try to buy fresh fish at sunset, but do not even think about taking any pictures of the people or the impressive array of seafood. Perhaps because of this apparent disdain for visitors, there is pretty, yet untrammeled coastal scenery. Hills rise inland, shrouded in mists, with leafy stands poking through and thinning into spiky coconut groves nearing the sea.

Nearby are two excellent swimming areas.

Before you continue around to the south coast, a rough gravel and dirt road cuts inland next to the police station. You follow it for three miles from Manchioneal, through banana farms and overgrown leafy foliage to *Reach Falls*. You will find no crafts market or jerk pork here, only a stunning waterfall at the base of a steep muddy trail. Reach is beautifully undeveloped except for a few foothold boards and cement blocks set along the path, along with several low bamboo rails to rest on at the water's edge. Frank Clarke and a few friends voluntarily take care of the minimal upkeep and attend to visitors for no charge, but "donations" are expected.

The waterfall can be climbed, and hikers can walk up the river valley to a whirlpool inside the Mandingo Cave, a half-mile hike through several river pools. You need a flashlight or a gas lamp inside the quarter-mile long cave. You can swim and bathe in the waterfall. Nudity, no problem. A heaven on a hot day. It is worth tipping Frank and his buddies, even if their cordial and possibly unwanted services smack of petty extortion.

Innes Bay is another under-utilized beach south of Manchioneal back on the main road. It looks like the South Pacific here, with coconut palms growing down from the mountains and enclosing a dramatic sweep of empty beach. Rough waters at the beach and very few people, ever.

MORANT POINT, WHITE HORSES & THE YALLAHS SALT PONDS

Morant Point is the extreme eastern tip of the island, marked by an old cast iron lighthouse. There is only one bad road to it through swampy terrain. Few tourists bother to make the ride, helping to maintain a dramatically isolated sweeping coastline.

Development is sparse on this end of the island. I always get strong feelings of truly being on the edge of the world here, and farther south, where cliffs drop away and the seacoast melts into briny sea foam.

Old Pera is a small town south of Port Morant Harbor, where another bad road preserves a small piece of untraveled coastline directly across from a string of tiny cays. Guaranteed, great swimming, no crowds.

Morant Bay is where you find an impressive statue of national hero Paul Bogle in front of the courthouse where he was executed for leading a slave rebellion in 1865. It was sculpted by Edna Manley, a leading figure in Jamaican arts, who also found time to be the wife of Chief Minister Norman Manley, who had Kingston's international airport named after him, and the mother of Michael Manley, Prime Minister from 1972-1980. Swim and snorkel here with Jamaicans, not tourists.

Rozelle Beach is just east of *White Horses*. It is the only breeding ground for the indigenous Blue Swallowtail butterfly. The beach is easy to miss, narrow and small, running along the road, next to the Zion Ethiopian Coptic Country Store. The Coptics are a religious sect who treat marijuana as a sacrament. The store is run by Lurleen Farquahrs and Shanette, mother and daughter, "not by birth, but by life." It can get noisy when trucks or buses run by. Other times it is just you, the sea gulls and a fishing boat or two, with the rest of the beach deserted. Good size waves for this coast, and there is small waterfall across the road, within easy walking distance.

The Salt Ponds are of interest to science for the variety of bacteria and micro-organisms that can survive their viscous depths. With up to ten times the salinity of the ocean, few living things can tolerate the conditions. Across the road are tall cliffs and the Gold Mine Camp and Club, in Green Wall, is the closest place with rooms for rent or camping spaces. A barren-looking stretch runs along the Salt Ponds for empty miles of beach populated only by shore birds and butterflies. Gold Mine Camp is also the best source of local information on swimming, snorkeling, coast trails, fishing, places to stay and eat along this overlooked but subtly intriguing area.

There are several more beaches between here and Kingston, but there are better ones elsewhere. The coast gets relatively dry and scrubby here, on the south side of the Blue Mountains, which block this shore from rains. *Cane River Falls*, east of Kingston and Port Royal, is a close-to-the-city spot for a swim in a river with a small falls. There are narrow beaches along the Palisadoes Road leading to Port Royal, just before you reach the capital.

PORT ROYAL & THE CAYS

Port Royal, the old pirate capital from the 1600's, is located past Norman Manley Airport, due south of Kingston at the end of the Palisadoes Road. You can take a ferry from pier #2 near the crafts market in downtown Kingston or drive out to the end of the road at the old pirate's Naval Hospital, next to the National Museum of History and Archaeology.

Alongside ancient brick ruins and modest modern homes, a dockside shanty town looks a lot like the "Popeye" set in the Altman movie. Odd boards are hammered at cross angles, tottering on the tipsy piers, all looking as if it is ready to topple. Fishermen here will carry you to Lime Cay for picnics, excellent snorkeling, nude bathing, and swimming outside the harbor. The cays and reefs south of Kingston are fish feeding and breeding grounds. Despite pollution in Kingston Harbor, there is good diving off the cays. Boats are also available for hire at Morgan's Harbor, a resort between Port Royal and the airport.

Country Roast Fish Center is a must stop in Port Royal, next to the bobbing wooden fishing dinghies. Food shops called Fishermans Cabin or Buccaneer Roast literally lean on each other, propped together so intimately that you are not quite sure who cooked the fish and who brought the cold beer, only that they appeared, eventually, and in due time for you to be transported into another dimension of the Jamaican experience.

In a dark shack perched on the pirate seawall, Simon Bryan has been cooking fish since 1951, oh so slowly, and with seasoned skill. His ramshackle kitchen takes forever to cook "escoveitched" fish in a vinegary pepper marinade. Deep fried cassava cakes, called "bammies," are a chewy side order to soak up the hot spicy fish. "Fish and bammy," a favorite Jamaican dish. Genuine Jolly Roger down here on the pier. Yo, ho, ho. . . .

KINGSTON

Kingston is one of the best places for experiencing the real Jamaica. It is, without a doubt, the most underrated tourist attraction in the country and brimming with adventurous possibilities. But you do not go to Kingston for its beaches. Skip Kingston for now.

HELLSHIRE HILLS, FORT CLARENCE

People from Kingston go to the beaches at *Hellshire* and *Ft. Clarence* that start a few miles past Kingston's newest suburban developments in Portmore. These are developed beaches. There are changing rooms, heavy security, crowds on weekends and holidays, numerous food stands. All kinds of Jamaicans from every social level visit these beaches, making the area a Kingston field trip destination, a living natural history museum. Fort Clarence reggae concerts are legends. The fisherman's beach just past there at *Naggo Head* is considered an even hipper destination by Kingston's beach freaks. "Fry fish and bammy" at Naggo Head is in the running for the island's best.

The Hellshire Hills, beyond the beaches, are a naturalist's delight. Low limestone hills swell out of long empty beaches. Uninterrupted coastal hiking through sandy trails and dry cactus scrub leads past salt ponds and caves. Two Sisters Cave, behind Ft. Clarence, has Arawak petroglyph carvings on one wall that are estimated to be 1000 years old. Although the beach coast leading into Hellshire from Kingston is likely to see more development, the north hills are equally likely to stay the same as they are now, kept as a nature preserve for plants and animals close to the capital.

The extreme south coast is mostly undeveloped and largely unexplored. From *Manatee Bay* to *Old Harbor Bay*, marshes and mangrove swamps rim the coastline. Dry limestone out-

---

Morgan's Harbour, Port Royal

crops and lack of rainfall add to the sparseness of the low forest of thorn scrub and columnar cactus found inland. *Wreck Point* and *Wreck Reef* hold interest for adventurous divers and snorkelers, but you will find no snack bars or rental gear near here.

GREAT GOAT ISLAND, LITTLE GOAT & ROCKY POINT

Port Esquivel is an alumina shipping port. Across *Galleon Harbor* are the two *Goat Islands*. *Little Goat Island* is uninhabited. *Great Goat Island* accommodated an American military base during World War II. Today, the mangrove-protected islands are virtually deserted, except for a few fishermen's shacks on Great Goat. Someday the islands will probably become an official wildlife sanctuary for the large indigenous iguanas living there. Get a fisherman to take you out.

There is little development or population between *Salt River* and the tiny fishing village of *Rocky Point*. The coastal area is the heart of a proposed site for a *Portland Ridge National Park*. The huge park would include the reefs, islands, and swamps adjacent to the Hellshire Hills, extending through the vast coastal marshlands from *Old Harbor* to *Portland Ridge*. It would incorporate the low coastal *Brazilletto Mountains* and the southerly portion of the *Harris Savanna*, following the coastline through *Jackson's Bay Beach* and on into *Macarry Bay*.

The designation of the National Park has gone no further than the proposal stage. There are no Jamaican National Parks. Recreation areas and forestry reserves have been designated in certain areas, but there is no comprehensive plan to preserve Jamaica's natural environments. Despite this lack of official recognition, the Portland Ridge area currently offers some of the island's most thoroughly deserted areas for fishing, swimming, hiking, camping and picnicking, along with unusual scrub vegetation. The region is filled with accessible caves and Arawak archaeological sites. The *Portland Ridge*

Lighthouse is surrounded by swampy lowlands and scrub reached by a single road.

MILK RIVER BAY, FARQUHAR'S BEACH, ALLIGATOR POND

Another proposed National Park would extend from *Round Hill*, on the Milk River, to *Great Pedro Bluff*. This would be a westerly extension of the Portland Ridge Park. It would include *Milk River Bay*, the swamp west of Round Hill, *Farquhar's Beach* and *Alligator Pond Beach*, as well as the dramatic cliffs at *Great Pedro Bluff* and *Lovers Leap*, 1500 feet above the sea.

The road, if it can be called that, from Round Hill, through *Gut Bay*, to the fishing village of Alligator Pond is a rugged joke. Cracked rocks form a parched, jolting pavement spiked by cactus. After a rain, deep potholes fill with water and the air turns thick with butterflies. Narrowing, the road completely disappears at times under uncontrollable scrub. Although it is flat a car can only move at around two miles per hour. The grass grows taller than a car, strong fibrous stuff so thick you cannot see through it. Pushing through here one October day, our guide whipped out his machete, serious about jumping out to hack and slash in front of the car to clear a path, but the road proved passable. It only looked as if it was not a road. This is primeval Jamaica, the hot and dry lost world part of the island, the *Long Bay* south coast, pocked with caves and Indian ceremonial sites, supporting thick lowland overgrowth of a small morass swamp. Local children gawk at a rare car and squeal "White man, white man," meaning no disrespect, but merely registering their shocked surprise. It is an adventure just being here, without even leaving the car. Few visitors or Jamaicans spend time in this area.

TREASURE BEACH

The central south coast is one headland beach after another, deserted stretches of five to eight miles long, fishermen's coves speckled with tidepools for swimming along mixed black and brown sand beaches. The hot sun is cooled somewhat along breezy stretches on coastal hiking tracks that wind through sharp coral and lava rocks. Jamaicans go barefoot here. You should probably wear shoes and beware of the undertow after bad weather. Otherwise, this coast is ideal for nude swimming, hiking, snorkeling, lobstering or scuba diving (bring your own gear—no rental shops here).

Treasure Beach is a top spot for secluded coastal beauty, along with neighboring *Great Bay* and *Calabash Bay*. When you are jostling around the airport in Montego Bay, or stuck in traffic in Kingston, it is hard to imagine that there is anywhere so pretty and calm left in crowded Jamaica.

Treasure Beach Hotel, the anchor of the local tourism industry, is "developing," according to acting manager Judith Mitchell. "The setting is what captures people," she says. The hotel does not offer a lot of man-made things to do. It currently has only a dozen guest rooms, small attached doubles with

Treasure Beach

ceiling fans, on a hillside running down to a swimming pool. You can hear the sea from the little patio in front of each room. No one minds if you pull the sheets off your bed and sleep down on the beach, with the waves to lull you instead of a humming fan.

A disco is planned, but there already is one half a mile down the beach at "La Corner Beach Club Restaurant." La Corner is a strange place. Most evenings men outnumber women by around 20 to 1. Recorded reggae and Jamaican pop screeches out of a tinny sound system and the men dance to it by themselves, balancing a beer in hand, shadow dancing. In the dark downstairs of the cinder block bunker of a disco, they do slow intricate steps. A shot of overproof white rum, called "John Crow Batty," and measuring in at a staggering 177 proof, is $2 Jamaican, under 40 cents US. A cold Red Stripe beer is $3 JA, a Pepsi $1.60 JA, or about 30 cents US. Few women seem to be hanging out, but an American visitor is offered companionship. The pitch: "You ever have a Jamaican woman?" Beach waves are the only sound you hear with more certainty.

Water sports are supposed to be added at the hotel. The restaurant is good and inexpensive. A lobster dinner is $50 JA. Breakfast of ackee with saltfish, boiled green banana, coffee and fresh fruit is $30 JA, a modest price for a hotel dining room where the waiter pours cream (actually sweetened condensed milk) into your coffee for you from a silver server. This is a lucky find for a purist's getaway. Isolated beaches, a good Jamaican hotel, relaxed seacoast people around, and few foreigners creates a sublime coastal environment in authentic Jamaican style.

BLACK RIVER, Y.S. FALLS

Black River was the first town in Jamaica to have electric lights in 1893. For years it was a busy sugar and slave port, with logging and fishing activity coming off the Black River, Jamaica's longest. It is a slow-moving river town and a special place for finding a bit of old Jamaica.

The river's 44 miles start in the southern Cockpits, in the

Parish of *Trelawny*, disappears underground at *Oxford*, then rises at *Siloah* in a blue hole. At *Maggotty*, a waterfall that is said to have been one of the country's prettiest is no more, replaced by a hydroelectric power station on the river.

After passing through Maggotty, the river opens into the *Upper Black River Morass*, an open swampy plain speckled with islands and separated by a narrow gorge at *Lacovia* from the *Lower Black River Morass*, Jamaica's largest wetland habitat. Lacovia is a big town on both sides of the river, where cashews are grown. Roadside sellers wave bags full of nuts at you when you drive by.

There is good river swimming along tributaries feeding into the Black, on the *Broad*, the *Y.S.* and the *Middle Quarters River*. One of the prettiest and most exciting swimming spots on the island is at *Y.S. Falls*.

The falls are located on a private 2000 acre cattle and thoroughbred horse property specializing in tropicalized livestock strains. The land has been in Tony Browning's family since 1887, and if you ask Tony, gray-haired and dignified, a white Jamaican gentlemen farmer in a button-down shirt and pressed jeans, he will tell you that only selected people are allowed access to the falls. Minutes later he will add that no one has ever been turned away.

Courtesy dictates calling ahead before you visit. There are insufficient roads on the property, as well as no insurance to operate the falls as a real tourist attraction. There is a 4-wheel drive road down to the falls, but you must get through several locked gates and have a vehicle with a high ground clearance to make it. The Browning's use the road. Visitors walk up the river in low water, or, in high, along the shore through sharp, tangly grasses that grab at your ankles, scratching your skin, itching, raising quick welts if you scratch or not.

The shortest walk in to the falls is two miles down a broad hill into the river valley, across several thorny fields and into a canopied Tarzan jungle setting. You must tramp around or over enormous knotted roots and fallen trees, through grubby, muddy trails, before reaching the misty, triple-tiered falls. Blooming orchids used to grow wild here. They were stolen during the 1970's. The Browning's think they were sold in

Miami. Even without orchids it is a site of profound beauty, from the sodden, mossy ground, to the overhanging vines draped from towering trees. In spring and summer there are enough flowers to make you forget about orchids.

The loud water crashes into piled boulders, dropping a transparent curtain over sheltered limestone caves behind the falls. You can hike around the edge of the falls, to their top, where you can look upriver and down.

Strong swimmers will definitely want to jump in. A powerful current and the fast eddying swirls at the base of the falls can really whip you around. Be careful. A lot depends on the speed of the river and falls. After rains, expect torrential flows, with predictably less turbulence after a dry spell.

As for why this is not a developed tourism site, Tony Browning's answer explains something of the growth problems facing the country in general, the tourism industry in particular. "Everything is safe in Jamaica," he says, his Rottweiler-Shepherd mix hounds at his feet, "but just because of a few strikes years ago we see that tourism is too chancy. I raise my horses and bulls. Manley is very popular again. What if he gets back in? Seaga's policies are working better than Manley's did last time, but he is not very popular. Not of the people. The people don't like him."

There is also political talk of damming the Y.S. River and installing a hydroelectric power station in place of the falls.

The Upper Black River Morass, only about two miles from the falls, is polluted due to pesticide and chemical fertilizer wastes draining into it from surrounding cane fields. Industrial waste from sugar production and the rum factory at Appleton pour in as well.

The Lower Morass is the biggest and most diversified swamp habitat in Jamaica and the entire Caribbean. Marsh forest and high canopy forest trees that are only found here line the banks of the river near Holland. Vines trail down from giant trees, birds singing and sailing above the shaded undergrowth.

Similar marshlands and forests are big tourist attractions in places such as Florida's Everglades. Here, they are devoid of tours yet brimming with lively activity, early morning fishermen, women doing wash, kids splashing around, cattle lazily drinking, insects humming. The marsh thickens into mangroves closer to the sea, aerial roots dropping into the river and the flooded soil below it, birds feeding, crabs scampering. Canoeists on certain serene stretches of the Broad river will find themselves passing through dark mangrove tunnels arching over the waterway. Flowering riverine plants include wild cane, wild ginger, bulrush, guaco bush and potato slip, blooming year round in the fertile morass and Jamaica's tropical climate.

The river banks support most of the heavier forest growth, while the lower morass opens into broad marshes covered in sawgrass and tall sedges. Birds and waterfowl frequent the Black and Middle Quarters River banks. Approximately 100 species of resident and migratory birds have been counted in the Lower Morass.

You can fish for snapper, mullet and snook in the lower reaches of the Black or Broad River, and the spicy pepper shrimp, really tiny crayfish, not shrimp, that are sold by women on the roadside in Middle Quarters, just north of here, come out of the Black River. Something else comes out of the Lower Morass infrequently and that is the American crocodile. They are called alligators here. Whatever you call them, this is home to one of the world's biggest concentrations of the critters in a natural habitat. They are not supposed to be a danger to man, man being the more dangerous to the crocs, hunting them close to extinction for their skins and meat. Fresh water turtles live in the morass, and edible frogs have been introduced commercially.

Fishing, basketry and canoe building methods based on African practices are the standard of life along the rural Black River. With shrimp pots dangling from dug-out canoes, shrimpers manage boat and pot handling skills nearly identical to those seen on the Niger River in West Africa. Pot designs remain virtually the same today as 300 years ago when they were introduced by relocated slaves.

Woven baskets for carrying the shrimp are made from thatch palms that grow out of limestone outcrops. The ingenious shrimp pots and baskets make swell souvenirs.

Families and fisherman in canoes use the waterway for

transportation through the town of Black River. Ask someone near the bridge in town to give you a ride up river into the morass. It should cost around $60 JA for a few hours. Aside from wetlands scenery, you can also look for hidden landing strips and irrigated ganja farms. A few years ago government money was allocated to promote a rice growing scheme in the soggy morass, but even in grain poor Jamaica, subsidized rice cannot compete for success with the weedy herb sativa.

BLUEFIELD'S BAY, SAVANNA-LA-MAR, BLUE HOLE AT ROARING RIVER

Bluefield's Bay is the port that Morgan, the pirate, sailed from on the way to capturing Panama City from the Spanish in 1670. The main road from Black River runs along the coast, past *Scott's Cove* (also known as *Seal's Cove*), *Whitehouse* and *Belmont*. This is prime fishing territory, less over-fished than the north coast. Many of the Jamaican spiny lobsters, as well as sailfish, wahoo, dolphin, bonito, kingfish and tuna sold commercially island-wide, are available every morning at the fisherman's beaches you can see from the road as you drive by, lining the way to the small town of *Cave*. This is a top stretch for hopping a ride with a good fisherman in a cotton tree canoe. The more adventurous may want to talk to a captain of a larger fishing vessel, one of a hundred, or so, that leave from Whitehouse for the Pedro Banks, seventy-five miles offshore. The wreck diving there is as good as the fishing.

This south coast stretch can also be recommended for particular roadside specialty foods, fish, of course, raw from the fishermen, or fish 'n bammy sold by assertive youngsters who thrust their hands into stopped vehicles. You can also buy limes in through here, water coconuts, mangos in season, cashews, other fruits. A non-food specialty of the roadside stands are the woven hammocks you will see offered for sale.

Past Bluefield's, the main coast road passes *Ferris Cross*, the most direct by-pass road back to Montego Bay. Farther on, *Savanna-La-Mar*, is a sedate old town, long-established as a sugar port, and somehow outside of the hustle and bustle found in other Jamaican towns of this size. There is no tourist industry here to speak of. There are several old schools and churches.

Savanna-La-Mar Hospital was the sight of a controversy during the Manley years. A team of Cuban MDs and medical specialists staffed the facility and offered free care to Jamaicans. The people loved it. Opposition government forces huffed and puffed about it. The point became moot after the election booting Manley out. Along with all the other Cubans in Jamaica, the medical staffers were off the island within 24 hours of the new PM Seaga's announcement of the official end of diplomatic relations with Cuba.

Mostly what you see in Savanna-La-Mar are well-dressed people and uniformed schoolchildren walking along clean streets, with pigs and goats grazing in many middle-class-looking front yards. Part of the reason for this image of prosperity has to do with the Frome Sugar Factory, five miles north of town, which is the main processing factory for the cane grown in the parishes of Hanover and Westmoreland. An estimated 10,000 Jamaicans earn livings directly or indirectly from the local sugar business.

You pass the sugar factory coming or going off the main coast road if you detour to the nearby source of the *Roaring River*, several hundred yards above the *Blue Hole*, near *Petersfield*, in Westmoreland. Situated at the end of a long series of unmarked roads north of Ferris Cross and Savanna-La-Mar, this small blue hole is magical to me, a remote, non-touristy Jamaican swimming hole the color of gem-quality emerald and close to the source of a cooling, fertile riverhead valley rising out of a wide plain of broiling canefields. Respite is possible, so long as you move slowly and stay clear of the midday sun.

Withering heat helps you understand Jamaican precepts, for example, the idea of "soon come." You hear the words everywhere. A rough equivalent is the Americanism, "don't get your shirt wet." Meaning? Stay cool, request in process. Do not

---

The Blue Hole at Roaring River

push and you will get what you want. Eventually.

The property next to the Blue Hole is known as the Ital Herb Farm, growers of organic varieties of Jamaican herbs and spices for the best island restaurants, exporters to Bloomingdale's and US health food stores. The good water and hot sun make them grow.

You have to ask directions to the Blue Hole, but if you can get close to it, anyone you meet will be able to tell you the way. Plan to take left-right directions with a sense of humor. Somehow, the two seem to get confused around here. Schoolbooks are expensive. Illiteracy is roughly 50%. You may have better luck watching the body language of the direction giver. The dips, twists and flapping arms will get you there if you can follow them, even if you cannot quite understand the country-quaint people.

You will certainly understand the sound of Jamaican laughter, and you will hear plenty of it, some, no doubt, directed at you. Lusty extravagance is the order here. A lavish sense of humor comes with Jamaicans' pride and it is the anchor that has secured them through an indifferent and often cruel history, as well as an economy reeling under conditions equivalent to the great depression of the 1930's—lasting for 25 years. Jamaicans have put up with so much for so long that they need to laugh and love pointing out each other's foibles and failings for a chuckle or a knee slapper. If they make fun of you it means they like you. You can feel honored.

You will know you are getting close to the Blue Hole when you pass by the giant silk cotton tree at the stone bridge. A tip-off here will be the swarms of young men and children who will surround a car or travelers. There is a cave here that can be explored, provided you are willing to put up with smoky kerosene soaked torches and the competition among local residents for the right to be your guide. A loose system has been implemented whereby groups of four eager guides work in a prearranged rotation escorting travelers through the caves. The scheme helps to eliminate fights among the boys that used to be a real turn-off to potential visitors, although the mostly verbal tussling was a cherished bit of authentic Jamaica for afficionados of the culture.

A tiny shop run by a soft spoken rasta named "Shaper" sits on the road at the end of the path to the cave entrance. Shaper started out selling cold sodas and snacks to cave visitors. Today, most of his business comes from pin-on coconut shell buttons and earrings that he makes and laminates with photos of reggae stars and other cultural tidbits, one shaped like a guitar, another the shape of the island, with a little map on it. Others are simply tiny coconut shell bars painted with red, green and gold rasta-colored stripes.

Desmond and Devon are two of the best cave guides under the cotton tree. Show them this page. They will take care of you.

The cave is a mile from the Blue Hole, up a skimpy dirt road, rocky and bumpy, a typically lousy country road.

Children will start pouring out of the small houses lining the way as soon as they see a car. By the time you pull up in front of the hand-painted sign for the Lover's Cafe at the Blue Hole Garden, the car will be surrounded once more, this time by smaller kids, the pre-teen and younger bunch, as compared to the older teens and young men at the cave.

It is a quarter-mile farther to the source of the Roaring River, where it bubbles up out of a leafy hillside, irrigating a thick bankside growth of floppy "elephant ear," dasheen leaves, a green spinach-like vegetable cooked in pepperpot soup.

A bright-eyed rasta named Esau runs the Blue Hole Garden with his wife, a French-Canadian born artist named I-Rise. They manage the small restaurant, the Lover's Cafe, along with two bamboo and thatch guest cottages on the river and a couple of rooms in a house perched on poles over the waterhole.

There is a service charge of $15 JA to swim in the Blue Hole and have access to the grounds, which include hiking trails and specialized herb gardens.

The restaurant is a bamboo structure, without window glass, so as you sit eating "ital" veggies and rice cooked without salt or meat, with all but the rice grain grown right here, you can look out over the Blue Hole and the rolling farm country across the valley. Esau's specialty is herbal tea. He mixes various concoctions, depending on the occasion, usually an iced tea, roots wine, or a multi-blend fruit juice. He is well-versed in the healing lore of the rural bush doctors, traditionally the only medical help available to country Jamaicans. "With the right combination of herbs, in the right proportion, and with diet, we can cure anything," he says.

After a drink or something to eat, Esau will show you his herb garden, or around the property. "The first time a white man coming up de road everyone come out behind the car, young, old, everyone," he says. "They thought it was the champion." Today, only the little ones come out to see a car with white men in this poor, remote farming valley. There is not much money for tourism promotion. "Everybody who comes here come on a word a mout' t'ing," according to Esau.

I-Rise paints, and has had shows and exhibits at the respectable Harmony Hall gallery, near Ocho Rios, as well as in Kingston. She will show you paintings, setting them out on the steep hillside, surrounded by rocks and plants, her work in bright Caribbean sea blues and clay earth reds, shining, reflecting a primitive Jamaican style. Or you can swim. The Blue Hole is heavenly, a small piece of paradise on a hot afternoon, a favored spot, visited by few, appreciated and kept virtually secret by those in the know. Local boys, "Jammin'," Wayne, or I-Rise's son Nicholas, will show you around if Esau or I-Rise are not there. Cottage rooms are available for rustic overnighting, or campers are welcome, too, and you can buy dried herbs or spices here, basil, hot peppers, thyme, coriander, lemongrass, for tea, peppermint, lime leaf, or many other organically grown varieties (an increasing rarity in heavily insected, heavily drench-sprayed Jamaica) depending on the season.

NEGRIL

Negril is the ultimate beach for many Jamaican visitors who travel only from the airport in Montego Bay to this one-time

Negril Beach

counter-culture and world class kick-back-'n-groove community.

Negril and environs essentially take up the island's west coast. The beach is seven miles long if you count an uninterrupted 4 1/2 mile stretch and the adjoining nude beach on *Bloody Bay*. Scuba operators line the sands close to the center of town. People snorkeling, fishing and going topless are usual. Total nudity is not uncommon, nor are spliffs the size of medium range weaponry. Mushroom tea is a local favorite, brewed with psilocybin from nearby cow fields. Many visitors rent motorbikes to putter around on, or bikes. In season there is live reggae on the beach most nights, with three or four bands to choose from on weekends.

Around the other side of town, running out to a 100-foot-tall, solar-powered lighthouse, are the west cliffs, 50 to 100 feet high in spots. Sharp limestone rocks face the extreme west coast of the country. The cliffs are less developed than the beach, with smaller resort properties, some quite plush, others with cold water outdoor showers only. Private homes and small guest houses accommodate fewer people than on the beachside.

Despite the lack of beach, swimmers, cliff divers and inflatable raft lovers find the cliffs fine for snorkeling, lobstering in private little coves, exploring sea caves.

Eighteen miles west of Savanna-La-Mar, 52 miles from MoBay, Negril feels nearly as far away from the mainstream as the high Blue Mountains. Until 1965, when the main road was completed, Negril had been isolated from the rest of the country by the 7-mile long, 2-mile wide *Negril* or *Great Morass*. This Morass is still largely unexplored, a mosquito breeding wilderness with fertile ganja islands amid soggy wetlands.

Around the time the road came through, so did the 60's generation, which found an amenable, gorgeous and inexpensive seaside community where they could get high, get naked and still be unnoticed. Tents or hammocks on the beach were and still are adequate housing. Bamboo beach huts are the next step up. Many of the "hippies" stayed in Jamaican homes, throwing down a sleeping bag on an empty bit of floor space. You can do it the same way today, but it will cost a few bucks more.

The beach is seven miles long, so it is hard to pick a best spot. Although there are hotels and cottages on the beach, the public has access to the entire stretch. The cliffs have more private property, but you can always go out to the lighthouse and climb down the stairs along 100-foot cliffs to the sea.

Licensed scuba operators also handle snorkeling, glass bottom boating and windsurfer rentals.

Ziggy's Watersports is at Rick's Cafe, on the west cliffs, Zavier "Ziggy" Chin, operator.

Richard Yesney is a licensed dive operator at *Hedonism II*.

Negril Scuba Centre is at the Negril Beach Club, Karen McCarthy, dive operator. Lessons are available twice daily, along with night dives. Also at Negril Beach Club, a good guy named Vince operates *Aqua Nova Watersports*. He has some of the beach's lowest rates for renting snorkeling gear and windsurfers.

Honey's is on the beach, Vincent "Honey" Gifford, operator.

Blue Whale Divers is on Norman Manley Blvd., offering scuba diving trips, snorkeling, deep sea fishing, river fishing, a sunset cruise and underwater camera rentals. Cecil Lloyd Brown is the certified scuba director.

There are other unlicensed operators in Negril. They may be light on experience, equipment checks, or insurance, for starters. Be careful.

Choice nude sunbathing locations are on the south end of Bloody Bay, at the all-inclusive resort called Hedonism II, funky Roots Bamboo or Firefly, all on the beach. On the cliffs, try X-Tabi, Drumville Cove, Lighthouse Park or Rock House.

The best snorkeling is off the cliffs.

There are beaches all the way back to Mo-Bay. You are never far from a place to swim off the main road, at places named *Orange Bay*, *Davis Cove*, *Cousins Cove*, *Lances Bay*, or *Mosquito Cove.*

"If you look at de' road an' say, 'it steep,' you Jamaican frien' will look at it, ponder a second, an' say, 'it not far.' "—Steve, Blue Mountains hiking guide, Jack's Hill.

CHAPTER FIVE

HIKING & BACKPACKING

The common image of Jamaica usually fails to encompass hiking trails and backpackers in remote country. Partly-clad beach-goers are more in keeping with the collective imagination, but have you ever thought of hiking naked to Blue Mountain Peak? It is generally warm enough. Carry an umbrella and a sun hat. Bugs will not even bug you up that high. And you only need sneakers, not hiking boots.

People walk everywhere in Jamaica, up and down main streets, back roads and rutted country tracks that look like goat trails. In the mountains, hills and coastal shorefronts there are thousands of footpaths. Some are relatively bustling with foot traffic. Others are long overgrown, scenic perhaps, sporting but impractical, or simply too remote to attract much attention.

You can hike for an hour, or a week, through all ranges of challenging terrain. American Peace Corps volunteers have helped keep certain Blue Mountain trails open, including the trail to the Peak, and the Canadian government has granted funds for trail upkeep and improvements. Properties administered by Kingston's Forestry Department have easy trails, some even sporting signposts.

If you really want to explore, sharpen your machete to carve trails through ancient Maroon hunting tracks in the John Crow Mountains, or the Cockpits. If you are up for it, you can hack your way through tangled south coast scrub and cactus, for ten hours daily, for days on end.

Only about 20% of Jamaica is not hilly. Half is forested. You can choose virgin forest tracks or well-worn trails for your hike. Mountain villages dot the relatively accessible south slopes of the Blue Mountains, facing Kingston and serviced by mass transportation. As remote as the area feels, you are never more than a few hours walk from residents who can help a hiker with directions, food, supplies, or a place for a backpacker to pitch a tent.

Certain parts of The Cockpits and the John Crows are virtually unsettled and unexplored. Maps do not exist for these areas. Long disused slave trails, built on Indian tracks in some cases, may be traceable if you are ready for serious arm swinging machete action, working bent over for hours on a hot, insect-infested trail, chopping your way through for the satisfaction of it. Pack your pith helmet and note that bumbershoots carried by smart Jamaican hikers are not dainty parasols but intelligent sun or sudden rain blockers. Function aside, the sight of a hiker wearing sneakers and a hat, and nothing more, beneath an umbrella, cannot help but make you smile.

Hardly anyone knows that there is good hiking within a few miles of Montego Bay, not in the rough Cockpits, either, but along the *Montego River.* The valley offers utterly secluded waterholes for swimming and no tourists anywhere, even though you can hop off a country bus at one end of a trail and back on another that will return you to Mo-Bay when you are through.

The trail system is among many being developed by the Jamaica Alternative Tourism, Camping and Hiking Association (JATCHA), a private marketing group representing more than 4,000 beds in "Alternative Tourism" properties, from high

Blue Mountain lodges, to hammock spaces swinging within easy reach of Negril's coastal hiking trails.

The Camping and Hiking Association lists accommodations that are available island-wide, at reasonable rates. Some are in relatively deluxe bamboo cottages or impressive restored "Great Houses" reflecting the elegance of the typical plantation house of the early sugar years. Others offer sleeping bag and tent rentals. The Association also helps maintain trails and lobbies for environmental protection and official National Park status for wilderness areas. They are an important single source for information, maps, and a reservation service, covering guides, transportation, accommodations, and adventure tours lasting several hours or several weeks. Contact PO BOX 216, Kingston 7, Jamaica, WI, or phone (809) 927-2657.

There may be no better way to get the feel of Jamaica than to walk its hilly roads. Jamaicans move with grace, a certain swing in the hips, a loose waggle in the shoulders, a light but sure hop in the step. When your feet hit these roads you soon *feel* it.

THE BLUE MOUNTAINS

The Blue Mountains are Jamaica's highest peaks, a botanical, scenic, and cultural delight to hikers looking for challenge without danger. The trails are steep and tiring, but never threatening.

The south slope system connects with Kingston. You can get off a plane, take an X97 minibus from the airport to West Parade, then a No. 54 bus to Barbican, at the base of Jack's Hill. A No. 12 bus will carry you to the end of the busline or ask for a minibus to Jack's Hill. If you prefer, you can walk up the three miles with the locals, hitchhike or talk an unregistered cabby into taking you for $25 JA.

Jack's Hill is a central starting point for hikes into the mountains and recommended because it is the location of the Maya Hiking Center. Maya is the home of Peter Bentley, President of SENSE Adventures and Founding Member of JATCHA.

Peter is a leathery-skinned white Jamaican, seemingly made up of equal parts boy scout and pirate. He favors wearing a camouflage bush hat, tattered running shoes and nothing else on hikes, when he can. At the same time he will spin your head with university educated details on Jamaica's flora and fauna as he leads you to one hidden and little known beauty spot after another. In a week or two on the island, Peter can show you places everyday that you would never find on your own during that time. The contacts with outdoor enthusiasts and alternative tourism operators that you can make through him are invaluable for successive trips you may want to make here on your own. You discover what is available on your first trip. Next time you know what you want to focus on.

Maya has a small reference library on hiking, camping and natural history, including country-wide accommodations information and maps. Guides are available here for around $15 US per day. You are expected to buy your guide's food and pay for accommodations. Arrangements can be made through Bentley. This will cost a little more than the friendly and well-meaning freelances you can negotiate with privately on Skyline Drive or Jack's Hill Road. Bentley's tours are better organized, although the group pace can sometimes run roughshod over individual preferences.

Check carefully on the composition of any group of strangers before you sign up for an adventure tour or you may find yourself left stranded taking photos on Blue Mountain trail while your cohorts race off to jump into the next coastal swimming hole. This has happened with Bentley groups. A straggler, losing a pre-paid 4-wheel drive ride down from the high mountains, and with only useless, large American travelers checks and insufficient Jamaican cash to pay for another, was forced to walk an additional eight miles, from *Whitfield Hall* to *Mavis Bank*, then to the nearest bus to *Papine*, finally taking a cab from suburban Kingston back to Maya.

The slow photographer was me. I had spent all my Jamaican dollars on Blue Mountain coffee earlier that day, figuring there would be no need for money at the Peak. The ride down was paid in advance and if you bring food up, as we had, there is nothing to spend money on up there.

On the trail I had stopped several times to take notes and the rest of Bentley's group did not want to wait for me. We separated, with an agreement to be down from the peak at a certain time. Chats with mountain farmers, shooting faces and vistas made me thirty minutes late, after an all-night, ten-hour hike. From the trail I could see the 4-wheel drive pickup, carrying my impatient tour mates, leaving without me. I was too far away for shouts to be heard. Left stranded, I stayed an extra unplanned night and walked out the next morning.

The improvised part of my journey took an additional 24 hours. I never did re-connect with Peter's tour. Sure, I was angry, but honestly, the extra walking time in the mountains introduced me to more of the countryside than I would have experienced from a car. The close glimpse into lifestyles of people living primitively along a populated foot path through the mountains was fascinating. Not having enough money in my pocket to buy a ride put me squarely on the level of hundreds of impoverished Jamaicans I passed and interacted with.

These unexpected changes in plans can be the best part of a trip. One thing I will say for Peter is that he believes in the possibility of magic. He left a note for me at Maya. It said, "Hope you had a good 'adventure.' " He never mentioned the hassles, uncertainties or missed connections, his way of helping teach me to see that the steep road be not far.

An advantage of working with Peter is that the JATCHA phone is in his house, and you can also get information on his tours from US tour bookers Sobek, Inc., Mountain Travel. He is the only mountain tour operator who can supply you with brochures and maps in advance. He charges $15 US for a customized information and reservation packet.

Once you reach Jamaica, any number of the freelances can be entertaining and proficient guides. Steve, Bucky, "Sweet Pea," and Denny are among young Jack's Hill guides who work for Peter. Some of the older men work on their own. Of these, two of the best guides and most entertaining companions are Leonard "Baps" Cole or Ken Moulton. Any Jack's Hill

---

Baps and Ken, Jack's Hill

resident can find them for you or you can write Baps at Rasta Perch, Jack's Hill P.O., Jamaica, WI.

Baps also accommodates campers at his home at Rasta Perch. It is exactly that, a perch, on a lush forest and garden-covered hillside. You reach his tiny shack by hiking a narrow trail off Jack's Hill Road for half a mile. Baps likes to sit in the doorless entrance, whistling on a bamboo flute as night settles over the hills, high notes floating over the ridges and valleys, neighbors' chatter drifting in, cooking fires glowing on adjacent slopes. In time the present disappears completely. You are sitting in the dark room, bare except for two mattresses on the floor, a flickering candle the only inside light. Baps, propped in the doorway, lifts a conch shell horn to his lips, pale moonlight casting a glow on his aboriginal silhouette and the ancient sea horn. The sound comes out as if from far away. If you let yourself go, the hollow wail calls you back to a slave shack, an Arawak fishing village or a Mandingo hut.

Maya Lodge and Sanctuary, situated on 15 garden- and fruit-covered acres bordered on two sides by streams at 2,000 feet, is also a hostel and guest house with a cafe. Tent campers can set up on level spaces on the shady grounds. You can cook your own meals in the kitchen for $2 US daily. Bring your own food from Kingston, or be willing to take your chances on what is on hand at Maya, or from Jack's Hill residents, which is likely to be modest rice and vegetables, if you have not made prior arrangements.

A lot of local people come and go through Maya. Something is always going on. The radio stays on 24 hours a day, playing near constant reggae broken only by BBC News. If you do not mind the noise, it is a good place for casual lessons in the conduct of people living in the "other" Jamaica, as well as for establishing a convenient mountain base, then making further plans from there. Harbor sunsets and Kingston night lights are particularly memorable from Skyline Drive, or climb the Jack's Hill water tower for a better view.

The Blue Mountain trail network branches off from Jack's Hill, *Mavis Bank*, *Guava Ridge* or the Pine Grove Chalets, a coffee plantation with the nicest Blue Mountain guest rooms and a good restaurant. You can start at any of these locations

Blue Mountain guide, Steve, at top of Blue Mountain peak

to reach Blue Mountain Peak and many other mountain trails pass through these spots.

Pine Grove is another good possibility for a mountain base near Kingston. It is more deluxe than Maya, with 360 degree mountain views, making it seem almost like a high tropical lamasery, but it is not as well set-up as a hiking center for distributing maps and information. Convenient mini-buses drive by Pine Grove on the road to *Content Gap* from Mavis Bank and Papine, and you can arrange for a plantation Landrover to drive you from the coffee farm to Whitfield Hall, another guest house at the base of the Peak trail.

For determined do-it-yourselfers, the best and only detailed trail guide to the Blue Mountains is called *A Hiker's Guide to the Blue Mountains*, by Bill Wilcox (Peace Corps Volunteer). The 1985 booklet is available through the Maya Hiking Center, or JATCHA, and Bentley sends a copy along in the info packet you get for $15. It covers long hikes, as well as short two-hour ones, such as from Jack's Hill to *Peter's Rock*, a good walk to get you used to the Jamaican mountain terrain, coastal views, numerous birds and a typical lung bursting finish, up a steep ridge, to Peter's Rock. If you are there in the right season (April-September), grab some mangoes on the way, or at least take in the shade beneath their branches.

From Peter's Rock, another two-hour hike, much of it along a dirt road, leads to Hollywell National Recreation Park. There are three cabins there, equipped with beds, stoves, fireplaces and refrigerators. Each cabin has four beds. Cabin rentals are in the range of $28 JA nightly (subject to change). Tent camping is permitted, if you pay the cabin rental first. Visit the Forestry Department at 173 Constant Spring Rd., Kingston to book a cabin, or phone 924-2667 for information. You must pick up your cabin reservation in person, in Kingston, so plan to take care of this matter before you reach the mountains, or arrange for Bentley or another Jamaican friend to help you out. Weekend reservations should be booked well in advance, as should Jamaican holiday periods. The rest of the time you can usually have the cabins, most of the park and nearby trails to yourself.

Near the entrance to Hollywell, at 4,000 feet, you can look down on the dipping and swelling contours of coffee plantations with bushes braided around receding hillsides. On one side lies the north coast. Other vistas reveal Kingston.

There are picnic tables at Hollywell and numerous trails, some marked by small signs, others overgrown. Several routes will lead you on short hikes to the *Wag Water River*, where you can swim, or up to *Oatley Mountain*, for more mountain vistas.

Another lengthy trail leads from Hollywell through *Hardwar Gap* to the north coast's *Buff Bay*, or you can follow it southward back toward Kingston via *Newcastle*, a military training ground for the Jamaica Defence Force.

The *Fairy Glades Trail* to Newcastle takes you through a variety of ecosystems. Tropical montane mist forest, composed of trees, shrubs, herbs, climbers and epiphytes growing on the surface of other plants, gives way at higher altitude to rare elfin woodland, characterized by stunted vegetation. The misty woods threaten to overtake cultivated coffee, bananas and citrus trees. Slender Caribbean pines brush clouds. Tree ferns, 35-footers, look like Kong-size house plants. Hundreds of other varieties of ferns thrive in the humid range, along with orchids, while songbirds and butterflies replace low-land insects. Newcastle itself was originally established as a refuge for resident British soldiers who were dying of mosquito-borne yellow fever at an alarmingly impractical rate in seacoast forts.

A montane rain forest covering the steep slopes of Mount Horeb in the vicinity of Hardwar Gap is thought to be "one of the most diverse ecosystems remaining in Jamaica," according to *A Hiker's Guide*. The road between Hollywell and Newcastle covers three miles of equally stunning tropical highland scenery. Look for miniature orchids, filmy ferns, lacy mosses.

The Old Stables Inn, a small shop above Newcastle, is a starting point for a number of trails. Walking down to it from Hollywell you have a choice of trails near *Woodcutter's Gap*. The fork to the right will take you to a paved road that will lead you in about one hour to *Catherine's Peak*, at 5056 feet, one of the highest in the Blues. A hard right will take you down to the 150-year-old stable. Rides back to Kingston are available in this area, either with private vehicles or buses.

The *Fern Walk Trail* and the trail to Catherine's Peak begin at the Old Stables. Both are easy, pretty and of special interest to birdwatchers and botanists for the plant and flower species found in this area and nowhere else in Jamaica—among them Spanish needle, Asian honeysuckle and Jamaica roses with their hanging red flowers. Throughout the Blue Mountains, as you reach higher levels, characteristic plant life is unique to these elevations.

Other tracks starting above Newcastle include the *Green Hills Trail*, which crosses the Kingston-Buff Bay Road above Hollywell and the *Silver Hill Gap Trail*. The Tuck Shop at the Newcastle parade grounds is a small food shop, selling cold drinks, cocoa buns and bullas (Jamaican snack pastries), hard dough bread and other snacks. It is one of the last places for stocking up, so if you are going higher, do any last minute provisioning here.

Silver Hill Trail will take you south through *Content Gap*, and down to *Guava Ridge*. You can stop in nearby *Gordon*

Fern Walk Trail, Blue Mountains

Town at Ian Sangster's "World's End." It is a distillery where they make "Old Jamaica" liqueurs. Free samples. Phone 926-8888.

Guava Ridge is where you meet the road to *Mavis Bank* and Kingston. Traveling north on the trail you meet a crossroads at *Silver Hill Gap*. The spot is within a few miles of *Clydesdale*, an old coffee plantation at 3700 feet, now another forestry preserve, with dorm accommodations and camping. If you take the Buff Bay Road to the *District of Section*, a stop is called for at the home of one grower of the finest coffee in the world.

James Dennis is typical of mountain smallholders. He lives on and farms three acres on a sunny southern slope of the Blue Mountains. His face shows its 55 years, although his wiry body looks many years younger. Today he works alongside his growing sons and daughters, planting, caring for, harvesting, curing and roasting those special beans that people all over the world are willing to pay dearly for.

Dennis harvests year-round, but unlike most coffee farmers, he prefers not to sell his beans to the big central coffee processing factories, such as the one at Mavis Bank. Instead, he sticks to old fashioned methods, picking ripe beans by hand, drying them on bamboo racks in the sun, then curing them by a special process that experts believe is what makes his beans special. He roasts coffee over a smoky wood fire in a dark, crooked, creosote-stained little shack on a Jamaica hillside, then sells it to visitors for half the price of the factory processed stuff.

You get your choice of whole beans weighed and wrapped neatly in plastic bags, or ground coffee that Dennis or one of the boys pounds to smithereens by straddling a hollowed log filled with whole beans. Grinding is accomplished by striking short but powerful blows with a stout hardwood branch, stubby on one end, with a tapered handle.

As soon as you enter Dennis's frame shack domain you are handed a cup of piping hot coffee. The scent of the place alone is like Summa Cum Coffee, the best of the best and overwhelming, especially considering where you are, in the heart of a virtual wilderness. There are always people hanging around Dennis's, sitting on a stone wall alongside the road, wandering in and out of his house next door, returning from the fields. The coffee is always brewed strong. It hits with ringing potency, what one might imagine it would feel like mainlining caffeine.

Backpackers may not want to carry the extra weight of pounds of cafe Dennis, but anyone else with the habit and a car to stash the beans in would do well to stock up on coffee here. There is one place for less expensive beans, but no place for better tasting ones.

Section is right in the middle of the rocky, hilly, bumpy and potholed five-miles-per-hour, Kingston-Buff Bay Road. If you have time and strong kidneys this is the most scenic north-south coast-to-coast road through the Blue Mountains. Roads in Jamaica are often jarring, always slow, with frequent curves, and the roads through the Blue Mountains are among the worst, very narrow, especially winding, one-lane only, no shoulders, and with little side clearance from unseen jutting

rocks or foliage-obscured branches. It gets extra tricky when it rains, but the road is passable, even when wet, in a decent front-wheel drive car, such as many of the island rental car companies can provide. Ask for one. Make sure the windshield wipers work.

You can pitch your tent in Dennis's yard for a few dollars, or push on up the road to Clydesdale. Make advance reservations for the dorm space there, or the single available cabin, with the Forestry Department in Kingston.

Instead of taking the Buff Bay Road from the Silver Hill Trail to Dennis's in Section, you can take the *Silver Hill Road* to Mr. Joseph Wolfe's farm and store at *Chestervale Bridge*, on the *Brook's River*. Wolfe is in his mid-60's, bald on top, but with long trailing dreadlocks and a curly gray beard tipped in sun-bleached red. He is a gentle-souled, opinionated rasta who alternately speaks scandalously or on religion, all the while selling fruits he grows and eggs from his free-running chickens, along with bananas and bullas. Wolfe also offers the least expensive Jamaican Blue Mountain Coffee that you are likely to find anywhere. Dennis sells for half the best commercial rate. Wolfe undercuts Dennis by half, sometimes offering the genuine stuff for under $2 US, or $10 JA per pound. Wolfe does not, however, put his beans through the extra curing step that Dennis swears by. His beans are good, but not as good as Dennis's.

Clydesdale is easily reached from Dennis's or Mr. Wolfe's, by trails or a road. It is set in an especially beautiful wilderness area with a high canopy of mahogany, mahoe, eucalyptus and Caribbean pine among the tall trees and thick timber of a steep-sided, lush, green outdoor palace. Several stone and heavy timber constructed buildings are on the property, along with remnants of an old slave-constructed aqueduct that once carried water to a now aged waterwheel, all overgrown with vines, but visible reminders of the busy coffee property this once was. Some of the attendants who live at the park grow coffee, but on a much smaller scale.

James Dennis, Blue Mountain coffee farmer

Below the waterwheel is a small waterfall and a pool that is a perfect spot for a picnic and a swim, in the nude if you like. Water gushes through a crack in the rock outcrops. The falls tumble over. You plunge in, cool mountain water washing off road dust, the towering forest enclosing you, birds singing, you wearing nothing but a smile.

An hour's walk from Clydesdale is the *Cinchona Botanical Gardens*, situated on a high ridge at 5,000 feet. You can hike on a road that is really too far gone for all but the bravest drivers and strongest vehicles. The ruts are big enough to trap a tire and hang up the frame of a car lacking exceptional ground clearance. In several spots passengers should be prepared to get out and push. I have seen a fearless rasta driver, a man who smokes his first spliff before he gets out of bed in the morning, actually say no to an offered smoke while he was trying to negotiate this road. Not only is it cratered, it is steep. A vehicle goes so slowly that while you are out pushing it is easy to imagine the vehicle flipping over on you or slipping backwards. But it is a splendid walk.

It is around two and a half miles from Clydesdale to Cinchona. There is another trail up to the gardens, starting farther down the road at *Top Mountain* and six other trails terminate at Cinchona.

If you plan ahead, the caretaker of the gardens will drive down to meet you in a sturdy Landrover that has proven itself on the road.

The gardens were devastated by Hurricane Allen in 1980, closed for years before that. The government is rebuilding, and there are even signs of construction equipment, but they have a long way to go. Eventually, the property will include guest cottages. And one hopes a new road.

Cinchona was established in 1874, one of three such places in Jamaica, along with Castleton and Hope Gardens, for the collection and study of plants and trees. The more than 100-year-old collection contains flora from every continent. These include Chinese Masson's pine, tea bush and weeping cypress, sacred Japanese sugi and Himalayan rhododendrons. Cinchona has the largest collection of Eucalyptus trees in the Caribbean, featuring two dozen varieties, some towering 150 feet tall.

Australia has contributed many trees, eucalyptus, blue mimosa and wild coffee among them. African yaccas and Canary Island pines, South Pacific Norfolk Island pines, South American rubber trees, North American pecans, Greek cypress, Indian oleander and many others share space with the Caribbean cinchona, a source of quinine, the Blue Mountain soap wood, billberry and woman wood, among other indigenous West Indian trees.

Azaleas, African agapanthus lillies, hydrangeas, dahlias, calla lillies, and orchids color this formal English garden high in the Blue Mountains with distinctive Caribbean highlights, all crowning the cloud-scraped views from the Grand Ridge of the Blue Mountains to Kingston Harbor.

The property today is reduced to thirty acres, without electricity, and including several old historic buildings in need of repair. The quiet and distance from "no problem" Jamaica, in the formal garden setting on the tall wilderness ridge, make Cinchona peaceful, almost otherworldly. The air is always cool, with at least a hint of breeze, the damp air sweet as honey with blooming scents. Compared to downtown Kingston, it is almost as if you had landed on another planet. Highly recommended, but walk, do not drive until the road is repaired.

From Cinchona you can hike down to *Westphalia* and across the *Green River* to *Penlyne Castle*, and from there to Whitfield Hall, the highest attended mountain accommodations and the best point of departure to the Peak. If you are driving from Clydesdale, you would follow the road down to Mavis Bank, where you would have to ford the *Yallahs River* at *Mahogany Vale*.

The road takes you through *Hagley Gap*, where there is a small store and rum shop, with cold drinks available. Jungle foliage partly obscures red, green and yellow rasta-painted houses with crooked tin roofs. Uniformed schoolchildren and raggedly dressed mountain people stare quietly at visitors. People wash cattle in roadside public taps.

There are very few cars up here in this land that would qualify as wilderness in any league. The steep mountains are packed with smallholdings. Bananas are planted strategically to shade the important coffee. The bad road gets worse higher up. It washes out in the heavy Blue Mountain rains, leaving serious gullies. Four-wheel drive or high ground clearance are necessary. If you bottom out and rip the oil pan off your rental car you will have a long walk back to a phone.

The eight-mile uphill walk from Mavis Bank to Whitfield Hall is a strenuous one that can easily take four hours. Unless you are able to make arrangements with a local resident for a place to stay, your best bet will be Whitfield, at the end of the road for motorized vehicles, at 4200 feet. The rustic guest house has five rooms and a loft, and tent campers are welcome outside beneath eucalyptus and citrus trees.

The cool air smells tangy at Whitfield. The scent of coffee is always in the air, along with fragrant flowers, and at night there are Caribbean hardwood fires burning. You get a bed and sheets at the guest house, but bring your own toilet paper. You can use the kitchen, but must bring your own food. Coffee is usually available by the pound or cup. This is the traditional starting point for the climb to the Peak, seven more miles up to 7402 feet.

If you are in good shape the hike from Whitfield should take three to three and a half hours. If you are in less than good shape, or stop to smoke a few spliffs on the way, or both, count on four to five hours.

It is common to see groggy hikers blindly wandering around Whitfield Hall at 2 AM after a short night's sleep. Usually by the time people reach the hostel, after a hike or uncomfortable ride, they barely have energy to prepare a small meal and tumble into bed. The 100-year-old guest house itself is interesting, with an antique pump organ that emits mordant wheezing tones, and stacks of yellowing guest books containing comments on the Blue Mountain hike by people from all over the world. You can leaf through some by the light of a

---

Blue Mountain wilderness

hissing kerosene "Tilley" lamp, the only nighttime illumination up here, other than candlelight.

Arrangements for a mule or horse to carry you to the Peak can be made at Whitfield, or down the road from there at the village of *Penlyne Castle*. If this is the way you choose to go, an animal and guide who comes along with it will cost around $20 US, and they will be waiting for you when you crawl out of bed in the middle of the night to begin the ascent. Ask for Sonny.

The peak trek is not a mountain climbing expedition by any means, but rather a steep hike covering a 3,000 foot gain in elevation in seven miles. Children can make it, along with the moderately fit. You need a flashlight and a warm jacket that you will peel off after a few hours. Hiking boots are unnecessary. Sneakers are adequate, and a poncho is a good idea. Getting out of bed at 1:30 AM is tricky, but not so bad once you are up, then you just guzzle some Blue Mountain and go.

The trail starts up half a mile from the dirt road that runs by Whitfield. A quick series of steep pitches and switchbacks provides startling views of Kingston's lights and scattered villages far below. In darkness you march through the cloud forest, up the rocky trail for two and a half miles to *Portland Gap*, site of a Forest Service cabin and a water tap.

Ridge after ridge unfolds from Portland Gap to the sea. Some hikers prefer to stay here overnight to make an easier two-day climb to the peak. The cabin must be reserved in Kingston, as must a similar cabin at the Peak.

Beyond Portland Gap the trail becomes steeper and more tightly closed in by the fern-draped tropical forest. You cannot see much of it at night, but on your way down in daylight you realize the surrounding tree cover is nearly impenetrable. Dead trees lean on live ones struggling upward to the sunlight, held tight by enormous vines. Competing ferns reach skyward, while crusty mosses cling to rocks or tree trunks. The higher you go the smaller the vegetation becomes, turning dwarf-like by the Peak, with pale blue, purple or tiny white flowers delicately coloring thickets of leathery and hairy plants.

The three and a half miles from Portland Gap to the Peak

are the steepest and most rugged. Seven minutes from the top a spot called "Lazy Man's Peak" is an especially steep, fern-encrusted slope that often is badly washed out by rains. Tired hikers sometimes want to turn back here, but those who continue are usually rewarded for the effort. Long views periodically open up along the trail, then, closer to daylight, the invisible forest comes out of the dark. At the Peak, if it is not socked in by mists, Jamaica awakens below you. There are shrunken and scrubby little trees up here and you can see lower peaks popping out of clouds.

Adjacent mountain tops are more dome-like than peaked. *High*, *Middle* and *East Peaks* are accessible by trail hikes from the top of Blue Mountain.

There are two graffiti-covered structures at the Peak, a bare, four-walled cabin and a caretaker's shack, both usually empty. Sadly, there are also piles of garbage up here, empty cigarette wrappers, bottles and cans. It sure would be nice if everyone who climbed to the Peak carried a little of the trash down with them.

On clear mornings, which are most likely from November to April and July to September, the north and south coasts are visible. Port Antonio's twin harbors appear in the hazy distance, 7400 feet below you and on the clearest days Cuba is visible 90 miles across the sea. A Jamaica sunrise is a colorful capper to the hike. Sunsets are equally inspirational.

On the way down, in daylight, you see everything you came through in darkness. Lush changing shadows of green hills ripple across the hillsides as the sun peeks in and out of moving clouds, many of them below you. Off the trail, the forest appears to be an impenetrable tangle of mossy jungle.

Below the high dense growth, farmers cling to impossibly steep hillside gardens, working on carrots, scallions, yams, onions and thyme. No one owns the land they farm. These are Blue Mountain squatters, far enough away from the mainstream to be left alone to grow their vegetables for Kingston's markets. These local farmers are a possible source of food should you forget or run out. You can usually buy enough from them to create a simple vegetarian meal, something you may be very happy to have back at Whitfield Hall, as soon as you kick off your shoes and get off your tired feet.

Here are some ideas for combining hikes to give you several days in the Blue Mountains above Kingston:

Day 1: Jack's Hill to Hollywell, where you spend the night.

Day 2: Hollywell to Clydesdale.

Day 3: Clydesdale to Cinchona to Whitfield Hall.

Day 4: Whitfield Hall to Blue Mountain Peak and return to Whitfield.

Day 5: Whitfield Hall to Mavis Bank to Jack's Hill.

Approximate times for certain hikes are:

Jack's Hill to Papine (Kingston), one hour (downhill).

Jack's Hill to Mavis Bank, five hours.

Jack's Hill to Hollywell, three to four hours.

Jack's Hill to Dennis's at Section, four hours.

Jack's Hill to Mr. Wolfe's, six hours.

Mavis Bank to Whitfield Hall, four and a half hours.

Jack's Hill to Blue Mountain Peak, ten and a half hours (the record set by four Jack's HIll guides for the thirty-five mile trek. They made only one twenty-minute stop to eat.)

As a general rule, allow at least twice as much time to travel uphill as down.

There are hundreds, if not thousands of other trails through the mountains and there is a proposal for a United Nations grant to complete a main trail along the *Grand Ridge of the Blue Mountains*, similar to New Zealand's Milford Track. This would make possible several days of continuous hiking, with sleeping huts or other accommodations along the way.

The western section of the trail is already open, with access points at Jack's Hill and Mavis Bank for the official starting point at Hollywell. The trail continues up Catherine's Peak to Clydesdale, Cinchona, *Morces Gap*, *Mossman's Peak* and Portland Gap to Blue Mountain Peak. Accommodations are in place for this portion.

The incomplete part of the trail would extend eastward to meet the *John Crow Mountains* at *Corn Puss Gap*, a distance of 15—20 miles, with access points at Corn Puss Gap, *Bath* and *Millbank*, deep in the heights of the John Crows and the Upper Rio Grande valley. Proposed accommodations through these areas would be simple cabins, similar to ones at Portland Gap or Blue Mountain Peak.

The Vinegar Hill Trail crosses the Blue Mountains from north to south starting from *Chepstow*, near *Buff Bay*. It traverses *Vinegar Hill*, then goes through Morces Gap, Cinchona, Catherine's Peak, Hollywell, Jack's Hill, and on into Kingston. This is an old trading route and the only high trail over the mountains connecting the north and south coasts.

JOHN CROW MOUNTAINS

There is a large wilderness area on the north side of the Blue Mountains which encompasses the John Crow Mountains to the east. Some trails are open. Most are overgrown. For example, it would take at least three days to hike from the Grand Ridge of the Blue Mountains to Port Antonio, hacking with a machete a good portion of the way, for up to ten hours daily, and definitely traveling with a guide who knows the area well.

There is a rugged trail near the east coast, starting at *Bath Fountain* (a mineral spa detailed in a later chapter), north of Morant Bay. The track takes you through a thick forest, across Corn Puss Gap, to Millbank, in Portland, about twenty miles south of Port Antonio. This is a minimum six-hour trek for the fit and healthy through Jamaica's last remaining rain forest.

Parts of the trail pitch down river banks into streams that must be forded, and which can be waist deep, or higher. It is a laborious fourteen miles through some of Jamaica's most incredibly untouched tropical scenery populated only by birds and butterflies, and decorated with orchids and ferns.

The rain forest is impassable after heavy downpours, which are frequent. An easier trail skirting around the overgrowth, affording more distant views of it rather than a path through the heart of it, starts at *Bath Village*, to *Hayfield*, *Cuna-Cuna Pass* and on to Millbank.

Another difficult John Crow trail leads from *Windsor*, in Portland, through more wet forests to *Nanny Town*, named after the Jamaican National Heroine and said to be inhabited by "duppies," a patois term for ghosts. Nanny and her Maroon followers used the remote trail to reach their hidden stronghold, from where they resisted slavery and British Colonialism. Carry a machete for this hike through parts of Jamaica's most rugged bush.

The Blue Mountains and the John Crow Mountains offer the best mountain hiking in Jamaica. The rest of the island also has good coastal and hill trails.

MANCHIONEAL to PRIESTMAN'S RIVER

The coastal wildlands on the eastern shore offer varied seacoasts of white sand beaches protected by small hills and rocky outcrops. Nearby is a main road, which means towns, food shops and supplies are available. Flag down a fishing boat for fresh catch to cook on the beach, or continue on to Boston Bay for jerk pork.

MORANT POINT

The lighthouse at the farthest eastern point of Jamaica is surrounded on one side by swampy lowlands, by the sea on the other. It is a dramatic, windswept coastal landscape where you will probably find no one. Great bird watching and good coastal hiking out here for those who enjoy being on their own. Plan accordingly for food, water and transportation.

HELLSHIRE HILLS

Close to Kingston, these limestone hills are best known for white sand beaches, not hiking trails, which is a distinct advantage to privacy-seeking hikers. You will meet few people out this way along the coastal headlands. The northern hills contain trails through a natural open-space wilderness area composed of an almost desert-like dry tropical forest. The region is spiked with cactus and thorny shrubs, the limestone terrain holding little fresh water.

Despite its proximity to urban Kingston and its close to one million population, Hellshire remains home to native plants and rare shore birds. There are no developments inland from the public beaches, no food or shelter, nor roads. You are never far from a beach, though, so you can always head down to the coast for a cooling dip in the sea. Deserted coastal hiking along many miles of beachfront is exceptional, although hot, and with no access to services it may be wise to plan a simple round-trip hike taking you in and out of the area in a day. If the heat does not slow you down you can make excellent time through here, covering many more miles in a day than, for example, in the Blue Mountains.

You could conceivably hike along the south coast from Hellshire all the way to Treasure Beach, or farther. The trails are rough and unmarked, services few and far between. The coastal plains and beaches are lightly populated.

TREASURE BEACH

From the Treasure Beach Hotel you can hike east or west along empty shorelines of coral cliffs and low rocky outcrops leading to miles of empty beaches. As far as trails go, there are not really any here, other than fisherman's tracks leading down to the sea. Away from the fisherman's beaches, there are few people or villages for many miles. The beaches have soft white sand and the part-rocky shoreline makes hiking interesting. Wear shoes. The coral outcrops can be very sharp. You may bump into a few loner-type fishermen out here, but few others. A great area for secluded day hikes out of Treasure Beach.

An easy hike south and east from the Treasure Beach Hotel will take you to the *Great Pedro Pond*, outside *Calabash Bay*.

North and west of Treasure Beach there are trails through the *Black River Morass* wetlands, as well as around the *Great Salt Pond* and the *Wallywash Pond*, Jamaica's largest body of fresh water. These areas are good for observing shore birds and

wetlands habitats. That means plenty of insects buzzing through here, so carry a reliable insect repellent and use it. Some of the insects attack flesh and leave you scratching till you bleed, with the nasty itching plaguing you for many days.

COCKPIT COUNTRY

North of Treasure Beach are the *Cockpits*, the Karst limestone region of steep hills and sinkholes. This is one of the few places in the Western Hemisphere where you can find this sort of topography that has been likened to an enormous egg carton. It is virtually unsettled, inaccessible to motorized traffic and challenging to hearty hikers.

Sharp limestone boulders are craggy and brittle. Steep honeycombed limestone hills drop precipitously into depressions 400-500 feet deep. Climbing up these near vertical hills is not unlike working your way up a razor-sharp ladder. The only way across some of the ravines is by fallen tree bridges. It is easy to turn an ankle or break a leg.

Certain valley bottom vegetation has been altered through tree cutting, primarily for charcoal production. Hilltops are, however, largely virgin landscapes. Naturalists can find trees such as broadleaf, mahogany, silk cotton, mahoe and Santa Maria growing to sixty feet high. Little trees, shrubs, orchids, ferns, mosses and lichens contribute to the ground tangle below. Bromeliads, called "wild pine," hold a pint of water, which can be extracted in an emergency. Plant species found growing on one hill will be absent from a neighboring hilltop. Growth at the bottom of hills will differ considerably from top growth.

No roads cross the Cockpits. The Kingston-Montego Bay cross-country train line diverts around the edge, only touching the Karst scenery between *Cambridge* and *Maggotty*.

Soil washes down from the Cockpit hilltops when it rains, so there is comparatively little growing up there, although some dirt manages to cling to cracks in the limestone cap and hearty plants grow horizontally out of the hollows. Sinkhole depressions are filled with mineral-laden soil and this is where the thick and practically impenetrable ground cover lives. Southern exposed hilltops sport one variety of palm, while at the shaded foot of the same slope the palms are another variety altogether.

Trails through the Cockpits are unmarked and hard-to-follow stony tracks, often covered in leaves and mud. Travel is slow over uneven ground and thick, thorny vegetation. Big rocks are wrapped with vines and roots. It is easy to slip on crumbly stone that breaks underfoot or on wet leaves. There is no one out here to help you if you get lost or hurt in a fall. Engaging the services of a guide is highly recommended, and if you travel without one, do not travel alone.

Early and late in the day mists float near the inverted Cockpit cones, swirling around the jagged rock outcrops and giving the place a smoky, sinister appearance. You hear constant dripping of rain water from the thick forest cover, although drinking water is scarce or non-existent. The region looks uninhabitable by any other than plant life, but you can also hear grasshoppers, crickets and cicadas. Parrots, red-crested woodpeckers, partridges, hawks, crows and hummingbirds of many varieties flit through the trees.

Take two to three quarts of water, per person, per day, with you. It gets hot during the day and rough going through the snag-and-bramble-covered ground saps your energy quickly. Catching drips from stalactites in caves is a possibility for finding water in an emergency.

Watch out for scratchbush, a green plant with serrated leaves. If you rub against it you will be itching for weeks. Ants and mosquitoes can be extremely bothersome. This is their heartland. Carrying insect repellent is essential. At least there are no snakes or reptiles to contend with.

Sneakers are adequate footwear. Take special care to watch where you are going to prevent falls into deep, leaf-covered holes. You really do not want to get hurt in here, miles from help.

The Cockpits range to 3,000 feet high, which means it can get cold at night. Be prepared for that with warm clothes. Cooler winter months are the best for traveling through here, as there is likely to be more water available.

If all goes well hiking the Cockpits, you can expect to cover a mile in an hour. It is not all machete-wielding territory, but some is and hiking high, winding paths onto mountainous cones, leading down into steep ravines and then up again takes a lot of time. Views over silent valleys and misty hills untouched by man give you a sense of pre-history and a special feeling of being alone that may, for some adventurers, be good reasons for hiking through here.

The best trails for self-guided trips are from *Quickstep* to *Deeside*, or from *Troy* to *Crown's Land* and on to *Windsor Cave.*

Guided access to the Cockpits can be arranged by Peter Bentley. He takes trips overland east of Montego Bay, marching through *Maroon Town*, and *Trelawny* parish, working through to the *Windsor Caves* and then north to the upper reaches of the *Martha Brae River* and *Falmouth.* Bentley's trips include transportation drop-off and pick-up at the end of the trail. It is a fourteen-hour hike and recommended only for the strong and exceptionally curious.

Another way to hike into the Cockpits is from behind the *Blue Hole at Roaring River.* Esau, who runs the Lover's Cafe, has lived there all his life and is an experienced guide.

NEGRIL

There is good coastal hiking here, although not of the most secluded sort. You can wander the seven-mile beach or follow tracks off the main road along the west cliffs. Inland trails lead to the *Negril Morass*, so bring your insect repellent if you head that way.

MONTEGO RIVER

Few people are aware of the number of trails that are open in this area east of Montego Bay. The best trails originate at Sign Great House. These lead through low hills and in and out of streams, with good spots for swimming, such as the Old Bridge, also known as the Dam. There are few houses back in this river-carved jungle, not many people, and the water is deep enough below the bridge remains for diving or even flips. Locals raise African perch and snook in the Barty River, which feeds into the Montego River near the *Upton Spring Pumping Station*, a hydroelectric plant. Girls and women wash clothes in the river while boys dive off the rocks.

Albert James operates machinery at Upton Spring. He does not see many travelers. "Don't get old," he told me, staring intently into my eyes, "just be cool. The Lord bless you, the love keeps you. You know Jimmy Swaggart?"

Watch out for scratchy plants, ticks and bugs.

Keep the love and walk good.

"... Oh, Mon, de river, she bad, BAD."—
Villager on the shore of the Great River, watching intrepid canoeists putting in for a first descent, 1983.

CHAPTER SIX

RIVER CANOEING & WHITEWATER

River canoeing came to Jamaica only recently, in 1983, when a team organized by California's Sobek Expeditions, one of the world's largest adventure tour operators, hooked up with JAT-CHA and expert canoeist Peter Bentley to scout the country's twelve major year-round rivers and 120 smaller ones. This was the first time that inflatable canoes were used here and the added flexibility enabled the explorers to travel on rivers that were previously thought to be unnavigable in dug-out or hard shell canoes.

The first trip traveled down the *Rio Grande* in Portland, a popular river on its calm lower stretches for bamboo rafting. Successive trips explored the *Great River Gorge*, southwest of Montego Bay, and subsequent trips have found numerous canoeable waterways. The catch is that all the rivers that are navigable are only so at certain times, depending on weather conditions that can change rapidly. It is possible to plan a river canoeing trip in advance, but you must be flexible as to which particular rivers you will be traveling on, and from which put-in points, with final decisions held up until you reach Jamaica.

As of now, Peter Bentley is the only Jamaican tour operator with specific knowledge of Jamaica's canoeable rivers. He has inflatable "Sea Eagles," made of a durable material that withstands the abuse of sharp rocks in Jamaica's sometimes very shallow waterways, and the shallow draft of the canoes makes them far more functionally maneuverable than hard-shell vessels.

The rivers themselves range from meandering flows to Class 5 whitewater, depending on conditions. Scenery varies from thick, tropical forest, as on the Rio Grande, to swampy lowlands, such as on the *Cabarita River*, near the south coast, north of Savanna-la-Mar. You can float gently, lying on your back, looking up at the trees and sky on the gentler rivers. At other times you will have to paddle furiously through whitewater rapids to stay afloat.

The most likely to be canoeable rivers are the following:

The Great River—The mouth of the Great River is just twelve miles from Montego Bay. This is the valley that the cross-country train follows to the edge of the Cockpits. The gorge is a nine-mile stretch that starts in a wilderness area few trav-

Watering cattle

elers know of. It winds through sharp-sided cliffs, under dense foliage, reaching the coast near the small town of *Unity Hall.*

There is a popular tourist attraction known as "An Evening on the Great River." This includes a short boat ride, dinner and a "native" show.

River canoeing here is a different experience altogether.

Nine miles up-river is a stone bridge at the village of *Lethe.* It is twenty-five feet above the river. Local people will tell you that in rough weather the river has risen over the bridge.

The first five miles down from Lethe are usually calm. If there has not been recent rain the water will be clear, reflecting blues and greens from the sky and trees above. Huge ferns and elephantine versions of northern house plants shade the cool gorge, with vertical rock walls rising dramatically out of the river. At several points there are modest Class 2 and 3 rapids, just rough enough to rouse you from a forest reverie to paddle through them, bouncing harmlessly off sharp rocks in an inflatable, something that would be impossible in a hard-shell craft.

There are numerous shady spots on the banks for a picnic, calm river pools for swimming, and few people living along this stretch. Jamaicans tend to come down to the river to do wash, bathe or swim. Few people live on the rivers. This is a good place to take off your clothes and try "canuding."

Half-way to the sea the river carves around a sharp right-angle turn and changes character dramatically. The lower half of the run consists of a string of as many as seventeen Class 4 and 5 whitewater rapids, depending on conditions.

This part of the river should be scouted in advance, from land, unless you prefer a dunking. There are ways through the whitewater, but without planning for them you are likely to wipe out. There is a runnable nine-foot chute along the way, a sure spot for thrills. The lower third of the gorge is the roughest water.

Negril River—This waterway comes out of the *Negril Morass.* It is not a whitewater route and is navigable by motor launch or dugout canoe. Fishermen in motor launches take travelers into the morass to view the wetlands and bird life. Make arrangements for the half-day trip at the mouth of the river near the crafts market and the roundabout at the center of town.

Cabarita River—East of Negril the headwaters of the *Roaring River* lead into the Cabarita. At times you can canoe along portions of the Roaring River, or else look for put-in points below numerous bridges spanning the Cabarita.

The course of the Cabarita is mainly gentle, unless there have been heavy rains. It winds calmly under foliage shade, through several short Class 2 whitewater runs, but do not let the gentle nature of the river fool you into complacency. The whitewater is extremely shallow and rocky. It is easy to dump an inflatable canoe, particularly because of the lethargy and lack of concern you will be feeling due to the calming nature of most of the trip. You have to pay attention through the swampy lowlands or you will be taking an unintentional swim, if not several dunks.

Y.S. River—When conditions permit you can put in at the base of the Y.S. Falls to come toward the Black River Morass. You have to hike in to the falls, set up the inflatables and shove off for Class 3 whitewater that will definitely attract your attention, although posing no threat to your safety. Foliage is astonishingly lush, overgrown giant leaves for cool shade in very pretty, picture postcard territory.

Many other rivers, as well as certain larger streams are canoeable for half day trips, mostly in areas near where they meet the sea and for short distances upstream. On larger rivers, such as the Black or Broad, you could make a trip of several days, camping along the way.

Black River—This is Jamaica's largest river, a year-round flow through swampy lowlands. Five rivers feed into it, and these too offer canoeing possibilities. Watch out for crocodiles! This is Jamaica's largest remaining crocodile refuge and the fearsome creatures can be seen close to the mouth of the river, near the town of Black River. Crocs ignore most people, so just steer clear of them and they will probably not bother you. As for other animals or wildlife you might encounter, there will not be much beside fish, the local shrimp, birds wheeling overhead and plenty of mosquitoes.

Broad River—This is one of the major flows leading into the Black River. It follows one of the gentler courses on the island, winding around slow curves through flatlands, for slow travel without hazards.

You can trace the Broad River to three blue holes in the *Santa Cruz Mountains*, where it bubbles up out of the earth, then travels calmly through cane fields and farm country to the morass swamp. It meets the Black River about a mile north of the town of Black River. Look for cashew vendors on the riverside bridges in through here. They grow the nuts in this region. You can lie back in your canoe, sunning yourself, munching cashews, and let the river carry you through the lowlands. Little shade in here, though, many bugs, hot weather. Dress lightly. Carry insect repellent. Wear a hat.

Rio Grande—The lower *Rio Grande*, from *Berrydale* to the sea, west of Port Antonio, is where the famous bamboo rafts popularized by Errol Flynn carry tourists on a slow journey through the heartland of Jamaica.

Rafting on the Rio Grande

This is one of Jamaica's few really touristy attractions that is worthwhile. It costs around $30 US for two people to be poled downstream by a barefoot raftsman who has served a long apprenticeship. Although there are several mildly turbulent spots, there is nothing dangerous about the trip and with the practiced raftsman the trip is usually trouble-free.

On the way you float past people washing clothes, swimming or bathing in the river. This is one of the more populous river stretches, probably because so many tourists come through. Vendors are set up on the shore to serve the river traffic, offering cold drinks from ice chests, wooden carvings, various supplies and souvenirs. Young musicians serenade rafters with energetic reggae or calypso tunes, trying for a tip. Others float by on their own rafts, coming right up to you to offer a cold beer or soda.

There are spots along the way to get out for a picnic and numerous swimming holes. Just look for the children playing in the river. They know the top spots.

The route was originally used to transport bananas to Port Antonio. Local legend has it that Flynn, washed up on Jamaican shores in his yacht during a storm, thought it would be good kicks to raft the river for fun. Voila! An industry was born.

The river is beautiful, passing through steep-sided gorges or meandering flats. The raftsman's pole splashes the water, the hollow bamboo clacking off the rocks below. The gurgling sounds and the resonating bamboo are nearly hypnotic. You can lie back in the sun, shoot photos, munch away on goodies provided by shoreline vendors, drift into another world. Wear a hat or rent an umbrella at the put-in point. The sun can be strong along the mostly unshaded six-mile route.

The raft trip takes about three hours, longer if you make frequent or lengthy stops.

Various arrangements are possible for land transportation. If you drive a car to Berrydale, you can have it delivered and waiting for you at *Rafter's Rest, St. Margaret's Bay*, where the river meets the sea. Package tours drop travelers and pick them up at the end.

This may not quite qualify as "adventure," but it is a pretty and peaceful river. Try to go in off season when the tourist buses from the big hotels will be absent.

For a truly memorable trip, the rafts operate on full moon nights. Take that trip with someone you love. The romance of the river is unbeatable under a glowing full moon.

As for river canoeing, it is possible and interesting on the upper Rio Grande above Berrydale. You travel on slightly rougher water than the lower stretch. After bouncing around through mild white water the lower six miles are tranquil in a rubber canoe, and a novelty for the locals who are used to seeing only the bamboo craft. A nice bonus here are the amenities offered for bamboo rafters, which are also available to canoeists. There are no peddlers selling cold drinks in the Black River Morass, but you will not have to go thirsty on the Rio Grande.

Martha Brae—Because of the popularity of bamboo rafting on the Rio Grande, a similar operation was started on the *Martha Brae River*. They use the same type of long bamboo rafts, but the trip is shorter, covering three and a half miles, in about one and a half hours, from *Rafter's Village* to *Rock*, east of *Falmouth*. This is perhaps an even more touristy operation, but again, the river is beautiful. Closed in by overhanging vegetation, you float past fern groves, bamboo, bananas and sugar cane.

Farther upriver, starting at *Good Hope*, location of a Great House whose owner once controlled most of the parish of *Trelawny*, decent river canoeing is possible. This is one of the largest rivers in the country, the largest in the parish and one of the twelve year-round rivers in Jamaica. The scenery is similar to the lower stretches., Pretty green parakeets flit through the trees, woodpeckers tap away. Orchids line the banks. You find moments of idyllic peace and quiet on the river. Then, when you reach Rafter's Rest, you can get out and avoid the river raft traffic, or continue on the meandering waters to the sea.

Most of Jamaica's rivers are still unexplored as far as canoeing possibilities are concerned. Stretches off the *Wag Water*

River, flowing out of the Blue Mountains toward *Annotto Bay* are sometimes navigable. The *Morant River* and the *Yallahs River* east of Kingston bear further exploration. The *Rio Nuevo River* between *Oracabessa* and Ocho Rios, on the north coast, is another possibility. And there are numerous stretches of the known canoeing rivers that have never been tried before. This all adds up to a special chance to canoe on a tropical river, and for trailblazers to cover the first descent of a previously untraveled river.

There are hundreds of flows waiting to be discovered in Jamaica if you are up for that sort of adventure. If not, the known canoeable rivers offer a variety of experiences and ranges of difficulty, ranging from the seventeen consecutive whitewater runs along the lower Great River, to the meandering pace of the Broad River through Jamaica's largest swamp.

"The trek begins innocently enough, along dirt roads and through the sugar cane fields that stretch from the mountains to the shoreline. But there's very little in the way of foothills. Before you know it your horse is aimed skyward and scrambling like an overgrown mountain goat up steep, rocky paths no wider than the horse itself. In a matter of ten minutes the temperature can drop as much as 15 degrees, and the clouds that perpetually shroud the mountains are swirling about you in a heavy mist. After a rest stop just past the half way point, the climb becomes slightly less steep and considerably less jungle-esque. Then you arrive at the top of the world, where the north coast of Jamaica spreads before you generously, taking your breath away as the horses catch theirs."—Tim Sayles, Editor, Polo Magazine.

CHAPTER SEVEN

HORSEBACK RIDING & MULE TRIPS

Horses and mules are standard transport in much of rural Jamaica. Few people can afford cars or gasoline. You see many farmers slowly traveling down country lands on the back of a swaying mule or a skinny horse.

There are stables island-wide for short trips of half a day or so. There is not much extensive trail riding or pack-tripping, but there is some, and you can see a lot of the country from the back of one of the animals. Special treats include seaside trots along beaches and for *Black Beauty* fans, you can even ride a horse *in* the sea, splashing along the shallows on a deserted stretch of shore.

The following operators can provide horses or mules for various excursions lasting up to several days:

MONTEGO BAY

L&M Riding Stable, 953-2002, offers free hotel pick-up service and a variety of rides.

A one-hour ride covers the *Coral Gardens* woodland trail ending in *Spring Farm*, a Mo-Bay suburb comprised of large upper-middle class houses. You get a brief fifteen-minute view of the countryside. Cost: US $12.

A two-hour ride continues beyond the end of the one-hour trip, up into the hills, valleys and pastures outside of town. The hilltop views are photogenic and then, you crest a low peak and wind down the other side of the hill toward *Tryall*, a

Beach riding

small village where refreshments are available. You pass the Half Moon Golf & Country Club, travel along the edge of the golf course, across a river and back to your starting point at the stables east of Montego Bay. Cost: US $24.

A three-hour ride follows the two-hour path and then veers off at the Village of Tryall, climbing farther into the hills to *Mount Zion*, a village overlooking the Rose Hall coastline. From there you head back to the stables. Cost US $36.

L&M also offers a beach ride along the main two-hour ride trail and then down to the sea from Half Moon Country Club. You can ride on the sand or in the water. Cost US $27.

Another ride extends beyond the three-hour trip, continuing on to Rose Hall Great House, a popular tourist site said to have once been inhabited by a witch. There is a waterfall nearby and you pass a house owned by country musician Johnny Cash, a part-time resident of Jamaica.

The Double A Ranch at Holiday Village, 953-2319, offers trail riding near the Holiday Inn on the north coast, east of Mo-Bay.

White Witch Stables, 953-2746, are located at Rose Hall Beach and Golf Club. Their trips cover the countryside nearby, including a ride to the Great House.

Good Hope & Trelawny Beach Hotel, 954-2289, rents horses at the beach or in the hills at the *Good Hope Great House*. The Good Hope Estate was once the largest land and slave owning property on the island and is now a private home. Horseback rides and plantation tours are available. You can ride past an old counting house, a slave hospital, sugar works, an ancient aqueduct, cut stone bridges built by slave labor and a water-wheel. Beach rides travel along the Falmouth coast.

OCHO RIOS

Prospect Plantation Stable, 974-2058, offers tours through a working plantation. Trails wander through citrus groves, coffee plantings, mahogany, bananas, cassava, allspice. Cattle are raised on the property. The ride takes you along the top of the *White River Gorge* and from *Sir Harold's Viewpoint*, named after a former owner of the property, you can see Cuba on clear days, ninety miles across the Caribbean.

Chukka Cove Farm, Ltd., PO Box 160, Ocho Rios, St. Ann, Jamaica, 972-2506, is the newest riding facility in the Caribbean, situated on fifty acres between *St. Ann's Bay* and Runaway Bay, on the sea coast. Rock cliffs line the shore and part of the property includes *Papillon's Cove*, an underground cave where scenes from the Steve McQueen-Dustin Hoffman movie were filmed. The property contains eight pastures and stables for forty-one horses. Tours lead along the seacoast or up into the hills of St. Ann's.

Trail riding on well-trained horses, with English tack, takes you through plantations featuring cattle, cane, bananas and coconut. Within an hour's ride you can scale hilltops overlooking the sea and work your way back down to the coast.

Instructions for beginners to advanced riders are available in dressage, cross-country riding and show jumping. There is a full-size polo field, with instructions available.

Seeing the interior on horseback

Bridle paths and forest trails take you across streams and into the surrounding hills. Among the standard rides offered are the following:

Mount Zion trek—The ride takes you from the sea to 1800-foot Mt. Zion through lush, garden-like scenery with good views at the top. The three-hour ride costs $30 US.

"Swim Your Horse Trek"—You ride through mountain paths to a deserted beach, unsaddle your horse and take the two of you for a swim. Some riders prefer to canter bareback along the sand. A guide re-saddles your horse for the ride back to the resort. Three-hours. Cost: $30 US.

Day trek to *Lilyfield*—You ride from the sea to 2,000 feet on a ridge overlooking thirty miles of coastline. This is for experienced riders. The narrow path is steep and winding. Deep in the hills you ride past cane fields, then through thick vegetation, orchids and tree ferns. Lilyfield is a coffee plantation, rare for this part of the island, and there is a stop at the 150-year-old farmhouse to observe the coffee production processes. The six hour ride costs $50 US, including lunch at the coffee farm.

Chukka Cove also offers an overnight trek to Lilyfield. It includes dinner and sleeping accommodations at the farm. In the morning, you ride to the edge of the Cockpits, to the little village of *Bamboo*. A resort vehicle carries your personal items for you so you do not have to worry about packing them in. Trips leave at 10 AM and return 4 PM the following day. Cost: $125 US.

Longer trips can be arranged and accommodations are also available at Chukka Cove, with various package deal possibilities.

There is also a stable at *Dunn's River Beach*, and horseback rides can also be arranged through Watersports Enterprises, 974-2244.

PORT ANTONIO

Priestman's River Plantation is owned by Patrice Wymore Flynn, Errol's widow. She has remained in Jamaica since the actor's death and operates a horseback tour of the plantation. Cost $12 US. Local hotels are able to book this ride for you, or Mrs. Flynn operates gift shops at the Marbella Club and the Trident Hotel, where reservations can be made, or phone 993-3294.

Rocky Point Stables, 993-3281, offers trail rides for novices and accomplished riders. They have ten horses and experienced guides, and they offer transportation from hotels. Contact Trina Delisser for information.

Frenchman's Cove Stables, 993-3224, offers horseback rides along another fantastic coastal stretch.

THE BLUE MOUNTAINS

In this area you are dealing with less formal riding programs.

Errol Flynn's property

Penlyne Castle is a small town high in the mountains, near Whitfield Hall and the starting point for climbing to Blue Mountain Peak. There are several mule and horse owners who will provide animals for the ascent to the Peak. This is a steep seven-mile ride, up through tropical montane and elfin forests, through some of the most remote and prettiest scenery Jamaica offers, and with some of the best views. Arrangements can be made by asking anyone in the village where you can rent an animal for the Peak trek. They come with a guide. You can also make arrangements at Whitfield Hall. Cost is approximately $20 US for the animal and guide. The round trip takes at least six hours.

MANDEVILLE

Located in the hills of central Jamaica at 2,000 feet, the city is a quiet one noted for garden clubs and popular with wealthy Jamaican retirees. The best riding trails are located around *Marshall's Pen Great House*. Contact Robert Sutton at Marshall's Pen, 962-2260.

Pamela Goodwyn, a one-time Jamaican horse-jumping champion, lives in Mandeville. She can arrange rides around a property called *Godfrey Lands*. Cost is $50 JA for a one-hour ride. She can be contacted through Diana MacIntyre Pyke, owner of Mandeville's Hotel Astra, 62 Ward Ave., 962-3265.

NEGRIL

Horseman Riding Stables, Ltd. are located on the cliff side, a quarter mile past the Shell gas station on the road to Savanna-la-Mar. One of the trips they run is a Hillside Plantation Tour for $15 US. Make arrangements through the Coconut Grove Hotel, 957-4216.

Red Ground Riding Stables are located on the cliff road beyond the Anglican Church.

Another option for good riders looking for adventure would be to simply approach country folk that you see riding horseback and ask them if any local people will rent you a ride. Freelance operators also ply the beaches at Negril and Montego Bay offering rides.

"Good luck and tight lines."—Joe Kieffer, Chairman Sir Henry Morgan Angling Association.

CHAPTER EIGHT

SAILING & FISHING

The north coast is a lot more over-fished than the south. Commercial fishermen are found mostly along the southern coast, but there is fishing all around the island, with commercial boats typically ranging twenty-five miles or farther off-shore. Outfitted sport fishing boats are available for charters in Montego Bay, Ocho Rios or Port Antonio, where deep sea fishing is popular. River fishermen should bring their own tackle. Otherwise, complete rental outfits are available.

As for sailing, there are a number of possibilities, from windsurfers to sloops, mainly available out of the larger tourist areas of the north coast.

MONTEGO BAY

Calico is a fifty-five-foot gaff-rigged ketch for day cruises leaving from the marina at the "On The Waterfront" restaurant. A 10 AM to 3 PM cruise sails daily, except Mondays. For $35 US, you get round trip transportation to and from the boat, drinks, lunch and use of snorkeling equipment.

An evening cruise from 5 PM to 7 PM, Wed-Sat, is $20 US per person, including drinks and round trip transportation to and from the pier.

This is a touristy trip, expensive by Jamaican standards, but a chance to go sailing on Montego Bay, which is a pleasing experience. Call 952-5860 for information and reservations or visit the ticket office at *Walter Fletcher Beach.*

The Mary Ann is a fifty-seven-foot sailboat offering day trips from 10 AM to 3 PM. You get fruits and drinks onboard as you sail across the bay to a marine garden of reefs and twenty varieties of coral. You can swim with the reef fish or snorkel, with masks, fins and snorkels provided for free. Cost is $30 US.

A sunset dinner cruise is $35 US.

Call 952-5505 for information and reservations or stop by the Montego Town Marina.

"Xanadu" sails from the "On The Waterfront" marina daily. 952-2578.

The LA Yacht Service operates sailing and fishing trips. Call 952-3290, or stop at the dock located next to Marguerite's Restaurant on Gloucester Avenue.

Bay sailing

Deep sea fishing charters are available at the following locations:

Stanley's Bay Marine is located near *Ironshore*, on the north side of town past the airport. Phone 952-3859.

Esso Marina is on *Mahoe Bay*, also near Ironshore, 952-2659.

"Bali High" docks at *Gunpoint Wharf*. No phone. Stop by to talk.

Windsurfer rentals are available at numerous Montego Bay locations, including:

Mo-Bay Windsurfing, *Doctor's Cave Beach*, 952-5505.

Whaleback Ocean Skills, *Cornwall Beach*, 952-2578.

The Montego Bay Yacht Club, at *Montego Freeport* is open to members of registered overseas yacht clubs. Proof of membership is required.

OCHO RIOS

The big tourism business in this town means there are many boats for hire and commercial touring craft.

"Fourth of July" is a sixty-foot ketch operated by Rum Runner Cruises from the Ocho Rios pier adjacent to the Ocean Village Shopping Center in the center of town. Cruises daily are at 10:30 AM and 3:30 PM. Cost: $25 US. Call 974-2323 or 974-2344.

Most of the big hotels along the coast offer some sort of boating, from windsurfer rentals to fishing excursions. There are so many vessels in a crowded harbor that sailing here hardly qualifies as adventure, unless avoiding water skiers and other vessels is your idea of kicks. Deep sea fishing, however, far off shore, can be good. Rates are around $250 US per half-day, for a crewed fishing boat, with bait and tackle provided. Contact the following operators for information and exact rates:

Watersports Enterprises is based at the Americana Hotel, Ernie Smatt, Manager, 974-2151.

Sea Jamaica, Ltd. is based at the Shaw Park Beach Hotel, east of town, Mike Draculich, Manager, 972-2382.

Sunfisher, Ltd., at Mallard's Beach, arranges charters.

Val Chung, in Port Maria, 994-2294, also arranges fishing trips.

A Blue Marlin fishing tournament is held yearly in September as a prelude to a major international deep sea fishing event held in Port Antonio in October. Contact the Jamaica Tourist Board for information.

PORT ANTONIO

This is *the* place for deep-sea fishing in Jamaica. The sea drops off more than a hundred fathoms only half a mile off shore. An International Marlin Tournament is held here every October to take advantage of the big fish. Fifty or more boats compete from all over the world. There is also a canoe fishing tourney held at the same time for those who have only small boats. The Tourist Board can provide registration and other information on the Port Antonio Tournament.

Marlin run best in these waters from August to October. On the south coast prime fishing time is from December to February.

Port Antonio is one of the most popular sailing and fishing spots on the island, but far less developed in other areas of tourism than Ocho Rios or Mo-Bay. This means there are fewer water skiers, jet-skiers or para-sailors, and so forth. Aside from the big Blue Marlin, some weighing five hundred pounds or more, these waters are home to yellowtail tuna, kingfish, wahoo and dolphin (not the "Flipper" kind). Many private boats sail into this harbor all year-round. There are also several charter fishermen always looking to catch a big whopper. Among the best is:

The "Coral Baby," a forty-one-foot twin diesel charter vessel operated by Roy Chin, 933-3086.

Huntress Marina is the place to go for most boat rentals. It is located at 16 West St., the main commercial street in the heart of town. Phone 993-3318. A number of different boats dock here, including a sixty-five-foot motor sailor, "The Huntress," which is available with crew for week-long coastal cruises. The catamaran "Lady Jamaica" makes daily harbor cruises.

Sailing off Port Antonio

Windsurfers, sunfish and day sailors are available, along with dockage, welding, showers and moorings for visiting boaters.

EAST COAST

The fisherman's beaches at Boston Bay and Manchioneal are possibilities for hooking up with local fishermen. You would have to hang around at the right times, usually early mornings, at dawn, and negotiate with individuals for a fishing trip.

KINGSTON

Royal Jamaican Yacht Club, at Port Royal, can arrange charters. The club is located on the *Palisadoes Road*, past the airport. They also offer club use privileges to overseas yacht club members with proper identification.

Morgan's Harbor, a hotel on the Palisadoes Road, also can arrange boat rentals and charters for trips to the harbor cays or farther out.

Port Royal fishermen will take you out to the cays to swim and snorkel, or for fishing. The dock is next to Country Roast Fish Centre and the Archaeological Museum.

OLD HARBOR

This is a decidedly non-touristy fishing and bauxite shipping harbor west of the Hellshire Hills. The semi-arid region is largely undeveloped and the fishing is good. Get there early to talk to fishermen about a trip.

ROCKY POINT

This spot is even more remote than Old Harbor, situated west of Portland Point in one of the least developed parts of the country. It has one of the larger fishing fleets, making it a good bet for a boat for hire.

ALLIGATOR POND

There are many more fish in the seas off the south coast than the north, hence larger commercial fleets operate here. This means you have a wide choice of sailors to negotiate a voyage with. This beach is one of the island's larger fishing centers, with many motorized boats, as well as the typical wooden dinghies and dugout canoes. Come here early in the day to work out a good price for a trip with local fisherfolk.

BLACK RIVER, WHITEHOUSE, BLUEFIELD'S BAY

These are all prime fishing beaches with numerous boats operating. At Black River you ask boatmen to take you out into the sea, or inland into the morass for freshwater fish or shrimp. Many fishermen in small canoes work out of the stretch north from Black River to Savanna-la-Mar, and many of the beaches can be seen from the road. Get there when the boats are ready to shove off. Most of the fishermen make very little money, particularly the ones with smaller boats, so it is usually possible to arrange for someone to give up a day's catch to take you out, provided the price is right. That price, by the way, will likely be considerably less than you would pay on the north coast.

NEGRIL

Negril is big on boating, with many dugout canoes lining the coast, especially on *South Negril Point* between the beach and the cliffs. You will not find many large vessels comparable to the north coast fishing boats, but more of the smaller dugouts, trolling canoes, and runabouts.

Most of the hotels rent windsurfers, sailfish or sunfish.

Ray's Parasailing, located on the beach between the Sundowner and Poinciana Beach Villas, does not offer quiet sailing, but they will take you up above the beach on a tethered line for around ten minutes of flying over Negril, for roughly $20 US.

As you travel along the coastline you will notice many other small fishing beaches with half-a-dozen or fewer boats beached on the sand. If you are looking for adventure just approach the fishermen and see if you are able to strike a deal.

Spearfishing is allowed on most reefs. You can dive for snapper, kingfish, mackerel and grouper. The fishing folk are generally friendly and well-informed as to the best of the local waters, and happy to help polite, inquiring travelers. Look people in the eye, address them as Mr. or Miss, ask good questions and you will get sharp answers that may surprise you with their cutting humor or honest clarity. Negotiating with a fisherman for a boat trip can be as valuable a learning experience as the fishing itself and can lead you to an unusual time on the waters.

"While in the Grotto's gloomy cells
We pressed the devious way
Through many a chamber that expels
With fretted roofs the day."—Robert Charles
Dallas, *Miscellaneous Writings*, 1778.

CHAPTER NINE

BIRDS & BATS: NATURAL HISTORY TOURING & CAVE EXPLORING

Jamaica has few indigenous animals. Most of the animal life found here was imported, either accidentally, as in the case of the rat, which arrived in the holds of merchant ships, or on purpose, as in the case of the mongoose, which was enlisted to get rid of the rats.

Native species include the coney, a nocturnal rodent that the Arawaks considered a dining delicacy, as well as more than twenty varieties of bats, called "rat-bats" (moths are called bats) by Jamaicans and found in the three hundred and eighty known caves beneath the surface of the island.

Butterflies are seen everywhere. Approximately one hundred twenty are known to inhabit Jamaica, with twenty-one species being endemic. The most impressive is the giant yellow and black swallowtail, with a six-inch wingspan. It is found mostly in the eastern Blue Mountains.

At one time there were many wild pigs in the mountains. These have been hunted to near extinction, although some survive in the most remote reaches of the John Crow Mountains.

There are twenty-seven species of native birds, along with another eighty or more part-time resident species.

BIRDS

Outdoor diners at open-air restaurants are targets for the little "cling-cling," a jet-black grackle that likes to hustle scraps of food. Long-necked Turkey buzzards, called "John Crow," are plentiful. The Jamaican national bird is called a "Doctor Bird." It is a swallowtail hummingbird with a green breast and black body. Its image is found on Jamaican twenty-five cent coins.

You can see birds everywhere, while floating in a raft down a wetland river, in the hills, or in the mud flats by a beach where shore birds congregate. There are also two notable birdwatching spots where you can chat with experts on the island's birdlife.

Lisa Salmon's *Rocklands Bird Sanctuary* is located south of Montego Bay, and *Marshall's Pen Great House* is located in Mandeville and owned by the Sutton's, an old Jamaican family.

Rocklands is situated a short distance past the town of Anchovy, approximately nine miles from Montego Bay. The feeding station has been in existence for thirty years. Opening time is 3:30 PM daily and feeding continues until dusk. Accredited members of birdwatching societies are allowed in at anytime, but the general public cannot enter until 3:30 and children under 5 are not admitted. Phone 952-2009 for additional information.

Doctor birds, rainbow-plumed mango hummers and tiny bee hummingbirds the size of bumblebees feed right out of people's hands. They drink a special sugar and water mixture out of little bottles, right on the porch of the main house. Quits, nightingales, finches, and many more species are observable, feeding in the yard in front of the house, and some one hundred species have been seen on the grounds, in the forest gar-

Birds are everywhere on the island

den, in bird baths, or up in trees. Miss Salmon is considered an expert on Jamaican birds. She can tell you exactly where to look for certain birds island-wide, particularly around Montego Bay.

Robert Sutton, Sr., at Marshall's Pen, is a gracious and extremely knowledgeable host as regards bird watching on his 200-year-old, 300-acre property, as well as other parts of the island. Birds around Mandeville differ somewhat from Montego Bay and Mr. Sutton can tip you to local varieties and best spots for birdwatching.

Marshall's Pen includes a cattle raising operation, hiking trails, horseback riding stables and gardens, as well as a bird sanctuary. The old great house is filled with leather-bound books, stamp collections, art works and antiques. Mr. Sutton and his son Robert Jr. are founts of encyclopedic information on Jamaican history and botany, as well as birds.

Other excellent birdwatching sites include the Black River

Morass and the rest of the island's swamps, the Cockpits, the Blue Mountains and the John Crow Mountains.

CAVES

The limestone areas of Jamaica cover around two-thirds of the island. These regions are pocked with caves and sinkholes. Most of the caves are inhabited by rat-bats. Although the creatures have little interest in man, Jamaicans make good use of the large amounts of bat guano for fertilizer.

Professor Alan Fincham of the Biochemistry Department of the University of the West Indies and the Jamaica Caving Club is responsible for a useful book for cave explorers. It is called *Underground Jamaica*, published by the University, and consists primarily of outlines of all the known information about explored caves, as well as whatever knowledge is available on unexplored ones. For specific caving information contact The Jamaica Caving Club, c/o The Department of Geology, The University of the West Indies, Mona, Kingston 7, Jamaica, phone 927-6661.

There are a number of "show" caves that are open as tourist attractions, with a far greater number of lesser known caves that offer serious challenges to the intrepid spelunker. A lot of the caves can be safely entered by novices, although care is necessary not to overstep the boundaries of good sense.

If you plan to go cave exploring carry lighting and spares. Many Jamaicans use kerosene-soaked rag torches, but if you use a flashlight, make sure you have extra bulbs as well as batteries.

Do not enter a cave by yourself. Make sure you leave word of your plans for caving so you can be followed if trouble occurs.

Be careful around water in caves. Levels can rise dramatically in a short time.

Watch your step. The limestone rock can be crumbly underfoot.

There is no specific cave rescue organization in Jamaica, so you will be pretty much on your own.

You will find the greatest number of caves in the Cockpits, the John Crow Mountains, the Hellshire Hills and the *Dry Harbor Mountains* between the *Cave River* and *Discovery Bay* in central Jamaica.

Many caves were used by Arawaks and one of the things you can do is search for Indian artifacts. Pottery shards and bones have been found by spelunkers. Arawaks used certain caves as burial vaults, others to get drinking water from.

One more word of warning. The Cockpits and the John Crow Mountains are still largely unexplored, or at best poorly documented. There are many caves in both areas, particularly the Cockpits. You enter at your own risk, so be careful before you climb into any cave. Even if someone knows where you are going it will be very hard to find you once you are underground if anything goes wrong.

SHOW CAVES

If you want to get an idea of the sort of caves there are on the island the show caves that are open as tourist attractions are good examples. These are among the more accessible caves and also the more dramatic ones. They are all well-lighted and guides walk you through, either official ones, or freelances who live nearby.

Two Sisters Cave is located in the Hellshire Hills near Fort Clarence beach, just went of Kingston. It is estimated to be 200,000 years old. Steps carved from rock take you down below the waterline to an observation platform. A carved Arawak petroglyph of a face is visible dimly across the water on the cave wall. Experts say the artwork is 1,000 years old.

Nonsuch Caves are located outside Port Antonio at Athenry. This is a well-lighted cave and you pay an admission fee for a guide to walk you through the passages. There are man-made steps and sidewalks inside that lead you to views of large stalactites and stalagmites. There are also numerous undersea fossils from when the cave was underwater. Next door are the *Athenry Gardens*, located in the hills with pretty views of the

Nonsuch Caves, Port Antonio

coast from neatly-tended flower beds, bananas, pimento and coconuts.

Runaway Caves, in St. Ann, one and a half miles east of Runaway Bay, have seven miles of known passageways through the limestone chambers that were once used by Arawaks, pirates, smugglers and runaway slaves as a hideout. The showcase of the cave complex is called the *Green Grotto*. Open from 9:30 AM to 5:30 PM daily, this large cave has guided tours through lighted paths, as well as a boat ride on an underground lake 120 feet below the surface, opening into a high chamber that glows with an eerie greenish light.

OTHER CAVE SITES

For the more adventurous:

Ipswich Cave is located along the train track south of Montego Bay, north of the town of Maggotty. A tourist train stops here on the way to the Appleton Rum Factory. Everyone empties out of the cars and parades down the steps into several chambers. If you want to go exploring deeper, go when the train is not around. This is the western edge of the Cockpits and there are many people around who try to sell things to the train passengers. One of them will help you through the cave. You negotiate the price.

Windsor Cave is located east of Falmouth on the northern edge of the Cockpits. The cave entrance is about a half mile from the Windsor Great House. A vaulted chamber at the end of a 200-yard passage near the entrance has large stalactites. Side passages veer off and the main passage continues to a drop-off point where a thirty-foot cliff hangs over a stream that is the source of the Martha Brae River. Numerous passageways through here can be followed for greater distances. Again, local guides can show you around.

Pantrepant Cave, Falmouth, has Arawak petroglyphs found in small difficult passages with low ceilings.

Wondrous Cave, at *Elderslie*, in the southern Cockpits, may one day be developed as a tourist attraction. There is an underground river and lake inside, as well as long convoluted passageways.

Oxford Cave, north of Mandeville, is among the largest of underground Jamaica. Although undeveloped for tourism, many of the chambers have been explored and locals can show you through.

Jackson's Bay Cave is situated on the south side of Portland Ridge in *Clarendon*, north of Jackson's Bay. This is an exceptional maze of water-filled passages and crawl spaces which lead to a large *Shamrock Passage* that opens into large chambers called the *Coliseum* and *Theatre*. This cave has been well-surveyed and contains 11,000 feet of passages. Signs of Arawaks are evident.

Crab Cave is deep in the bush near Portland Ridge. Old bottles have been found far inside, indicating that the subterranean chambers were used long ago as some sort of hideout, possibly for runaway slaves.

Gourie Cave, near *Christiana*, on the eastern edge of the Cockpits, is thought to be the island's longest cave system, but many of the passages are underwater.

Mountain River Cave, north of *Spanish Town*, holds numerous Arawak cave drawings believed to be well over 1000 years old. The Archaeological Society of Jamaica is working with the Smithsonian Institution to document the representations of birds, fish and Indians. Experts have noted similarities with African designs, as well as other West Indian art. Local guides will show you around. Despite the site's historic value, it has not been developed as a tourist attraction.

Three Finger Jack's Cave, east of Kingston, on the *Cane River*, above the falls, is thought to have been a hideout for a famous highwayman. When Jack was finally done in by bounty hunters in 1781, his head and tell-tale hand were cut off and preserved in a jug of rum until the reward-claiming evidence of his demise could be delivered to the territorial governor.

Riverhead Cave in St. Catherine's opens to the earth in a canal that can be followed inward to a lengthy dry passage. A man-made dam a quarter mile inside indicates that the water was once used for irrigation.

Coffee River Cave, in *Auchtembeddie*, in Manchester, has been carefully explored by the Jamaica Caving Club. A river passage leads into a complex of tunnels. More than 9000 feet of passages have been mapped, with about half of that under water.

Roaring River Cave, Westmoreland, is located three miles from a Blue Hole and the underground source of the Roaring River. Steps lead down to several tall chambers above an active streamway. Local guides will help you here.

"The motorcyclist may have a problem with the loose gravel and potholes on some roads, but my wife and I, who have done a lot of bicycle touring in the northwest of the United States, find Jamaica is an almost ideal place to see by bike."—Respondent to cycling survey sponsored by Jamaica Camping and Hiking Association.

CHAPTER TEN

BICYCLE TOURING

Jamaica is perfect for bike touring, from an island circuit of 435 miles, to shorter day trips, mountain rides, seacoast tours, or just for transportation. The scenery is gorgeous, the weather agreeable and traveling distances typically manageable. The island roads are narrow, though, without shoulders in most spots, and definitely lacking bike trails. Drivers can be erratic, veering around corners into oncoming lanes, traveling fast, not expecting to see bicyclists. Several sideswiping incidents have been reported, so care is necessary to insure a safe time.

There is relatively little motorized traffic on country routes, and this helps. City riders should exercise special caution.

Many hotels can provide bikes for guests. Rentals are available in Montego Bay, Negril and Ocho Rios, but these are not touring bikes. The equipment is unsuited to lengthy rides or rough terrain. If you really want to explore Jamaica by bike, consider bringing your own with you. Contact your airline to make arrangements for shipping. The charge is not great and the airlines provide shipping cartons.

Loose gravel and potholes can be hindrances to riders, particularly in the steeper mountainous areas.

Jamaican roads can be an adventure

It is smart to travel as lightly as possible, just in case you have to swerve fast to avoid oncoming traffic or an unexpected crater in the middle of the road as you are wheeling fast around a tight curve.

Travel in single file only. The roads are too narrow for anything else.

Wear a helmet. It will help keep the sun off and give you valuable protection.

Coastal roads are mainly level, without too many steep pitches. Mountain trips are a different story, but the rides through the high country are magnificent, cool, pretty and powerful exercise.

A rider could spend days in the Blue Mountains and a truly expert off-road rider might even want to try to tackle the Blue Mountain Peak trail on a solid mountain bike. This would be a real challenge. We are talking adventure here. What it lacks in sheer altitude it more than makes up for in steep, slippery track and wild country. Just be sure to bring repair equipment with you, a patch kit and so forth.

You can easily plan a multi-day trip with overnights at various camping facilities, guest houses, or even cushy hotels. Most of the camping sites can provide tents and sleeping bags, if you reserve in advance, so you will not have to travel loaded down with lots of gear. Markets or small restaurants along the way can provide inexpensive food.

Plan on taking ten days to two weeks for a leisurely circuit of the island. This pace will allow time to enjoy yourself at stops, without too strenuous a schedule. Shorter trips of seven days will cover good portions of the island. Day trips are possible.

Plan on covering fifteen to thirty miles daily without too much trouble. A lot of the going is slower than you might think from looking at a map. The bad roads, friendly people, rum shops, beaches and mountain vistas are all out there to slow you down. Take your time and enjoy yourself. This is one type of adventure travel that someone unfamiliar with Jamaica can handle alone without a lot of hassles.

Bike rentals are offered at the following locations. Call to see what sort of equipment is available.

MONTEGO BAY

Montego Bike Rentals, 21 Gloucester Ave, 952-4984.
Village Rent-A-Bike, Holiday Village, 953-2872.

OCHO RIOS

Sunnyride Rent-A-Bike, Content Garden, 974-2130.
Just Rent-A-Bike, Main Street, 974-2800.
Vacation Wheels, Ltd., Carib Ocho Rios Arcade, Shop #3, 974-5021

NEGRIL

Leonard's Bike & Bicycle Rental, West End Rd.
Island Bicycle Rental, West End Rd.

The following is a recommended bike trip itinerary that can show you all the way around the island, or any part of it.

Day 1: Montego Bay to *Lucea*, an old fishing village on the northwest coast. No tourists here, other than those passing through. A decent place for cyclists to stay is the inexpensive *Tamarind Lodge*, a casual old Jamaican house with porches overlooking Lucea Harbor. Camping is also available.

Day 2: Lucea to Negril. There are good beaches for cooling swims on this route, as well as many places to stay in Negril. Numerous beachside camping spots are available, as well as inexpensive accommodations, or you can spend a night in a relatively plush Negril hotel.

Day 3: Negril to Black River. Good beaches. No tourists. Inexpensive guest houses and restaurants, or sleep out and buy fresh fish on the beach.

Day 4: Black River to Treasure Beach. The ride from Negril to Black River is around fifty miles. This leg is under twenty miles, allowing a relaxing stop here to take advantage of the superior beach and easy-going people.

Day 5: Treasure Beach to *Milk River Spa*. The south coast roads are unbelievably bad. You may have to stop to slash through tall grass where the road is supposed to be, but you will have a chance to see Monarch butterflies and these most remote southern plains and beaches. Expect hot, hot weather along this coast. Milk River Spa has hot mineral baths (see Chapter 11) where you can soak to rest your tired bones after the difficult travel. There are guest rooms, as well as a restaurant.

Day 6: Milk River to Old Harbor. Camp on the beach in this fishing village or rent a room from a local family.

Day 7: Old Harbor to Kingston. Stay in the city or continue through it for a short distance east into the Blue Mountains.

You can stay at the Maya Hiking Center inexpensively, with camping available, as well as maps, meals and good advice.

Day 8: Kingston to *Great Salt Ponds.* Camp out along the beach or under the high cliffs. The Gold Mine Camp & Club has inexpensive rooms. Good fresh fish.

Day 9: Great Salt Ponds to *Bath.* The Bath Hotel and spa is another mineral spa that you may enjoy after days of riding. There is a good restaurant and inexpensive, but nice rooms. It gets busy on weekends, with Jamaicans, not foreign tourists.

Day 10: Bath to Port Antonio. You may want to stop sooner, at Boston Beach or along the secluded east coast. Numerous choices of accommodations around this area, from camping on the beach to luxury hotels. Good restaurants. Pretty rain forest scenery.

Day 11: Port Antonio to Strawberry Fields. Camp on the beach or stay in a small cottage. The rugged, undeveloped coastline is perfect for side trips to waterfalls and secluded beaches. If you prefer a fancier place to stay, push on a little farther to Casa Maria Hotel in Port Maria.

Day 12: Strawberry Fields/Port Maria to Ocho Rios.

Day 13: Ocho Rios to Falmouth.

Day 14: Falmouth to Montego Bay.

JATCHA puts together several bike trips, making all your reservations and helping plan your route according to your special interests. No one else on the island is currently putting together bike trips. If you ask the Tourist Board for help there is a good chance they will think you are nuts.

Some nice inland trips include:

Buff Bay to Kingston. This forty-four-mile route takes you through the heart of the Blue Mountains, into coffee country and back to the city. It is steep in many parts and the roads are terribly rutted, but the scenery is tropical forest superb, the people along the way friendly and open. You can visit forest preserves and coffee plantations. Camp overnight in Section at Dennis's coffee farm to split the trip in half.

Be careful: You can fly on the downhill run into Kingston. Few cars use this route and the road is so bad that they have to go slow. It is quiet enough so that you can hear any cars or trucks coming from far away, so you do not really have to worry too much about oncoming traffic.

Port Antonio to *Bowden Pen* is another excellent bike route. This trip takes you up high into the upper Rio Grande valley, through the John Crow Mountains and Maroon country into the fertile heart of a rain forest. Incredible tropical forest scenery, few cars, fewer tourists. It is a strenuous ride up, a breeze down. Watch for potholes.

"You jes' drove t'rough one million black faces."—Leonard "Baps" Cole, on the far side of Kingston's Coronation Market.

CHAPTER ELEVEN

TOURIST SITES MOST GUIDE BOOKS LEAVE OUT

If you follow the advice of most Jamaica guide books, the places you visit will be great for meeting tourists and paying top dollar to be hustled through a watered-down version of island culture.

There are many other sites to see and things to do in interesting places where you meet mainly Jamaicans, not your neighbors from New Jersey. The adventure is in plugging into the culture and learning how Jamaicans live, rather than experiencing what commercial-minded Jamaicans think foreigners want to know.

Most of the sites and attractions in this chapter do not host many tourists, Therefore the residents and proprietors are likely to be somewhat less polished and also less jaded toward visitors. If your mind is open when you mingle with Jamaicans, these spots are bound to introduce you to friends.

Kingston

KINGSTON

The capital city is one of the most exciting places in the country and one of the best for learning how the culture operates. Many guide books recommend skipping the city altogether, citing dangers and playing on urban fears.

Kingston is obviously not a beach fry resort. It is a big city, and just like any other, it has its problems. Many people think New York City is disgusting, but few would deny that it is also energetic, exciting and a valuable stop for visitors.

If people came to Jamaica for its culture, rather than for its beaches, Kingston would be the country's greatest tourist attraction. If you are here for adventure and learning do not skip it. And do not worry extravagantly. Take normal precautions. Look both ways before crossing a street. Hold your bags tightly. Stay alert about your personal security. This is a fast moving, crowded, growing city, a teeming Caribbean cauldron filled with 900,000 people doing the best they can to make things work.

Being in Kingston is an adventure. City crowds, traffic jams, heat and typical Jamaican hustle can be intimidating at first. Goats wander the streets near downtown. People are walking everywhere. Fast cars and crammed buses careen around narrow potholed streets, jostled arms and heads hanging out of windows, gears grinding, noise at a high pitch.

Colorful produce stands packed with vegetables and fruits line sidewalks. Heavy handmade wooden carts block traffic.

Children in school uniforms look like part of an invading army.

Colors blur in the humidity and mix with discordant urban sounds, all of it cooking in the heat. Radiated warmth bounces off concrete highrises. The air feels as if it is escaping from an oven.

And of course, you stand out here. Everyone knows you are not a local and therefore, to some, you will be a mark. Say no, if you have to, and keep moving. Rough characters who will try to hustle and hassle you are a minority.

Pay attention to warnings about certain areas. Do not walk alone at night or down dark alleys, but then, you probably would not do that in your home town, either.

There are a lot of things to see and do here. Curious travelers through Kingston will find favorite spots and attractions with personal appeal. A visit to the following sites will launch you on your own adventure.

The Victoria Crafts Market, at the end of *Harbor St.*, is in all the guidebooks, but is nevertheless a good spot to gauge the tempo of the city. It is a square block of permanent shops and semi-permanent indoor stalls where you can buy every kind of knick-knack and touristy souvenir offered in Jamaica, as well as some unusual stuff, one-of-a-kind carvings, log drums, pottery, and so forth. This is where you can get the best prices on the more ordinary souvenirs. Most of the weavings, straw goods, baskets and t-shirts you see offered all over the island are manufactured in Kingston. They sell for less here than in Ocho Rios, Montego Bay or Negril, making this a good place to hone your haggling skills for the real thing, the street dealing and interactions you are bound to encounter.

Two blocks west of the market, on Harbor St., is a big bus terminal, a main dispatching point for transportation island-wide. This is the real thing. Numerous sidewalk vendors line the streets, selling cigarettes for 35 cents JA each, matches, candies, anything to turn a buck. You probably should not try to take photos here, unless you do not mind scowls, verbal abuse, money demands and possibly threats from the hard-working, long-suffering people. Wandering through here, whether for a stroll or to get a bus, will bring you face-to-face with the hard core of a tough part of the real Jamaica, in no uncertain terms.

Pier #2 is a few blocks south of the market and bus stop. This is where you get the water taxi to Port Royal. It costs under $1 JA for the short harbor cruise, with seven departures daily, twice that number on Saturdays. You will find more haggling here, desperadoes too, some rough characters and memorable local color.

The National Gallery is on Orange St., in the West Building, part of the *Kingston Mall*, phone 922-8540. Open 10 AM to 5 PM. Admission is free. Donations are accepted. Most people give $1 JA.

The gallery houses a prominent collection of Jamaican fine arts, mainly establishment-oriented pieces, as opposed to people's arts. Some of the collection is boring, and a lot of it is top notch.

The Bob Marley statue by Christopher Gonzales that was commissioned for the National Stadium stands in the lobby, where you can see it through the front window, without going in. When it was unveiled, people simply hated it, so it was stuck in here and another statue was hastily ordered.

Bob Marley Statue/National Stadium. The stadium is located between Old Hope Rd. and Mountain View. This second commissioned official memorial statue is the one everyone likes, a bigger-than-life-size guitar-playing Marley, the reggae star

Bob Marley statue

and cultural hero, the man who brought Jamaica to the world with his music.

The Bob Marley Museum, 56 Hope Rd., is inside the old Tuff Gong studio where Marley worked and lived. It became a museum in May 1986.

There are all sorts of Marley memorabilia inside. One room is wallpapered in news clips, others in posters and album covers. Gold records are on display. Incense is kept burning inside, with Marley tunes piped-in. You can see a small kitchen upstairs. It is next to Bob's old bedroom from before he hit it big enough to afford the mansion his family still lives in on Jack's Hill, high above Kingston at 2,000 feet.

Records and t-shirts are sold downstairs. No photos or tape recording are allowed on the property, which includes an Ital fresh juice bar.

Admission is $7 JA for adults, $2 for children. Caution: Tour buses filled with Japanese visitors have been sighted here. The museum is still relatively unknown but is bound to become a major tourist draw in years to come.

Ziggy's on Marcus Garvey Drive is the Tuff Gong recording plant. Named after one of the Marley children, you can watch records being produced on a free tour. *Very* heavy dudes hang out here, tough looking men with dreadlocks and time to scowl at you. This is, however, a good place to get the hottest reggae records or tapes, and the best place to get Marley t-shirts. They also sell rasta crafts of more unusual designs than typical schlocky souvenirs.

The Institute of Jamaica, 12 East St., 922-0620, holds different types of records, namely Jamaican history books, maps, nautical files and slave registers, all part of the National Library and a small museum. The Institute also publishes *The Jamaica Journal*, a cultural magazine, and conducts archaeological and Afro-Caribbean research.

Survey Department, 23 1/2 Charles St, 922-6630. This is where you get the best maps of the country, including a new 1/50,000 topographical series that includes hiking trails, small roads and various hard-to-find natural sites. These maps are highly recommended if you are going into the bush on your own. Cost is about $12–$15 JA per map, with a series of 12, in color, covering the whole island. Survey Department maps have omissions, and roads and trails wash out due to weather conditions, but these materials are the best sources for topographical information short of hiring a driver or guide. The maps can be a help too if, say, your guide is from Montego Bay and you want to get around the Blue Mountains.

University of the West Indies, at the old *Mona* sugar plantation, is a big school and research facility in east Kingston, in the shade of the Blue Mountains. Look for the colorful building-size outdoor "Year of the Child" mural depicting Jamaican life. University Hospital is here, in case you need medical help.

Hope Gardens, is a 150-acre botanical gardens just north of the University. Pretty flowers bloom all year round, and there is an extensive collection of indigenous and imported trees, as well as a small zoo.

Stanley Motta, N. Odeon Ave., 922-6951, is an electronics and appliance dealer with several stores in the Kingston area. This is not a tourist site but a place where wealthy Jamaicans shop for high-priced import goods. Of possible interest to visitors is a camera repair department. If you have equipment trouble on the island this is the only place where you have a chance of getting it fixed in time to record your trip. Talk to Mr. Quest or Mr. MacKenzie.

Coronation Market overflows North and South Parade, spilling over onto King St. and Queen St. This is the biggest island market, a place where you can buy anything that is available in Jamaica. Young boys push wooden handcarts stacked high with sugar cane, cabbage, carrots, bundles of fresh thyme, seasonal fruits and every other sort of produce that grows in Jamaica. Other vendors sell from rickety wood stalls. Racks of clothes are everywhere. A lady stands on a corner with a mountain of bras draped over her arm. Cars honk mercilessly through gridlocked traffic, buses pushing slowly through the crush, pedestrians weaving among stalled traffic.

The busiest days for freshest foods and best selections of everything are Thursday to Saturday.

One thing you will rarely see here is a hotel tour bus.

There are few tourists anywhere near here. It is far too

rough of a scene.

Remember at all times that you are not expected here, making it extra important for you to keep your wits about you, or be smarter and come with a Jamaican friend.

You might want to try driving through here the first time just to check it out and see if it is a place that you really want to visit. If you do walk through you will find the best deals on everything from papayas to panties to bamboo brooms. A visit to Coronation is truly an unforgettable cultural expedition. Highly recommended. Bring patience, but leave naiveté home. Watch yourself and watch all around you in the busy crowd.

BATH

You turn north off the southeast coast at Port Morant to reach the *Bath Hotel and Spa.* The road is bordered by thick overgrown jungle with fresh fruit dropping off trees and littering the way to this neat, old, secluded end-of-the-road hotel.

Guest rooms are comfortable, not fancy, but people come mainly for the mineral baths. They flow from two natural springs, one hot, one cold, both slightly radioactive and said to offer "A cure for rheumatism and kindred ailments and especially for treatment of the skin infections."

The level of radioactivity is 4.9 x 10-10 curies per liter in the hot tank, .09 x 10 -10 curies per liter in the cold tank.

Questions to the staff about the dangers of radioactivity elicit blank stares.

There is no doubt the clean mineral baths feel good. As to whether they do good for you, you will have to decide that for yourself. For information call 982-2132, or 982-2315.

Note: Rugged hiking trails leading through the John Crow Mountains or westward into the Blue Mountains can be picked up here.

SPRING GARDEN

One-mile from the town of *Spring Garden*, on the north coast road to *Skibo*, is a 156-acre property called *"Crystal Springs."* Eventually there will be guest quarters, but for now there are only large gardens, coffee plantings, bananas, gunga peas, as well as an old waterwheel and a canteen/store under construction.

Sylbert Moore manages the property and he will show you the Doctor Bird feeders filled with a sweet strawberry syrup to keep the hummers coming around. You can understand why the birds are wanted when you hear their chirping songs in the cool garden air.

For now this is just a pretty spot to visit and spend a little time wandering among the trees and flowers. Its location close to busy north coast tourist centers is bound to make it a popular, laid-back spot to stay once accommodations, some planned with private kitchens, are finished. Camping is currently allowed for a small charge.

CASTLETON GARDENS

If you do not mind breathing heavy road exhaust, this is a pretty botanical garden on the main road midway between Kingston and Annotto Bay. The Junction Road parallels the Wag Water River and winds over and through the western edge of the Blue Mountains.

Heavy mountain rains contribute to the lush growth in the shady fifteen acres, including tree ferns, azaleas and mahogany. The place is a little run-down these days, but worth a stop if you are passing by, particularly since the winding road is a tiresome, heavily trafficked one. Camping is allowed, on request, down by the river.

ORACABESSA

Ian Fleming's "Goldeneye" estate is located here. There is not much to see other than the sea view and the outside of the house where the author wrote several James Bond thrillers. He took the name for his fictional hero from the author of a book on Jamaican horticulture. Dennis Mills, at the Nucho Restaurant in Ocho Rios can give you information on the Fleming villa, which rents with a cook and gardener, for privacy seekers, or you can drive up to to see the place and a little bit of Jamaican and literary history.

Three miles west of Oracabessa is a road up to Noel Coward's "Firefly Hill." This was that writer's dream retreat, high on a hill, 1000 feet above the coastline. It was originally owned by the pirate Henry Morgan, but Coward bought the property in the 1950's and spent his final years here until his death in 1973. It is the ultimate in secluded writer's habitats, with a long coastal view and a simple house surrounded by sloping lawns and gardens.

Coward's study is a room with an open, glassless wall overlooking the seacoast. Today the property is owned by the government and is considered a tourist attraction, although few people climb up to it. The road twists up the side of a steep hill, through shaded switchbacks. A four-acre plateau at the

The view from Noel Coward's study

top of the road, above *Blue Harbor* and *Galina Point*, is idyllic, a romantic spot, lit by fireflies at night that gave the writer the inspiration to name it. Coward is buried here.

FERN GULLY

This is a road leading south from Ocho Rios, eventually passing through *Spanish Town*, to Kingston. It is home to hundreds of Jamaica's estimated 550 varieties of ferns and in the cool shade of the steep-sided gully it seems as if it is always raining, which it frequently is. There is usually plenty of traffic, as well as many touristy shops and food stands beneath the big leafy trees and ferns, but the three-mile stretch where you find the most copious growth is still worth a visit. It is pretty, reminiscent of a deep redwood forest in California, only more lush.

ST. ANN'S BAY

Marcus Garvey Statue. Yes, it is here, near his birth place, a statue to the Jamaican national hero, a criminal in his lifetime, later to be made a recipient of the highest national honors. Check it out and the Caribbean feel of an old courthouse and a parish church built in 1866. There is also a statue of Columbus in town. The Garvey statue is in front of the library.

NINE MILES

This is a tiny village south of Runaway Bay, between *Philadelphia* and *Alexandria*, and missing from most maps, where Bob Marley is buried. His tomb is something of a national landmark, the final resting place of the young superstar who carried Jamaican consciousness to the world.

The singer and musician was born outside the town, in the central area of the "garden parish" of St. Ann, named for its fertility. The tomb sits on a hill in a tiny chapel with stained glass windows in rasta colors of green, gold and red. Fans turn out for Marley's April 6 birthday and play his tunes all night long. Ganja is growing in a garden outside the crypt.

MONTEGO BAY

This is probably the single most visited area by tourists, yet it has several interesting sites for the more adventurous traveler.

Sam Sharpe Square is in the center of town and notable less for its historic value than for its position in the heart of the local culture. The setting of statues in the heart of downtown attracts a few tourists and many more Jamaicans. Pay respects to the national hero, then buy sugar cane or steamed peanuts from a street vendor while you mingle with the locals.

Governor's Coach is the name given to a popular tourist train trip that leaves Montego Bay and takes you to the Appleton Rum Distillery and back to town. Many hotel guests take

Governor's Coach tour, Montego Bay

the ride which carries you through the hills outside of the city, into the Cockpits, through the town of *Catadupa* where the streets are lined with bolts of colorful cloth. Ladies there measure you for a shirt or a dress that you pick up custom-tailored on your way back from the booze factory.

The ride costs around $40 JA, which is more expensive than a first-class ticket from Mo-Bay all the way to Kingston, but it is worth it. You get to see the edge of the Cockpits, visit the Ipswich Cave, drink rum punch with a box lunch and tour the distillery. And then there is the slow ride. A Calypso band comes along, and even though that music came from Trinidad, the entertaining trip is definitely a taste of Jamaica.

Be forewarned: It is a long trip. It takes all day. I was unaware of the length of the trip and thought it was going to be a short sightseeing run around the outskirts of town. The trip takes seven-eight hours on the slow train. Be smart and bring some munchies along. You can buy bananas and fruit from street sellers in Mo-Bay before you leave in the early morning. The box lunch is not too good and the sweet rum drinks can work with the swaying train to make you sick on an empty stomach.

Bob Marley Centre. There is not much to see here most of the year, but every summer this is the site of Reggae Sunsplash, the year's premier musical event.

NEGRIL

The Lighthouse is located out past the west cliffs. It is solar-powered. There are steep ladders leading down from the cliffs to the sea and the 100-foot-tall lighthouse gives you good coastal views. Caretakers live on the property, but call ahead to make sure you can get up to the top.

MIDDLEQUARTERS

Bamboo Avenue is in all the touristy guides, but this roadway is still worthwhile. Bamboo stands were long ago planted along the road and when they are full and well-watered in rainy season a tunnel effect is created. The thing I like best about the bamboo is the sound it makes in the wind. The hollow clattering and ponderous creaking of the thick woods are primal Jamaican percussion, a source of Jamaican music. The wind rhythms are part of a subliminal attitude that infuses the sound of the best island tunes with a magnetic appeal that moves you with it when you hear it.

MANDEVILLE

This is a slow-moving town, well-to-do because of nearby Bauxite works and favored by wealthy Jamaican retirees. It is popular with gardeners, birdwatchers and the more sedate wealth of the island. Despite the slightly snobby appeal and lack of fast action, there are good things to see here.

Cecil Charleton's House. Charleton was the Mayor of Mandeville for more than twenty years until his defeat in 1986. He also owns numerous thoroughbred race horses and legal Jamaican betting parlors, all of which have made him a very wealthy man.

Free tours are conducted of his octagon-shaped house, a huge mansion with eight bedrooms on a hill overlooking the city. The tour takes you through his kitchen, as well as his bathroom and bedroom closet, showcasing lots of suits and evidence of conspicuous consumption in the midst of great poverty all around. An outdoor pool that is a lot like a moat flows under his living room. You can walk down steps from the house into the water, then swim outside. Cockatoos and parrots sit in cages guarding a circular driveway.

Strange politics here. Fine arts are prominently displayed, along with heavy carved wooden furniture, gaudy designs, with photos of the mayor on almost every wall. One room is unoccupied, with every furnishing in white, for the gentleman's daughter. I liked a photo of the horseman standing with shady-looking characters at Florida's Hialeah racetrack where his horses ran. Another personal favorite is a photo of Charleton in pompous military garb, with huge epaulets and a hat that looks as if it was borrowed from John Paul Jones. Most impressive for the inequity of it all.

The Bammy Factory is located in Clem Bloomfield's house, at 40 Greenvale Rd. You can watch ladies grinding cassava into flour that is then shaped into squares and baked or deep fried. There is no wheat grown in Jamaica. Bammies are a starchy bread substitute, a little heavy but good with fried fish. Phone 962-2821 for information.

Pic-A-Peppa Factory, on Shooter's Hill, offers another factory tour, this one showing where they manufacture the Jamaican equivalent of Worcestershire Sauce, a sweet, pungent mix made from tropical fruits and spices. Jamaicans pour it on everything they eat, from eggs at breakfast, to fish at dinner. Phone 962-2928 for information.

Pioneer Chocolate Factory is in neighboring *Williamsfield.* Watch chocolate being made from Jamaican cocoa. Phone 962-4216 for details.

High Mountain Coffee Factory is also located in Williamsfield. You can smell this place as you drive by. It is the only coffee factory in this area. They specialize in High Mountain coffee, as distinguished from Blue Mountain, which grows only in that region, and at certain altitudes. High Mountain is lighter and sweeter in taste, and also a very good coffee for a lower price than the more renowned stuff.

Some people like to blend the two coffees. They vacuum pack most of the beans or ground coffee sold here, but they will bag fresh beans for you on request. High Mountain was recently selling here for $35.58 JA per pound, with Blue Mountain going for $55.75 for a half-pound tin, $75.35 JA per pound. Obviously, you are better off buying your coffee from a farmer, if possible.

MILK RIVER

Milk River Spa is another healing mineral spa located at the end of a long, dry road through canefields and scrub close to the south coast, two miles from the sea. The waters here flow from rocks above the hotel and spa, at a constant 120 degrees F., and have been test proven to have the highest levels of radioactivity known to occur naturally on earth.

The World Health Organization says the baths are safe for short dips of fifteen to twenty minutes, twice daily.

Again, no one here questions the dangers of radioactivity and part of the standard treatment includes drinking a tumblerful of the murky, warm water. Bottoms up?

Many people claim to have been cured of arthritic complaints, muscular problems, skin diseases and a wide range of ailments. You will no doubt hear stories about people dragging themselves in here on crutches and then throwing the crutches away after a week of baths. The spa director believes the radioactivity allows the high magnesium, calcium, sodium and other mineral content to penetrate and heal the body.

Radioactivity has been measured at 160.2 x 10 -10 curies per liter. This equals nine times the radioactivity of the Bath spa in England, fifty times the levels of the Vichy spa in France, three times more radioactivity than the Karlsbad spa in Austria, and fifty-four times the radioactive content of Baden spa in Switzerland.

Jamaicans consider the place a retreat and weekends bring busloads here from Kingston. Weekdays are usually uncrowded. Few Americans know of this place although European and Canadian visitors are common. Package tours include a bus ride from Kingston, two baths and lunch, for $80 JA, $40 for children under 10. The baths alone cost $4 JA, $2 for children.

An attendant knocks on the door to the private baths after fifteen minutes to get you out. The bath chambers themselves are none too fancy, dark and with cracked tiles, but the water feels good—that is, if you can relax in there. I took one nervous quick soak, but could not stop thinking about the radioactivity. You float easily in the heavy, salty water. Does it cure? I was not ill and cannot say. Other guests were convinced of the healing powers. A girl with phlebitis thought it was fantastic. For information call 925-9544.

SPANISH TOWN

This is an old Jamaican capital city. There are a lot of architecturally significant buildings representing a fair amount of history, but I find the area depressing. Many people line the crowded streets. Not as dirty as it once was, it still feels claustrophobic and intimidating to me. This is just a personal feeling. The best places to visit are the *National Archives*, several old churches, a *Folk Museum* and a *People's Museum of Craft & Technology* in the *Old King's House*, as well as the *White Marl Arawak Museum.*

"Everyt'ing's gonna be alright. Everyt'ing's gonna be alright."—Bob Marley, "No Woman, No Cry."

CHAPTER TWELVE

REGGAE, MUSIC & DANCE

In Jamaica, reggae is called the "heartbeat of the people." The thumping, bass heavy rhythms derive from American blues, as well as African chanting and tribal drumming, spiced by the tempos of the Caribbean that you hear in the hustle of the ghetto, the patter of rain on a tin roof and the creak of bamboo in the wind. It frequently features lyrics about protest, cutting to the bones of inequity, then in the next breath turning to celebrate existence and survival, singing with the power of the oppressed to persevere despite hardships heaped on cruelty.

There was a time when you could hear reggae blasting from concert-size speakers on every corner of every decent-sized Jamaican town. This is less common today. Listening to Jamaican radio you hear a lot of pop-reggae, the same as what you hear on American top-40. "Dubbing," or rap music is very popular, with its repetitive strains competing for airtime with the best of traditional "chanting," the name given to the fundamental roots music of electrified reggae, which sounds a lot like blast-away rock n' roll.

Of the latter style, the most popular exponent was and still is Bob Marley, the late and lionized music star who virtually transformed the island-bred music into an international phenomenon. In music shops, vegetarian "Ital" restaurants and rasta vendors' stalls you see posters of the dead musician. His popularity here, since his death in 1981, is comparable to Elvis in Memphis—gone but in no ways forgotten, practically deified and spoken of lovingly, in reverential tones.

Marley's old house and studio, called Tuff Gong, is located at 56 Hope Road in Kingston, and it is still something of a center for the most serious reggae being produced today. Rita Marley, the singer's wife, runs the business now. She is a popular star in her own right, performing with the "I-Threes," former Marley back-up singers, along with Judy Mowatt and Marcia Griffiths. The Marley children, Ziggy, Sharon, Cedella and Steve are into the act, too. They have a group called "The Melody Makers."

How popular is reggae and the Marley legend? Tour buses visit Tuff Gong these days, taking the short museum tour through Bob's old bedroom and kitchen.

"Foreigners like real Jamaican music. Jamaicans love foreign music," according to Paul Kelly, one of the managers of the Marley Museum.

Oddly, this seems to be true, as more and more Jamaicans strive for a homogenized, Americanized existence, trying to separate themselves from their roots in poverty and slavery by emulating the styles and tastes of a powerful white establishment. Americans and Europeans jaded by their own provincial tastes are looking for something new and different, with reggae filling the bill as an exotic import. The grass is always greener. . . .

One of the gate guards at Tuff Gong is a tall rasta named "Bragga," who grew up in Kingston's *Trench Town* slums with Bob Marley. He traveled from the deepest ghetto to the heights of international acclaim with his friend, and back down to the guardianship of the reggae castle on the star's death. This is a man to talk to if you are looking for the real thing in live reggae. Few spots in Kingston offer live music nightly. Bragga knows about all the sessions that go on unadvertised every weekend. He may not offer this information to everyone. These all night jams are private, family-like affairs. But you can try.

Once a month, or so, there is a big reggae show in Kingston. These are advertised on radio and by handbills pasted up all over town. Watch for them.

The biggest stars today include Toots and the Maytals, Bunny Wailer, who played with Marley, Rita Marley and the I-Threes, Peter Tosh, another ex-Marley bandmate,* Third World, The Mighty Diamonds, Burning Spear, Dennis Brown, Jimmy Cliff, Sly Dunbar and Robbie Shakespeare, Leroy Sibbles and the lyrical poet Mutabaruka. The biggest dubbing star is an albino disc jockey called "Yellowman", followed closely by Linton Kwesi Johnson.

There are hundreds of local bands all over the island, particularly around Kingston and Negril. Many of these are good. After all, music is one of the only ways for young people to get out of the ghetto.

Once you start listening to reggae you will probably find yourself tapping your foot to it, then the rest of your body sort

Ipso Facto, at Reggae Sunsplash

*Tragically, Tosh was murdered in late 1987.

of falls into the groove. When you hear it after you get home from Jamaica, it transports you right back to the island, in your heart at least, and in your body as it seems to involuntarily step and sway to the tune.

Amazingly, despite the presence of all this good music, discos proliferate all over the island, playing recorded music, often re-playing rap songs over and over again in a destructive hypnotic manner that numbs your senses as much as good reggae lights them. So much for mass taste.

You can hear live reggae on weekends at Fort Clarence, on Hellshire Beach. The shows are popular, crowded colorful and exciting when the music is hot. As for local clubs, the best known one is called *Skateland*, located at Half Way Tree, a major Kingston intersection. Other clubs have occasional live performances, but mostly the discos proliferate, filled with scratchy sounds and hookers.

For top-flight information on what is going on around Kingston musically, stop by *High Times, Ltd.*, at the Kingston Mall, around the corner from the National Gallery. Definitely see Delroy Bailey or Betram Brown, nice guys and knowledgeable ones. If you hear some recorded music you like, but do not want to carry around an LP, they will record any record in the shop on your blank tape, and they can give you the inside scoop on the local music scene. This is also one of the best record stores on the island, with one of the widest selections of classic reggae and new tunes, too. Occasionally you can meet recording artists here promoting their records. A must stop for reggae fans. Shop 42, Kingston Mall, phone 922-5538 or 927-7453.

Tuff Gong (927-7103) also sells reggae records, mostly Marley stuff and other artists working for their label. Ziggy's, the Marley recording studio and pressing factory on Marcus Garvey Drive sells records. Bunny Wailer's *Cash and Carry*, on Orange Street, *Music City*, on East Queen Street, and *Aquarius*, on Half Way Tree, are among the numerous record stores in Kingston, all with varying selections. There are record stores in Montego Bay and Ocho Rios, but the best ones are in Kingston.

Reggae Sunsplash is the biggest reggae event in the world, drawing 50,000 people to each show for four nights in August at Mo Bay's Bob Marley Centre. It is a powerful cultural scene as salespeople hawk all kinds of ital foods, curry goat, bammy and fish, jelly coconut, sugarcane, fruit juices and drugs to the glowing crowd that walks in with cold buckets of Red Stripe beer to help them through long nights listening to top stars.

Everyone who is anyone performs at Sunsplash. There have been reports of hassles, but in the last few years these have diminished as people seem to come in peace from all over the world to hear the ultimate expression of this type of music and make the scene. Montego Bay gets super-crowded and places such as Damali Beach are filled with campers for the week-long bash surrounding the nights of music. Plan far ahead if you want to attend. Flights and accommodations are booked solid for this annual Jamaican version of Woodstock. And get

At Sunsplash

your rest before you come. The music goes on until dawn and the parties last longer than that.

On Sunday nights in Mo-Bay you can usually find an outdoor dance outside Chin's Bakery and Global Travel in Sunshine Plaza, 2 Church St. These tend to get a bit raunchy, so watch yourself.

A reliable Mo-Bay hot spot is *Lyle's Intensified Inn*, a combination restaurant, hotel, nightclub, wholesale liquor store and disco. You can buy fresh Jamaican pastries, fritters, fish and bammy, or you can drink white rum for $2 JA per shot. "Restaurant & Bar—Eat—Drink + ?," says the "Zap Comix"-style sign out front, at 36 Barnett St., 952-4980. The next line on the sign says "NO LOAFERS, Prostitute & Pimps Read & Run or Else?"

Despite or because of the colorful sign, there are plenty of hookers and pimps. Inside you can watch dancers in string bikinis performing slightly lewd acts while caressing metal rails on a little stage in the center of a dark dance floor.

There are also wholesale bulla cakes and inexpensive meals. Late at night, the combination of services makes for a crowded scene. The restaurant serves good, authentic Jamaican foods at low prices and the whole operation exemplifies the loosest of Jamaican nightlife. People drink and hoot at the dancers. The dancers come on to all the guys. Located next to Oneness Plaza. Be careful, but check it out. It is quite a happening scene, particularly on weekends.

Several other bars line Barnett St. Lyle's is the biggest and busiest. Other interesting clubs nearby include *The Jokers Club*, on Orange St. and Love Lane, where there seems to be a perpetual game of dominoes going on. Next door is the *Solidarity Pub and Tailoring*, "Prop. Prince Brown." Stand back and watch a loud game of emotional dominoes, drink white rum that will knock your socks off, chat with nightlife cruisers, hookers and pimps.

The Far Bar and *Sir Winston's*, both on Gloucester Avenue, cater mainly to tourists. The first has loud recorded music. The latter often has a live show.

There are several record stores in Montego Bay, all carrying selections of reggae. A lot of the records they sell are not shrink-wrap sealed and many are badly warped. Bring blank tapes and pay to have them recorded.

Negril is often the site of live reggae shows, usually outdoors, on cement bandstands along the beach, which is a pretty fantastic place to listen and dance under the stars. Try *Alfred's* or *Roots Bamboo*, or check for signs plastered around town. Weekends are best for live music.

Port Antonio is the site of the famous *Roof Club*. Music starts at 7:30 nightly and goes on until dawn. Guests at Navy Island, across the harbor, report being kept awake by the Roof Club sounds, which usually come from recorded music, not live, including lots of dubbing and not so much reggae these days. After a while it sounds as if the same song is being played over and over again.

Another jumping spot for Port Antonio nightlife is the *Centre Point Club*, a bar and restaurant up a small hill on the east side of town. Good seafood, loud music. Several other clubs in town include the *Blue Jay Club* and the *City Club*. Expect loud music, rarely live, played until dawn.

Ocho Rios has clubs, too, although only infrequent live reggae sessions. Bigger hotels have shows, but rarely decent reggae. Listen for the sounds at night or ask locals around the clock tower where the best music an be found.

Dancing in Jamaica is a natural extension of the powerful music, ranging from classical Caribbean dance troupes, to mesmerized, drunken slow-stepping to hypnotic dubbing, to loosey-goosey grace generated by top-notch reggae.

Reggae, in particular, seems to infuse people with a special rhythmic signature. It practically forces long-limbed bodies to sway in suspended time, as if motivated by a pre-historic internal drive mechanism. Jamaicans look strong and fit when they dance to their music. The reggae flows through the casual dancers, the disco goers, the concert dancers, connecting each individual to a heritage of movement so deep it defies conscious memory.

There is also a Jamaican National Dance Troupe that performs primarily in Kingston. Forget the fire-eaters or the limbo dancers gyrating to imported calypso. Jamaican artists have their own dramatic sensibility, a unique blend of Caribbean hot-life and African history that combines to produce the commanding, graceful expressive movement of Jamaican ballet.

The National Dance Theatre Company performs in Kingston in July and August, and again in November and December. More formal than street dancers or reggae partygoers, this troupe nevertheless captures a sense of the island spirit in stylized movement.

Other uniquely Jamaican performing artists participate in a *National Pantomime*, a seasonal showing of satirical vignettes that runs from Christmas to Easter in Kingston. Local regional theatre fills in the gaps during the rest of the year.

Christmas-time also sees "Johnkanoo" celebrations, featuring street dancing, parades and parties island-wide.

The Barn Theatre and the *Way Inn Theatre* at the New Kingston Hotel in Kingston offer amateur productions. Even the National Dance Theatre members hold down full-time jobs in employment-poor Jamaica, despite the fact that they have performed to critical raves all over the world.

There are many other reggae clubs throughout the island, from the small *Treasure Beach Disco*, right on the isolated beach, where you can hear waves crashing into the shore in one ear, dubbing playing over and over in the other, to *Ringo's Club*, at Jack's Hill, a tiny local hangout where you drink your Red Stripe and sway in the darkness to a scratchy collection of reggae classics, with Kingston's city lights glowing far below you.

Drinks in these places are usually cheap, $2 JA for a beer or a shot of 177 proof rum.

The company is most often congenial Jamaicans out for relaxation.

The music varies from masterpieces to horrid, scratchy dubs. The experience is, however, surely a part of your Jamaican adventure. Get out and boogie with Jamaica. As long as you are here, you owe it to yourself. The music and dance will entertain you with a lyrical sense of Jamaica you will long remember.

"The great thing was being able to see ourselves as Jamaicans in Jamaica."—Edna Manley, artist.

CHAPTER THIRTEEN

ARTS & CRAFTS

All you have to do to see art in Jamaica is poke around roadside souvenir stalls or look at the outrageous signs and paintings on the sides of buildings.

Artists come in all forms, from roadside rasta wood craftsmen to fine artists who display their work in the National Gallery. As with reggae and music, the arts are an expressive form of release. Colorful paintings and proud carvings, cunning jewelry designs in shells and hard black coral all reflect a bond with the ancients as well as the newness of the country. The exuberance of recent independence combines with an African heritage. Some of the work is presumptuous, some is touching. A lot of it is bad or easy, but most is at least spirited.

Kingston is the center for the highest standards in the fine arts. The National Gallery has many interesting artworks, including the largest intuitive section on the island. These primitive works revel in fundamental individuality. Color and exuberant forms are similar to Haitian art. See this and more here, as well as at *The Frame Center*, a gallery at 10 Tangerine Place, 926-4644, and *The Mutual Life Gallery*, 2 Oxford Rd., 926-9025, on the corner of Old Hope Rd.

For excellent craft work, visit *Devon House*, 26 Hope Rd., 929-6602. The buildings here have architectural interest for their restored Georgian designs. Goods for sale are costly, also

SWABY'S
COOL
JOINT
WELCOM

Mural, Assembly Hall Building, University of the West Indies

skillful. *Upstairs Downstairs Gallery*, 108 Harbor St., 922-8260, has works by famous artists at high prices.

For the less formally inclined art fancier, check out the graffiti scrawls on urban buildings and the colorful signs and murals adorning shops and restaurants. Personal favorites include wall art outside *Swaby's Cool Joint*, a restaurant and bar south of Montego Bay on the road to *Petersfield*, the cartoon art outside Lyle's Intensified Inn, in downtown Mo-Bay on Barnett St., the all-Jamaica "Year of the Child" mural on a building at the University of the West Indies, in Kingston, and literally hundreds of other interpretive paintings, most done in bright Caribbean flower colors, or in the red, gold and green emblematic colors of the rastas.

The common thread in these highly individualistic works seems to be boldness in colors and stylized subject matter reflecting a pride that surfaces despite the hardships many art-

---

Swaby's Cool Joint

ists experience, made even rougher by the harsh conditions of living in a place like Jamaica.

The thing that saves much of it from pomposity is a sense of humor. Jamaicans work hard under trying conditions, yet do not take things too seriously. This is the heart of the survival instinct that gives so much of this "yard art" the look of comic book art, as well as a nobility in laughing at itself when it would be just as easy to cry.

This yard art is everywhere, from Kingston's bleakest bombed-out looking ghettos to the country inn dining room of the Hotel Astra in sedate Mandeville, where a large intuitive painting depicts Jamaican agriculture. The informality and lack of pretense establishes a presence that is admirable and undeniable.

There are many imitators, numerous lousy wooden carved birds or mass produced paintings. All the tourist strip shops sell those.

There are really nice galleries, too.

Jamaican yard art

Harmony Hall west of Ocho Rios, is always worth a stop. *Joe James Gallery* in Rio Bueno, on the north coast, has a lot of paintings, drawings and sculptures priced from $80 JA to $100,000. James has had US exhibitions at Washington, DC's Calvert Collection. He recently opened a small gallery in Miami's Coconut Grove. *Heaven's Art Gallery.* 52 Barnett St., Montego Bay, 952-2852, often has nice work for sale.

Other well-known artists include the late Edna Manley, the wife of a Jamaican Prime Minister and the mother of another Prime Minister. Her specialties include sculpturing and promotion of Jamaican arts and artists. She created the powerful Paul Bogle statue in Morant Bay.

Another famous statue is the Bob Marley piece outside Kingston's National Stadium. The original work that was conceived by Christopher Gonzales drew such public criticism and threats from the people of the county that it was whisked away from this very public spot. Another artist was commissioned to create a new Bob. You have to go to the National Gallery to see the Gonzales piece.

John Dunkley is another famous name in Jamaican art. It is almost impossible to buy one of his paintings today. The former barber originally decorated his haircutting shop with his artwork. Today, many of the pieces hang in the National Gallery, as well as in private collections. Carl Abrahams, Sydney McLaren and Mallica Reynolds, who paints under the name of "Kapo," are among the best-known island artists, intuitives, primitive explorers of colors and shapes that identify the Jamaican psyche and reality.

Paintings on walls probably date all the way back to the Arawaks. They left their designs inside caves. Some are still visible today, 400 years after their demise as a living race.

Many Jamaicans are little-known for their work, but their work no less reflects the integrity of their spirit. I-rise, as mentioned earlier, is the name of a Canadian-born artist who lives at the Blue Hole at the Roaring River. Her paintings are gaining recognition and are special because they come from a newcomer to Jamaica, looking at this country with fresh eyes, a Jamaican by choice, not by birth. Her work is on display at Harmony Hall and several Kingston galleries, or you can meet her at the Blue Hole. She will pull out a selection of recent work and set paintings up outdoors, propped on rocks or against tree stumps for your viewing pleasure. A little down the road from here, *Shaper's Store*, at the base of a 300-year-old silk cotton tree at the entrance to the Roaring River Cave, is filled with coconut shell art, carved buttons and paintings done in a rasta motif, primitive for sure, completely honest, too.

My friend Baps, in Jack's HIll, carves wooden flutes. No great art involved here, just simple design creating pure Jamaican sound. You can buy one from him for a few dollars.

In Port Antonio an interesting thing happened while I was traveling with my wife. I had recently brought her custom-made black coral earrings from Tonga, in the South Pacific. One of the little black stars always seemed to come loose from the post it was glued to. She lost one of the stars in Jamaica.

We were having breakfast at the *Bonnie View Hotel* when a young man approached us trying to sell his designs in Jamaican black coral jewelry. I asked him if he could match the star that was left. He assured me he could do it. He wanted $60 JA for the job. I said $30 JA. He said okay. We gave him the one earring and left for another appointment, telling the jeweler we would return later that evening. My wife was a little nervous about this casual arrangement. She was attached to the little earrings and even though one was lost she did not want to lose the other one.

After traipsing around the countryside all day we returned to the deserted-looking Bonnie View after dark. Within minutes Tony Maxwell appeared with two earrings. It was impossible to tell which was the duplicate and which was the original. $30 JA is around $5 US—for a custom-made black coral earring. Look for Tony if you like the black coral.

Another Port Antonio artist is Renford Stewart. He has a small studio at 5 William St. where he paints and sculpts. Nothing fancy here, just the bright colors of the Jamaican countryside, done in oils, the result of twenty years of self-taught expression. He charges from $40 JA to $300. "My price small, my painting inexpensive," the humble artist explains.

You really cannot miss at those prices for an original oil painting.

If you venture into the surrounding Portland countryside, up toward the village of Millbank, deep in the John Crow Mountains, look for a friendly man named "Peggy Laura." His real name is Roderick Searchwell and he sculpts out of the local hardwoods. He favors rasta-inspired carved heads. It may not be the greatest art but it certainly is legitimate self-expression, and far from the commercial stands of Ocho Rios or Montego Bay.

There are literally thousands of street artists in Jamaica, mass producing souvenirs or junk found in Kingston's crafts market, to the real things you can buy from Peggy Laura or I-Rise. The museums and best galleries hold classics. The streets hold the breath of today, as fresh as the morning and as fleeting as the mist. Grab it while you can.

Plentiful Scottish-inspired rasta tams are colorful hand-made crafts. You can buy a decent-sounding mass-produced

Wood carver

bamboo drum emblazoned with ugly paint drippings and the tacky tourist logo of "Jamaica." You can have your choice of thousands of wooden doctor birds or sea turtles. The craft markets in Montego Bay, Negril, Ocho Rios and Kingston are filled with them, along with flour sack clothing, t-shirts, straw bags, lathe-turned wooden goblets and bored higglers selling the least artful of the crafts available. You can look a little farther and come up with unique expressions at Muriel Chandler's *Caribatick Factory*, on Rock Wharf in Falmouth (954-3314) at Shaper's or even in one of Baps' bamboo flutes. He is short on tools. The Flutes are made by heating a piece of scrap iron over a wood fire and burning in the finger holes. How much more intuitive and authentic can you get?

"Jamaica has numerous secrets. . . . "—Peter Bentley, President, Jamaica Alternative Tourism Camping & Hiking Association.

PART III

MONEY SAVING ALTERNATIVES

It is easy to spend more than you want to on a trip, a skill to spend less without sacrificing comfort or pleasure.

Knowing where to get the best deals on good food, whether you cook it yourself or eat out in restaurants, the best rates on accommodations, from camping in your own tent to staying in a ritzy, staffed villa (in off-season for value seekers), as well as how to make the most practical transportation arrangements, can save you a bundle.

Cutting costs and doing all the things you want to do, is an acquired talent.

Tour operators take responsibility for choices and sell you packages, sometimes before you know what you want to do. Independent travelers on tight budgets often face unanticipated spur-of-the-moment cost-cutting compromises.

A plan, however loose, and the information to carry it out, helps you take the adventure out of paying your bills and leave it where it belongs, in the things you do, the sites you see, the people you meet and interact with.

This section deals with the basics of travel, eating, sleeping and getting around, and includes hints on dealing successfully and economically with Jamaican commerce.

You may want to ride a bike around the country, at no cost for transportation and then stay in top hotels, or you may want to skip the hotels altogether, spend your money on a rental car and stay with Jamaican families. Whatever your preference and comfort level you require, these listings will provide safe and economical alternatives to winging it completely or buying into a package plan that suits no one completely. This is where you get the background to make good choices for yourself from far away, at least enough to get you started in Jamaica until you can find your way on your own.

Americanized hotels are fine if you are in the US, but if you want to experience the unique qualities of Jamaica, these leads will show you things relatively few foreigners are aware of. You can try some or all of them and be assured of finding good value and interesting experiences in an adventurous mode as Jamaica unveils its secrets for you.

"Underneath the mango tree, my honey and me. . . ."—James Bond, "Dr. No."

CHAPTER FOURTEEN

FOODS & DINING

Jamaican foods include a lot of fresh vegetables and fruits grown here, as well as throwback foods popular since colonial days prior to refrigeration. Salting of fish and meats has retained popularity from the days when this was necessary for preserving foods on long ocean trips. Fresh fish are primarily prepared for visitors. Many Jamaicans prefer salted cod, which is neither fresh nor local. Other heavy spices are also used. Hotly seasoned foods make you sweat, which actually helps cool you down in steamy tropical weather.

Major hotel dining rooms and pricey restaurants in tourist areas still try to cater to visitors' tastes by flying in steaks (there is hardly any local beef) and canned green beans, but more of these places are starting to offer local foods as well.

For the traveler who wants to get a taste of Jamaica, smaller eating establishments are more authentic, as well as less expensive. Roadside vendors that you see everywhere are another source of fresh local foods, from coconut water served by a machete-wielding rasta, to the famed hot-peppered shrimp thrust through your car window in Middlequarters. Other quick stops can net you jerk pork, Red Stripe beer, mangos (in season April to early October), paw-paw (papaya), dried fish and yams, and of course, bananas are everywhere.

Roadside vendors work everyday. Village markets are generally open every day, except Sunday, although the busiest market days for the best selection of fresh foods are Thursday to Saturday, when all the farmers from outlying villages come into Montego Bay, Kingston or any of the bigger towns to peddle their crops.

Mangos, avocados or breadfruit can sometimes be picked off trees for free, but the island is crowded and most of the arable land is being farmed. Most of the foods that are growing belong to someone. Ask first. The sale price for a piece of fruit might be something like 20 cents JA for a banana, 50 cents JA for a mango.

Aside from eating out or buying fresh food to prepare yourself, there is a third option in the numerous local cooks who will whip up a meal for you at nominal rates. If you plan ahead, they will usually buy the food for you, or you can bring your own, or take pot luck. I have gone this route many times and never regretted it. Something is always cooking and Jamaicans, males and females, are inventive chefs.

Drinking water is generally purified and safe to drink. If in

Hot peppered shrimp

doubt, go for a Pepsi or a Red Stripe. The hot sauces and spices may be more dangerous to your health. Caution is advised.

A lot of the local food and drink may sound and taste unusual to travelers. The following is a run-down of some of the things you will encounter.

Ackee is the national vegetable, a standard when served with salted cod for a classic Jamaican breakfast. It grows on a tree and has a hard shell, which, when cracked, emits a poisonous gas. You let the gas escape, then boil or saute the yellow fleshy insides with scallions and tomatoes. Cooked ackee looks like scrambled eggs, takes on the flavor of the spices it is cooked with.

Bammy is a bread substitute made from cassava flour.

Bird Pepper is a little red and yellow pepper—super hot.

Breadfruit was introduced by Captain Bligh of the famous mutineers ship, "The Bounty." It is a starchy vegetable, another bread substitute, served fried, roasted or boiled.

Bulla is a small, sweet spice cake, a snack food you can buy in bakeries or rum shops by the roadsides.

Callaloo is a big green, leafy vegetable, also called dasheen, or elephant ears. It tastes like spinach and is used in pepperpot soup.

Cheeseberries are small, sweet, yellow berries that grow wild in the Blue Mountains, free for the picking.

Cho-cho is a squash-like vegetable, pear-shaped and with a prickly skin.

Coconut water is the liquid you get out of the big green coconuts sold by roadside vendors for a dollar or two. They first cut a hole in the hard shell for you to drink from, then, after you drain the sweet liquid, they whack off the top with a machete. You can use the hard piece of shell as a spoon to scoop out the meaty inside.

Cow cod soup is made from bovine genitals and said to increase virility. "It build de' back up for de' man, keep you going long in de' night, right t'rough de' night."

Curry goat is a spicy, curry stew served with rice and cooked green bananas. Watch out for bones!

Dragon Stout is a locally brewed dark beer, similar to Guinness Stout.

Escoveitched fish is fried in spices and vinegar. Eat it with bammy and have a cold Red Stripe nearby to put out the fire in your mouth.

Fish Tea is made by boiling fish and vegetables with allspice and hot peppers.

Ginger is a valuable export crop. Jamaican ginger is world famous. Here, it is used as a seasoning or brewed in a tea that is supposed to aid digestion and ease stomach upsets. Many rum shops also sell home made ginger beer.

Guava is a sweet fruit with hard seeds. Eat it fresh or try the jelly made from it.

Hard dough bread is Jamaican white bread.

Irish Moss is a thick drink made from seaweed, sweetened condensed milk, nutmeg, and vanilla. Said to be a boon to sexuality.

Janga are the little river crayfish used for making hot-peppered "shrimp" or, as Jamaicans say, "swimp."

Jerk pork is the barbecue style of slow cooking marinated, spiced meat over green pimento wood. Chicken and fish are also jerked, but pork is the classic meal.

Johnny cake is a fried dough ball made from white flour.

Mango is a succulent, messy fruit with soft flesh filled with sticky juice. Some are stringy, others smooth, some sweet, others tart. Of the more than two hundred varieties growing only in tropical climes worldwide, sixty to seventy varieties are found in profusion throughout Jamaica. They can be eaten straight off the blessedly shady trees, or prepared in chutney or preserves. Some people like to eat unripe, hard green mangos with salt. The sap on the outside of the skin is related to poison ivy so wash your hands after you handle it. The skin is edible, although not usually eaten. A cold mango on a hot day can go a long way toward explaining why Jamaica is thought of in some circles as a paradise. Look for different varieties in different regions.

Mannish water is a thick, spicy goat soup served to energize grooms on their wedding day. Made from goats' heads, tripe and feet.

Matrimony is a fruit salad made from star apples, which are a green and purple fruit, along with oranges, grapefruit and condensed milk.

Mushroom tea is made from psilocybin mushrooms. Depending on who makes it and how much you consume it can be a strong psychedelic drug. It is legal. The mushrooms grow beneath cattle manure.

Naseberries are also called sapodilla. The size of a peach, you can eat the fuzzy brown skin of this fruit along with the sweet pulpy inside.

Old Jamaica Liqueurs are made in the Blue Mountains from local produce combined with rum. Varieties have flavors of pimento, coconut rum, wild orange, and ortanique. When you take the free factory tour at Ian Sangster's World's End, you get thimble-size samples of all the different liqueurs.

Ortanique is a Jamaican-bred cross between an orange, a tangerine and the word unique.

Otaheite apple originally came from the South Pacific. Red on the outside, with a big pit in the middle, the white fruit inside is sweet.

Patties are meat pies in a pastry shell. The meat is of indeterminate nature, heavily spiced. Jamaican burgers.

Paw-paw is papaya.

Peas are what Jamaicans call beans. Red peas or "gunga" peas are served with rice as a staple meal.

Pepperpot soup is made from leafy green vegetables such as kale and callaloo, combined with pig's tail, salted beef or ham hocks and yams. Add allspice, scallions, thyme, garlic and scotch bonnet peppers. The secret to making the best soup is adding grated coconut just before serving.

Pic-a-Peppa Sauce is the local variant of Worcestershire Sauce. It is sweet and spicy and Jamaicans douse everything with it.

Pimento is the Jamaican name for allspice, combining the flavors of cinnamon, nutmeg and cloves. The best in the world is grown here.

Plantain is similar to a banana, though less sweet and usually served fried rather than eaten raw.

Pumpkin soup is made from green Caribbean pumpkins, "ca-

labaza," along with yams, coconut, tomatoes, marjoram, thyme, scallions, pimento and hot green pepper.

Red Stripe Beer is the locally brewed favorite. Many Jamaicans prefer drinking it "hot," at room temperature.

Roots is a concoction of various bush and tree roots mixed into a rum-based tonic, sometimes called "roots wine." The exact blend is usually a brewer's secret and may include ganja root, among others. Generally it looks like a muddy liquid with twigs floating in it and tastes something like witch hazel. It is said to be a good tonic for cleansing your insides. Swilling the stuff bravely is considered a sign of virility.

Run down is a fish custard made from mackerel, coconut milk, peppers and scallions. It tastes better than it sounds.

Rum is everywhere, a product of all the sugar cane grown here. A syrupy sweet rum punch is served free to everyone getting off a plane at Montego Bay's airport. Recipe: One measure sour–usually lime juice; two sweet–fruit syrup or sugar; three strong–rum; four weak–water.

There are numerous brands of light and dark rum, including home brew. The most potent is called "John Crow Batty," a white rum that checks in at a dizzying 177 proof. Make sure you do not have far to fall before you start drinking it.

Scotch bonnet is a powerful hot pepper.

Solomon gundy is a heavily spiced pickled herring.

Soursop is a green-skinned fruit with a rough outer texture. The inside is flaky, like broiled fish, and the taste is like a sweet-sour citrus.

Sprats are greasy little fried or roasted fish sold in rum shops.

Stamp 'n Go is a breaded fish fritter.

Star apple is a round purple fruit, with seeds inside in the shape of a star.

Sweetsop is similar to soursop, but sweeter.

Tamarind is an acidic fruit with a brittle brown shell. You can eat it fresh or in fruit drinks. It is one of the main ingredients of Pic-a-Peppa sauce.

Tia Maria is a coffee liqueur made in Jamaica.

Market stall

Ugli fruit is a citrus hybrid bred from crossing grapefruits and tangerines.

In addition to these foods, health-care-poor Jamaicans grow numerous herbs that they brew into "bush teas" for home-made medicines. There are hundreds of varieties of common and unusual plants used by the rapidly dwindling ranks of "bush doctors." Among these are lemongrass, fevergrass, leaf of life, sorrel, dandelion, basil, thyme, "come search me heart," colormint, peppermint, lime leaf and of course, the famous cash crop, sinsemilla, which is dried and smoked or brewed in tea. Any country-born Jamaican will have at least a passing acquaintance with the healing herbs. City-folk are less likely to have that knowledge. Among the best sources for detailed information on bush medicines are Ken Moulton, of Jack's Hill, and Esau Kerr, proprietor of the Lover's Cafe and former manager of the Ital Herb Farm at the Blue Hole on the Roaring River.

FOOD SOURCES

The following is a guide to the best restaurants, markets and roadside vendors all over the island.

MONTEGO BAY

The city has its share of over-priced restaurants and hotel dining rooms serving aberrant Jamaican foods that do no justice to Jamaican cuisine, nor to the American or Continental tastes they mimic badly. There are also many decently-priced restaurants serving the real thing in Jamaican cooking, as well as dozens of street vendors serving delicious creations.

Bevin & Barnett Sts. is a busy corner from 4 PM to 2 AM. Street vendors come out in force, selling sugar cane, water coconut, steamed peanuts from loud whistling carts and some of the best jerk chicken in town. The chicken is barbecued in a steel drum smoker by a quiet chef who did not want to tell me his name. He thinks nothing of keeping you waiting, either, letting the chicken slow cook in its own time, to perfection, before he will serve it. Cost: $8 JA for a half-chicken. He sets up on the small island in the center of the intersection. Soak in the local color while you wait for your food.

Damali Beach has a good restaurant and a jerk pork stand in the parking lot.

Whitehouse Village on Kent Ave, behind the airport, has a string of good bars and restaurants on the beach that only locals go to. Try fresh fish.

Wexford Grill in the Wexford Court Hotel is open 24 hours. It looks fancy, and the waiters do serve rolls with tongs, but the prices are reasonable and the food is pretty good. A lot of local business people wearing suits eat here. Good air conditioning. If you are traveling with a finicky child, this is where you can get pizza or burgers.

China Doll Pastry Shop is located behind Sam Sharpe Square. Good variety of cakes and snacks. Inexpensive.

Royal Dainties is an "Ital" restaurant across the street from the main post office. Vegetarian foods only, including fresh fruit drinks, but with plenty of sugar added. You can get a meal of rice and vegetables for around $1.50 US.

A nighttime vendors' market forms by the bridge just north of Sam Sharpe Square.

Charles Gordon Market is near the south end of town on Fustic St. People sell their herbal concoctions, fruit juices, breads, vegetables, cane stalks and other produce out of shopping carts. This is a busy, busy place where you can get anything, including religious revival meetings, domino and bingo games at night.

Lyle's Intensified Inn, 36 Barnett St., has good food, low prices, downstairs on the street below a raging upstairs disco.

GREENWOOD

Turtles Inn is on the main road at *Long Bay*. Mrs. Edna Stephenson serves a lot of fresh seafood, six varieties of turtle prepared in soup for $10 JA, stews and turtle steaks for $25 JA. She also serves curry goat, $25 JA, Chicken, $20, lobster, $70, shrimp, $70, steam fish $25, conch soup, $10, fish tea, $7.50, mannish water $7.50. She gets most of her fresh fish from Savanna-la-Mar on the south coast.

DUNCANS

Sober Robin is right on the main road east of Falmouth. It is a noisy spot but the prices are good for the heavily touristed north coast. A dinner of Jamaican spiny lobster is around $35 JA, other dinners are around $20. There are also a few guest rooms for $70 JA nightly for two.

RIO BUENO

Lobster Bowl at the Gallery Joe James serves grilled or broiled lobster and other fresh fish, but the prices are high, around $90 JA for a lobster dinner.

DISCOVERY BAY

Columbus Park Patty Stand has good patties at this touristy spot commemorating the landing of Columbus, even though this is probably not where he actually first set foot on Jamaica.

RUNAWAY BAY

Northern Jerk Pork definitely serves some of the best jerk pork on the island. It costs $10 JA per half-pound, and they have a unique way of preparing it, deep frying the meat first, then slow cooking it over a traditional wood fire. They also serve fried chicken, have a bakery and a bar. You can eat in the dining room or take out.

OCHO RIOS

There are a lot of expensive and mediocre restaurants in this town, and also a few good ones.

Village Jerk Center, on Main St., across from Turtle Towers in Ocho Rios cooks good jerk pork and chicken.

Lobster Pot, west of the crafts market, is the cheapest restaurant in town for seafood. Steamed fish is $16 JA, curry lobster is $35, steamed lobster is $50.

Jeff's Drive-In has dinners for $30 JA and up. Located in the shopping center near the Burger King.

Parkway Restaurant is located on the square by the clock tower. Not exactly touristy, but not really inexpensive, either, with the lowest priced dinners at $30 JA.

Road Runner is an ice cream shop on the strip west of the crafts market, in the Ocean Village Shopping Center, featuring fresh Jamaican fruit flavors such as mango or lime. This is

An adventure in dining—one of many

a big chain, with shops in Kingston, Montego Bay, Spanish Town and Savanna-la-Mar.

The Ruins is overpriced but in a beautiful setting, with an outdoor patio for dining next to a waterfall.

You can also eat Kentucky Fried Chicken, Burger King, and when you are done go shopping at Woolworth's. Ocho Rios is the Gatlinburg, Tennessee of Jamaica, tacky, touristy, too little for too much money. The most vulgar and commercial part of Jamaica.

MARKING STONE

Around a half-mile east of Annotto Bay is a small cluster of roadside sellers offering roast fish, cooked lobster, raw conch, sea shells, stalks of sugar cane, boiled corn on the cob, saltfish and yams, peppered shrimp, Irish moss and seasonal fruits. The vendors are a little pushy, but traffic is brisk so the food is fresh.

DEVON PEN

Aquarius Specialties/Fantasy Pub is a tiny take-out joint in a small village on the road between Kingston and Annotto Bay, not far from Castleton Gardens. They serve something they call "Tahitian-style fry chicken" and it tastes great, fresh and served hot, cooked to perfection. Cost $6 JA for a half-chicken. The shop is clean, the crowds constant.

BUFF BAY

Rosa's Cantina is a small restaurant behind a rum shop and grocery store. The prices are better than the food, but you can get a hot meal for $1–$6 JA. Rosa serves rice and peas, chicken with sliced tomato and hot green banana. Curry goat and escoveitch fish are top dollar here at around $10 JA.

HOPE BAY

Errol's Easy Going International Coffee Shop. Frankly, I never ate here but I love the name. There are not a lot of restaurants in Hope Bay.

PORT ANTONIO

Aside from the good and expensive restaurants at the bigger hotels, such as the Trident, there are a lot of small restaurants and take-outs in town.

Daddy D Snack Center, on West St. serves patties for $1.50, meat loaf patties for $1.30. You will have to ask Daddy D what the distinction is. A lot of Jamaicans eat here.

Atlantis Restaurant on George St., in the alley next to the Bank of Nova Scotia has good "janga" soup, made from crayfish, for $3 JA. Dinners of curried goat, fried chicken, pork, or steak are $12 JA. Pork stew, stew peas or oxtail are $11 JA. Breakfasts are $6 JA.

The Upper Place Restaurant is located upstairs at the City Centre Plaza, next to the Jamaica Tourist Board office. They serve bacon and eggs for $10 JA, curry goat for $13 JA.

Coronation Bakery, *Three Star Lion Bakery*, or *CC Bakery* sell hard dough bread, 3 lbs for $5 JA. Also look for fresh bullas and cocoa buns.

Mandala Restaurant on West St., upstairs, near the noisy Roof Club disco, serves creole chicken for $15 JA, steam fish or fish and coconut for $20. Lobster is $50–$60. Pizza is $4. A breakfast omelette, with toast and coffee, or tea, is $9. Red Stripes or Dragon Stout are $3. Heineken is $4. Cold soda is $2. Fresh fruit juices, orange, banana, paw-paw or soursop are $5.

Early Bird Restaurant is a jumping spot with locals. A big chicken dinner is $9 JA. Take-out or there is a small, hot dining room in the back.

Try-Me Restaurant had only chicken livers for breakfast two times I stopped by. A sign outside says "It's finger licking."

Kingsley Bar & Restaurant is on West St., directly across from the mini-bus terminal and taxi stands. It looks like only a bar from the street, but there is a dining room in the back that is always crowded with local people. Count on unusually fast service and loud noise inside. It has the cheapest breakfasts in town at $6 JA for ackee and saltfish or scrambled eggs. Coffee is served in the dark dining room with sweetened condensed milk. It is hard to find fresh milk anywhere, including many of the best hotels. Fresh food at Kingsley, best in-town prices.

A city produce market is busy Thursday through Saturday on West St. Located in the center of town, in front of *Musgrave Market* where you get crafts and souvenirs, a few doors down from Kingsley's. Bananas are around 20 cents JA each, $2.40 JA, or less than 50 cents US per dozen.

BOSTON BEACH

In the shadow of the John Crow Mountains, where rebellious Maroons first barbecued wild pigs, the epicurean standard for jerk pork is established at *Boston Beach*. The cooking fires and open air butcher shops are mere yards from the roadway, with several firepits going all the time from early morning until late at night. Pork, fish, chicken, goat or pig heads, feet, sausage, "chit'lin's," nothing is wasted and it all gets the treatment, being soaked in a secret hot pepper marinade, then slow cooked for hours over green sticks and under cover of a section of metal roofing material. The first cooked meats are done around 10:30–11 AM.

Among other experts, Harris Grace, also known as "Lawless," makes some of the most potent hot pepper sauce you will find anywhere. This is the famous blend that sets Boston Beach pork apart from the rest of the jerk cooking on the island. He sells re-filled ketchup bottles of the salty stuff for $8–$10 JA, and this amount will last for many months at home. Try it for lighting up a Bloody Mary. Cheers.

MORANT BAY

There are not many restaurants around this area. Try *Chef's Seaview Restaurant & Lounge*, west of town, on the beach. It has a disco, too.

ROZELLE BEACH

Aside from the *Zion Ethiopian Coptic Store*, which sells mostly tinned food supplies, *La Rozelle Beach Club & Restaurant* prepares sea food. They usually have lobster, roast fish and fish tea.

BLUE MOUNTAINS

There are few commercial dining rooms in the Blue Mountains. If you plan to spend time on your own in this area, hiking or camping, or even driving by yourself, it is a good idea to note the rare markets.

Papine Market, in West Kingston has the last good shopping before you enter the Blue Mountains. There is a big outdoor market near the University of the West Indies on Thursday and Saturday, also supermarkets, drug stores, liquor stores, bakeries and a lot of little restaurants open every day.

Maya Hiking Center at Jack's Hill has good food. It is best to call ahead to make sure there is food available, or bring your own. Someone will cook it for you. Pot luck might net you rice 'n peas, with scallions, a sliced tomato, carrots and a glass of herb tea or Blue Mountain Coffee. On a lucky night you will find a beer, or you can walk up the road to a small store that usually has only liquid refreshments.

Meals at Maya usually run between \$1–\$6 US, although unsuspecting guests have paid as much as \$2.75 US for two slices of toast. That is not as bad as the German guest at Maya who took a cab from *Constant Spring* downtown to Maya, only to be driven to Whitfield Hall instead. He paid \$300 JA for that

J's Soul Centre

ride, then it cost him $200 JA more to finally get all the way back to Maya. A mistake like that can cost you your food budget for a week, or at least make you lose your appetite for Jamaica.

These are not intended to be scare stories. If you are alert that such things happen, you can prevent the same thing from happening to you. Ask first before you order. As for the cab, negotiate a flat rate in advance and check maps so you know where you are going. Ignorance is no excuse in the eyes of the law or in a poor country.

Pine Grove Chalets is a nice place to stay and there is a great restaurant with a bar. Take your meal on the patio overlooking Kingston's night lights. Try the pumpkin soup. Moderate prices, higher than the least expensive, a lot lower than the most expensive restaurants.

Blue Mountain Inn, on Gordon Town Road, 927-7400, is one of the highest priced restaurants on the island. They have served the British Royal family and once served supper to Lyndon Johnson. This is the ritz of the Blue Mountains, listed purely for those looking for somewhere to splurge.

Tuck Shop at Newcastle is a small shop with cold drinks and snack foods.

Mr. Wolff's on the Brooks River is a farm and store. He always has bullas and bananas, usually other fresh fruit.

Mavis Bank is a centrally located mountain village with several stores. It is not uncommon to find no cold drinks in the entire town. There is a chicken farm where you can get eggs or fresh chicken, not frozen. They taste the way chicken tasted in the US twenty-five years ago.

There are small stores at *Redlight* and *Hagley Gap*, mostly specializing in drink, but if you are hungry and have the time, ask if someone can cook you a meal. You can usually buy fresh carrots, scallions, cabbage, mangos, bananas and other produce directly from local farmers.

KINGSTON

Kingston has more people and more places to eat than any other city. The fundamental to the lavish, and everything in between, are represented. You get it a little quicker, a little less lovingly here, but you can find plenty of good food for good value.

Minnie's Ethiopian Herbal Health Food was shut the last time I visited, but promising to reopen at a new location at 170 Old Hope Rd, in *Liguanea*. It is listed anyhow because this restaurant used to serve the best food in Jamaica, all fresh, vegetarian "Ital" style, huge servings cooked to order at reasonable prices. Fresh fruit juices, too, along with friendly service. The old Minnie's used to be a thatch roof bamboo cottage in a busy east Kingston neighborhood. Menu specials include roast or steamed fish, fish balls, callalou, vegetable stew, red pea stew, gunga pea stew, banana and yam "dumplin," or festival (fried sweet bread), along with juices from beet root, soursop, june plum, pineapple, paw paw, guava, or cucumber. For beer drinkers, choose from ginger beer, Red Stripe, or Heineken.

Gino's is also on Old Hope Road. It stays open 24 hours for relatively greasy but tasty Jamaican food. Inexpensive.

The Princess on the corner of Old Hope Rd. and Hope Rd., in Liguanea, serves inexpensive Indian food.

Lyn's Vegetarian Restaurant Ltd. and Performing Arts Auditorium, 7–9 Tangerine Pl., advertises "Eat the healthy happy way."

Pronto's Jerk Pork, 165 Constant Spring, in Kingston is one of surprisingly few places for jerk pork in Kingston. Jerk cooking is available, just hard to find. Pronto's proprietor, a Mr. C. Willy, prepares a tender variety of pork that comes out like stew meat, tastes like beef.

Other places to try for a square meal include *Parkview Restaurant*, on the Parade close to downtown, and *Hammond's*, on the corner of Queen and Duke Sts., open 24 hours. *Devon House*, with its arts and crafts displays, and Colonial architecture, is a nice backdrop for a relatively high-priced restaurant. The cafeteria at Norman Manley Airport does not have the greatest food, mostly steam table fare, but it is legitimate Jamaican cooking, serving rice 'n peas, curry goat, and so forth, with meals starting at around $9 JA.

MT. DIABLO, EWARTON

Mt. Diablo is the highest point the main road crosses between Ocho Rios and Spanish Town. You see a lot of fast cars tooling through here, Toyotas, Hondas, Mercedes, Volvos, all mostly racing back toward Kingston from north coast resorts, playing pass and slow down with big trucks. There are a lot of little stands along the road, particularly closer to Ocho Rios and in Fern Gully, but not a lot of places to stop for a meal.

Ewarton is a fairly large town, with many people lining its roadsides, children walking to school, others waiting for buses. It has a couple of decent, not great, but okay restaurants.

The Bamboo Corner Restaurant, 47 Main St., has nice people

Kitchen at Minnie's Ethiopian Herbal Restaurant, Kingston

ON TOUR
JIMMY CLIFF
BUD BROTHERS
CALIFORNIA INDICA

running it, mediocre food. Breakfasts here could be better, but in a pinch you can get a container of processed fruit juice and coffee. The jerk chicken is ready around 11 AM.

Restaurant/Snacks across Main from the Bamboo corner, next to the big rooster sign, has better food, as well as a quicker turnover of customers. A breakfast of two eggs, bread, sliced tomato and coffee runs around $10 JA for two people.

MANDEVILLE

Hotel Astra, 62 Ward Ave., rates a special mention for growing much of the food they prepare in the family garden of the owners, the MacIntyre's. Not inexpensive, but reliably good.

Capri Restaurant is next to the Odeon Theatre. Good for meeting local characters. Live bands several nights a week.

Spotlight Restaurant is in a converted bus with a colorful paint job.

Crazy Jim's is not fancy, but it is good and inexpensive.

Bill Laurie's Steak House is on a hill overlooking the town. Pretty view, nice antique furnishings, pricey. Stop for a drink instead of a meal if you are on a tight budget.

MIDDLEQUARTERS

This is where you get roadside service for the famous hot peppered shrimp. These are really small crayfish from local waters, roasted with salt and country pepper. Women vendors swarm over a car, sticking their arms through the windows to offer bags of the greasy, delicious critters for $2, $4 and up to $20 JA for a big bagful. You can sample different offerings to choose one you like best—free samples. It is hard to drive and eat the crunchy devils at the same time. Do not drive away without buying drinks. You will need them quickly to put out the fire in your mouth.

TREASURE BEACH

Treasure Beach Hotel serves excellent food at low prices for a hotel. Lobster is $10 US or $50 Ja. Breakfast is pricier, but you get legitimate Jamaican cooking at $30 JA for ackee and saltfish, green bananas, coffee and a plate of fresh fruit.

Le Corner Beach Club Restaurant is within walking distance down the beach from the hotel. Cheaper food available here.

Markets at *Great Bay* and *Calabash Bay* are busiest on Fridays. Fresh fish are available from fishermen along the beach daily.

BLACK RIVER

Waterloo Guest House was the first house in Jamaica with electricity. A fish dinner is $15 Ja, lobster is $50 JA. Curry goat, $13 JA, cowfoot, $11.

Friday and Saturday are main market days in the town of Black River.

WHITEHOUSE

Fresh fish at the beach market every morning. Vendors sell prepared food all along the road from *Scott's Cove* to *Bluefield's Bay.*

NEGRIL

The beach and cliffs are packed with restaurants. Some charge double the going rate for sodas or beer. Some are gems.

De Buss is a restaurant inside an old converted double-decker bus that was used as a prop in a James Bond movie. Joy Gentles Logan serves the best jerk chicken on the island. And she allows camping on the beach. Highly recommended.

Miss Brown's moved from her landmark position next to the

roundabout to an out of town location, but she is still in business serving world famous mushroom tea for around $1.50 JA per cup. One cup is a mild buzz. Two cups are an experience. Three, and you may need help to walk. The mushrooms are of the psilocybin variety. A colorful way to see Jamaica.

Wharf Club is a funky bar on the curve between the beach and the cliffs. Conch chowder, $1.50 JA.

Evans Restaurant is the first shack next to the bridge at the crafts market. Run by two Melvins, one young, one old. Older Melvin Hyatt brings out a Red Stripe case filled with psilocybin mushrooms he grows himself. He lets you pick through the box for the ones you want for your cup of tea. He always throws in one or two extra mushrooms. The restaurant food is also good, inexpensive, and the price of the mushrooms decreases with the more you consume (or at least it seems that way).

Country serves good "Ital." So do *Desi's Dread* and *Happy's*.

Negril Beach Club has a huge breakfast buffet with an omelette chef in white, cracking eggs without a single drip. Expensive. Around $8 US for a mammoth breakfast buffet featuring Jamaican fruits and dishes, along with ham, bacon and eggs.

Rick's Cafe has an expensive restaurant and a famous outdoor bar for sunset watching. Trendy atmosphere.

Market sellers line the bridge daily with fresh fruits and vegetables. Fishermen are all along the beach. Almost every shack on the beach or cliff road sells something to eat. There is a supermarket in the shopping center near the roundabout. Local cooks will whip you up a meal. Many accommodations come with kitchens.

Sundowner serves Jamaican food. Moderate to high prices.

There are several towns and restaurants between Negril and Montego Bay. *Lucea* is a non-touristy town, with a few cheap restaurants. Your choice here is limited by what is open on any given day. There is a big market in the center of town where you may have more luck.

There are thousands of parts to eat in Jamaica that are not listed here. The ones included here, as well as several mentioned in other parts of this book and not repeated here, will hold you nicely while you discover your own favorites.

"Stay in old 'Great Houses,' Jamaican-style hotels, guest houses, luxury villas, cabanas, cabins, simple rooms with families, or camp midst numerous beaches, cliffs, streams, rivers and waterfalls, caves, forest-clad mountains and on out-islands."—Peter Bentley, President Sense Adventures

CHAPTER FIFTEEN

ACCOMMODATIONS

Depending on the degree of luxury you are looking for there is a tremendous variety of accommodations on the island, including around 8,000 beds in traditional hotel rooms and another 4,000 beds in alternative-style accommodations such as the ones mentioned in the quote above. At the top of the line villas you will be waited on by cooks and maids. At the lower end beach tents you will be competing for space with creepy crawly insects. In between you can find comfort and a more intimate experience of Jamaica than what you ordinarily encounter in the predictable sameness of a luxury hotel.

The following listings cover the whole island, considering value, authentic Jamaican style and access to adventure. Big hotels have heavy ad and PR budgets to promote their interests. They also routinely add a 10% service charge and a government room tax of $4–$12 US per day. Campsites, cottages, guest houses, not-so-touristy hotels and Jamaican homes are a lot less expensive and harder to find unless you know where to look for them. This is where to look.

MONTEGO BAY

Sign Great House is one of the best unknown places to stay near Montego Bay. An old Great House, it was abandoned for years and recently refurbished by American owners who have taken care to maintain a Jamaican-style ambience in private bungalows and rooms. This means you can find peace and quiet in the hills six miles east of the busiest and noisiest tourist town in Jamaica, and still have easy access to beaches, shopping, nightlife, as well as a forty-acre property, hiking trails and the Montego River. The open air restaurant is good, service conscientious, and rates reasonable at $30 US per single, $40 US per double. Camping is $7.50 for one person, $2.50 for each additional person.

You can take a bus from downtown to Sign. Cicadas, cows mooing and the buses tooting their horn to let people know they are coming around the sharp mountain road curves are the only noises you hear. Highly recommended. Tennis, pool. Phone (800) 545-4141 ext 577 for toll free information, or local number 952-0028.

Wexford Court Hotel is on Gloucester Ave., across the street from the beach. It is comfortable, air conditioned, conveniently located and has a 24-hour coffee shop. Rates on request. Phone 952-3679.

Caribic House is a small, clean hotel across the street from the beach on Glouchester Ave., in downtown. Cheapest in-town rates, no air-conditioning, ceiling fans only, for around $20 US per single, $25 per double. Phone 952-5013.

Damali Beach has camping by the sea. $10 US per night in your tent, $12 in their tent. Changing rooms and showers. Great snorkeling, calm water, bar and restaurant open 8 AM to 2 AM. Phone 953-2387, or a US phone (215) 471-0884. Ask for Parchi or Arnold.

Ironshore and Sunshine Villas are booked through Parchi at Damali. These are staffed, luxury digs, two bedrooms, two baths, with kitchens and pools. April to December off-season rates are around $100 US per night, $350 weekly per couple. High season December to April rates are about double. More private than a hotel. You can get free transportation to the beach or into town for dinner.

Mountainside Guest House, on Queen's Drive and Federal Ave., 952-4685, offers a great view overlooking the airport. Pool, some rooms air-conditioned. Nudists welcome. Rooms for singles are around $25 US, doubles $35. Camping $5 per person.

Richmond Hill Inn, Union St., 952-3859, is an old plantation house with a pretty view overlooking the bay. This is a gracious small inn, a little more expensive than some of the guest houses, yet less than the big hotels. Single rates around $38 US, doubles around $50–$80. Air conditioning, private baths, pool.

Ocean View Guest House, on Sunset Ave., 952-2662, is close to a bus stop and the airport. Wayne Matthews charges around $25 US per single, $35 per double. Private baths, air conditioning. 10% service charge, no room tax.

Seville Guest House, also on Sunset Ave., 952-2814, has air-conditioned rooms for around $30 US per single, $45 per double, as well as costlier apartments and villas. Ask for Wesley Barrett or Easton Powell. 10% service charge, no room tax.

Kirlew Guest House, Reading, St. James, 952-1473, is a small guest house three miles west of Montego Bay. Six rooms, ten beds. Rates around $20 US per single, $25 US per double. Private baths.

Chalet Caribe is just past Reading, south of town, 952-1364. Specializing in scuba diving packages, with reasonable hotel rates, around $36–$48 US per double, from April to December, 25% higher in high season, and there is a government room tax of $6–$12 US per day added, along with a 10% service charge.

DUNCANS

Sober Robin has noisy rooms near the roadside for $70 JA nightly for two.

DISCOVERY BAY

Spanish Court Apartments, 972-2235, are furnished with two beds and a couch, with kitchens, for $65 JA nightly, or $375 JA weekly. Pool. Not a busy place, you might be able to talk down the price.

OCHO RIOS

Not noted for its inexpensive or authentically Jamaican-style accommodations, there are still several neat places to stay in the area.

Crow's Nest is the home of Audrey Barned. Located two miles east of the clock tower on the main highway, this is the least expensive accommodations so close to town. Two rooms in Audrey's house are around $20 US per night, for two. She also has camping space and will cook meals for you, and there is a small bar. The rooms are not fancy, the bathroom could be cleaner, but Audrey is a fount of information on interesting things to do and things to see in the area. Stop by for a drink and a chat even if you do not stay overnight. One block from the beach. Phone 974-5188.

Murphy Hill is a real find, situated at 1750 feet and up several rough back roads off of Fern Gully, the site offers panoramic views of Ocho Rios, along with clean, antique-furnished rooms for $20 US nightly per person. Swimming pool and fishing pool on site, horseback riding. Jamaican-owner Neville East does no advertising. You can share a kitchen or meals run from $20–$40 JA. Top price is for steak or lobster, which can be served in your room or on a pretty outdoor terrace. Take the turn-off for *Lydford*, or Spring Mountain Road to get here. Highly recommended. Phone 922-0440 in Kingston for information.

Friendship Farm is another fascinating place to stay. This is a working 600-acre farm, in *Walker's Wood*, on the opposite side of Fern Gully from Murphy Hill, about 7 miles from Ocho

---

Shaw Park Gardens, Ocho Rios

Rios, with accommodations available in converted buses. Flowers are planted all around the painted buses, and though the rooms are small, reminiscent of a boat, they are well-kept, with beds, showers, toilets and outdoor barbecues for cooking. There is also a restaurant, as well as the gorgeous property of rolling grasslands, ponds and a swimming pool with a stunning coastal view.

Jack Wilmot owns the property and he provides tours of cattle paddocks, a duck pond, root crop and fruit cultivations, plantings of gunga peas, breadfruit, plantain, bananas, yams, sugar cane, naseberry, otaheite apple and much more, including tropical spices such as peppercorns, nutmeg, pimento and ginger. Animals such as nubian goats, sheep, rabbits, pheasants and ponies roam the grounds. You can fish in stocked ponds, swim, horseback ride or just enjoy the quiet peace. Children's facilities include a playground and supervised horseback rides, as well as a summer camp for children 8–15, from July 4-Sept 4.

Rates are around $15 US per person nightly in the buses. Phone 972-2465 for information.

Several reasonably-priced guest houses in Ocho Rios proper include *White Table Guest House, Christopher's, Jeff's Guest House* and *Anancy's Web.*

CASTLE GARDEN

This is a village you miss if you blink driving through. Situated between Oracabessa and Port Maria, there are two inexpensive places to stay.

Sea Lawn Coral Beach has camping for $5 US per person. Mike Higgins runs the place and he will take you out snorkeling nearby. His wife cooks breakfasts and dinners.

Trevor's is directly across the street from Sea Lawn, up a steep driveway. He has one room available for $45 JA nightly.

PORT MARIA

Casa Maria Hotel is a little more expensive than the cheaper guest houses, but it is a palatial, quiet place on a hill outside of town. Sedate and clubby, eight miles east of Ocho Rios, singles are $47.50 US nightly, doubles are $50, plus 10% service charge and $4–$12 US room tax. Breakfast and dinner are available for $18.75 US daily. Two-bedroom, two-bath cottages that accommodate four to six people are $340–$390 US weekly, including maid service. Phone 994-2323.

Mannings Hotel is in Port Maria. Rooms with shared bathrooms are $10–$15 US nightly for one or two guests.

Strawberry Fields is approximately eight miles east of Port Maria, but the road to it only comes through from Annotto Bay, around fifteen miles east, then five miles back in. It is an isolated beauty spot, with secluded beaches along the road leading to a shallow cove. Camping spaces are $5 US per person, and there is an inexpensive restaurant and bar. Hike nearby, bathe in waterfalls, climb coastal cliffs. Cottages are overpriced at $30 US for a single, $50 US for two. Several platform tents with cots are available for around $20 US per person nightly. All rates include breakfast.

BUFF BAY

Fish Done is a single cabin with two bedrooms at the end of the Vinegar Hill Trail over the Blue Mountains from Jack's Hill. The actual location is midway between *Chepstow* and *Skibo*. Pretty swimming holes on a river, excellent hiking. The large cabin can accommodate up to ten people inside at $10 US per person. Camping is $5 US per person nightly. A cook is available. This is really off the beaten track.

Sydney and Rachel Munroe operate several bed & breakfast properties in nearby *Spring Garden*. Contact them c/o Ketto PA, Westmoreland, Jamaica, WI.

HOPE BAY

Rio Sol Mar is the home of Mrs. Paula Espeut, located at the point where the Swift River meets the sea. Great beaches, hiking, river or seacoast swimming. The site is a little noisy due to cars and trucks speeding by on the road. Rooms in the house are $12 US nightly. Two nicely furnished apartments are available, without a kitchen for $12 US nightly, with a kitchen for $15 US. Big beds, a short walk to the beach through a stand of palm trees. No restaurant, but housekeeper Ruby James will cook for you at negotiable rates. Women washing clothes in the river, fishermen floating by, cars and trucks buzzing along the road make it seem like a busy spot. Ronald Dunkley, the caretaker insists the area is safe. "No molested down here," he says. "We don't allow it."

Content Farm advertises "for the physically fit or those who want to be." Guests stay in bamboo huts that sleep up to three people, for $140 US weekly. Vegetarian breakfast and dinner are included, with coconut water and fresh fruit available at any time. Fresh fish are available on request. There is no running water or electricity, just pure rustic beauty amid lushly foliated scenery. You bathe in mountain streams. It is a two mile walk to the river, six miles to the beach. For information contact Sister P., Content, Hope Bay PO, Portland, Jamaica, or Parchi Parchment, Sunshine Villas Ltd., PO Box 61, Montego Bay, Jamaica; phone 953-2387.

NORWICH

One and a half miles west of Port Antonio, and another mile and a half into the hills are two mountain chalets called *Friends*. Good views from the one-bedroom loft houses, with living room, bath, kitchen and TV. Two can sleep in a loft, more in the living room. Rate is $50 US daily, optional maid service $5 US daily. Call Ken Ramsey, 925-6738.

PORT ANTONIO

Several of the nicest and most expensive luxury hotels and

Ronald Dunkley and Ruby, at Rio Sol Mar

villas are in this area, and there are also top-notch bargain digs, full of local color.

Scotia Guest House, 15 Queen St., 993-2681, is an old Jamaican house with a high veranda overlooking West Harbor and Navy Island. Rooms for two to four people are around $10 US per person nightly.

Hope View Guest House, 26 Harbor St., 993-3040, is right on the main street in the heart of downtown. Some of the rooms share a bath. Cost is $35–$60 JA per person nightly.

Ivanhoe Guest House has single rooms for $60 JA, doubles for $65. Breakfast is $8 JA, dinner is $15.

DeMontevin Lodge is a famous Jamaican-style hotel. Most guidebooks include a picture of its antique and crystal Victorian architecture with gingerbread trim. It is neat looking, but for relative value, the prices leave something to be desired. The beds are soft or the mattresses are thin. They shut off all the water from 10 PM to 5 AM. At other times hot water is often only a trickle. The location at 21 Ft. George St. is convenient to town and a little quieter than some of the downtown guest houses, but not by much.

Rooms with a shared bath down the hall are $75 JA for a single, $105 for a double. This includes threadbare towels. Rooms with a private bath are $85 JA for a single, or $135 per double. A room with a private bath that I stayed in had no towels and no bathroom light. There was, however, a 1911 copyright edition of *Ethan Frome*, along with a Bible in the room.

Meals are available featuring Jamaican cuisine. Breakfast is $14 JA, dinners are $28–$60 JA. These meals are served by a waiter in a white shirt and black tie, in a room full of old crystal, lace doilies and antique furniture. The food is good, but not much different than what you can get in town for half the price. This is a well-known place with a good reputation not lived up to.

Bonnie View Hotel, Richmond Hill, 993-2752, is set on a working plantation surrounded by greenery on a hilltop affording a panoramic view of Port Antonio, its twin harbors and the coast in either direction. Rooms with private baths and hot water are $37 US per single, $59 US per double.

Meals are served on a stone patio perched atop a million-dollar coastal view. Breakfast is $22 JA, dinners are $33 JA and up. Much of the food is grown on the property, including breadfruit, bananas, ackee, plantains, yams. Manager Bertram Wee Tom insists all the food is fresh, never frozen.

Remember to add in a 10% government tax, $6 US room tax and a 10% service charge. Definitely go up for the view, maybe for a meal or a drink, even if you do not stay overnight.

Way Valley Guest House, 11 W. Palm Ave., 993-2753, has inexpensive rooms and a cocktail lounge for in-house nightlife.

As for the luxury accommodations, *Trident Villas at San San* come with a cook who will prepare meals if you buy food, for $120 US nightly, per single, $190 per double. The *Trident Hotel* charges $245 US per single, $295 per double, with ultra-gourmet breakfast and dinner included. $8–$12 US room tax is added on daily.

Frenchman's Cove charges $97.50 US per single, plus $6 room tax and 12% service charge. Doubles are $130 US plus the extra charges. Breakfast and dinner are included. Nice beach.

The Admiralty Club at Navy Island is very private. Summer rates for cottages and villas are from $55 US to $155 US, for two to six people plus 10% service charge. Winter rates are $95 US to $200, plus 10%. A cook is available for $5 US daily. Breakfasts are $27 JA, dinners from $77–$97 JA. A US toll-free information number is (800) 423-4095, or outside the US call (312) 883-1020.

One of the more unusual places to stay in this area is twenty-two miles up into the John Crow Mountains from here, offering absolutely complete privacy in the rainiest part of the country surrounded by the heaviest foliage. *Rainbow Valley* is a modern-looking guest house located in *Bowden Pen* and owned by a white-haired, bearded American lawyer named Royce Brimson.

You have to travel deep into the bush to get there, and if you make a wrong turn you end up in *Moore Town* and *Cornwell Barracks*, both Maroon villages. I asked a group of idle young Moore Town men if there was really anything different about Maroons. "We at de' tail end a' dat t'ing," was the answer.

Moore Town is the site of *Bump Grave*, where National Heroine Nanny is buried.

The road to Bowden Pen follows the prehistoric Rio Grande River valley, framed by the largest tree ferns and most dense foliage in Jamaica. The one lane road gets narrower the farther you go, in places barely wide enough for a car, finally becoming a classic "Ramar of the Jungle" environment. Men and women with machetes walk up and down the road carrying heavy burdens on their heads, bunches of bananas, and one woman was hauling large stones up from the river to rebuild a washed out portion of the road for the Public Works Department.

The last five minutes to Rainbow Valley, with cattle and goats running ahead of you, looks as if a car will not make it. It is possible, although not recommended in wet weather.

This is possibly the least visited area of the country, aside from the Cockpits, deep in the island's last remaining rain forest. Numerous trails fan out from here, with one leading over the mountains to Bath, others heading into the Blue Mountains, another leading through heavy bush to the legendary lost village of *Nannytown*. Donkey rides and guides can be hired in small villages.

Rainbow Valley is situated on seventy-eight acres surrounded by forty square miles of green, mountainous terrain. You can swim in the upper Rio Grande, or just take in the wide views from the breezy porch. A bus from Port Antonio goes as far as Millbank, and it is about a one-hour walk from there to the guest house. Rates are $20 JA daily for campers, $75 JA daily for a bed and fresh vegetarian meals of greens, root vegetables and local fruits.

Birdie Bifield's house is about a mile farther up the road from Rainbow Valley and it is even more private. The road disappears into a wooded thicket about a quarter mile past Birdie's, just beyond a small waterfall where you can swim or bathe. Birdie is a spry Jamaican lady who rents out a room in her house for $5 US nightly, with longer stays at negotiable rates. She will cook for you if you buy the food.

The last store is in Millbank, but they may have little more for sale than bananas. Bring food with you from Port Antonio.

Comfort Castle has a slightly better stocked store. You may be able to buy a cold drink there, or possibly at the D&T Store in the village of *Ginger House*. I asked there who "D" was. Answer: "D' girl." "Who's d' girl?" I asked. "D' girl for d' shop," I was told in terrifically confusing Abbott and Costello style. Be prepared to fend for yourself up in this neck of the woods.

BATH

Bath Fountain Hotel is attached to the radioactive mineral spa, located on a small river on the other side of the rain forest from Bowden Pen. Several hiking trails start at the hotel. Rooms with shared bath are $30–$40 JA. Rooms with private baths are $40–$50 JA. Rooms with private baths and a balcony are $50–$60 JA. All rates include use of the mineral baths. Room tax of $4–$8 US and 10% service charge are added.

Meals are available in the dining room. Dinners range from $20–$35 JA. Miss Olive Haik is the manager. Phone 982-2132 for information, or after 8 PM call Miss Haik's home, 982-2213.

MORANT BAY

Morant Villas are airy suites on the beach, thirty-two miles east of Kingston. Each suite has a bath and kitchen, as well as a patio with a sea view. You can cook or walk three minutes down the beach to Chef's Seaview Restaurant, open 24 hours. Rates on request. Call 982-2422 for information, or in Miami, (305) 279-8298.

GREEN WALL

Gold Mine Camp & Club is one of the rare places to stay along the southeast coast. Joe Corniffe runs the place and is an expert on the St. Thomas area. He can tell you how to get to the nearby *Cane River Falls*, the 1000-foot-high *Judgement Cliff*, the *Yallahs Salt Ponds*, as well as many miles of deserted beaches. Rooms for one or two are around $10 US nightly, camping is $5 per person.

THE BLUE MOUNTAINS

Maya Hiking Center and Sanctuary has cabins with mattresses on the floor for $12.50 US for one person, $20 US for two. A dorm space in a room with four beds is $7.50 US. The bathroom is down the hall and shared by one and all, but it is clean and there is hot water. Tent spaces are $5 US, $2.50 more for each additional camper. Tents can be rented for $2.50 US nightly. The 15-acre parcel abuts a residential area with a tremendous view of Kingston 2000 feet below. Phone 927-2657.

Rasta Perch is a house in the low rent district of Jack's Hill, the home of Leonard "Baps" Cole. You have to walk half a mile from the road to his tiny shack on a hillside. This is about as primitive as Jamaican hospitality gets in these parts. Cost: $5 US nightly to pitch a tent outside or to sleep inside on a mattress, rasta lore and magical time with a Jamaican version of Don Juan, the sorcerer, included. For information, find Jack's Hill, ask anyone for Baps.

Pine Grove is a nicely-kept working plantation and coffee farm surrounded on three sides by mountains, with the fourth side unveiling a panorama of Kingston. Great food in the dining room, quiet mountain people up here at 3700 feet. Hot water baths, color TV. Clean rooms, with kitchenettes are around $75 US for up to four people. Phone 922-8705 for information.

Hollywell is the forest reserve with modestly furnished cabins, equipped with beds and kitchens, available for $28 JA nightly, for up to four people. Camping is possible, but you must pay the cabin rental. A receipt is required and this can only be picked up at the Forestry Department in Kingston, 173 Constant Spring Rd., phone 924-2612. Weekends tend to be booked at least a month in advance, weekdays, no problem, mon. Hiking trails, flowers, views from 4,000 feet make this as

Cabin at Hollywell Forest Reserve

scenic as an American National Park, only a lot less crowded. You must arrive before 4 PM when the manager leaves for the day. Bring food. The kitchen has utensils, but there are no shops nearby.

Clydesdale is another forest reserve with accommodations that must be booked in Kingston. There is one furnished cabin available for $28 JA nightly, or dorm space for around $15 JA.

Section is where you can find James Dennis and family, expert coffee growers. Dennis will let you camp on his property for around $5 US per person. There is always something cooking here. Purchase coffee, negotiate for food. Good cooks. Great folks. Best coffee.

Wildflower Lodge is presently only open in the summer as a camp. Located in the high Blue Mountains, it is an alternative to Whitfield Hall. If you get this far you can inquire as to rates and accommodations, which should be reasonable.

Whitfield Hall is the traditional starting point for the climb to Blue Mountain Peak. This is an old guest house, without electricity or hot water, but with a lot of charm. There are five rooms and an upstairs dorm. John Algrove, the owner of Whitfield Hall, does not approve of ganja, so please smoke it outside. Phone 927-0986 for information and reservations.

Beds with sheets and blankets are provided at Whitfield, but you should bring your own food. It is an hour's walk to the nearest store. You get use of the kitchen with a room.

Up here you use kerosene gas Tilley lamps from England, candles and a roaring wood fire, which is needed in the cool mountain air. Very rustic, very Jamaican, quite nice under tall eucalyptus trees and with Blue Mountain peak looming above. Bring your own toilet paper, too.

This is one of my favorite spots in Jamaica. Rates are $30 JA per person nightly inside, less for campers. Old books, guest registers with comments on the Blue Mountain climb, and an antique pump organ are cared for by heavyset Cynthia Warren and her staff. I call Cynthia the Queen of Whitfield. This is an enchanted place.

Portland Gap is the site of another Forestry Department cabin, at 5200 feet, this one banked in flowers and mist-shrouded views of the lowlands. $28 JA nightly. Contact the Kingston office or bring a tent and camp out. Water available here. Bring food.

Blue Mountain Peak has another Forestry Department cabin, at 7402 feet, funky, graffiti-covered, but with a fireplace to keep warm, which you will appreciate. It gets cold up here, sometimes 40–50 degrees. Bring water along with food. There are barrels for catching rain water, but they usually have bugs floating in them. I doubt if anyone will bother you if you camp out up here without paying in advance.

KINGSTON

Kingston is where a lot of Jamaican adventures happen in a big city with nearly a million people. If you cannot find adventure here you are not looking for it. There are good hotels with fancy amenities and prices to match, such as the *Wyndham* in New Kingston, or the *Jamaica Pegasus*, where you can count on spending at least $100 US nightly for a double room. Or you can stay at colorful spots with lower rates, memorable characters and slightly less in the way of indulgent pampering, incredibly more in the way of unforgettable experience. Try for a hotel with air conditioning. Kingston is a hot town.

Mayfair Hotel, 4 West King's House Close, 926-1610, is well-located for access to main roads, Hope Road and Constant Spring Road, yet on a quiet side street with a mountain view. The colonial-style hotel is a bit frayed around the edges, but the wear gives it a mysterious air. This is the sort of place where you expect to see foreign correspondents lurking about in trench coats. Rates are around $35–$45 US per single, $40–$50 per double, plus room tax and 10% service charge. Fresh flowers brighten the dining room. Swimming pool, air conditioned.

Indies Hotel, 5 Holburn Road, 926-0989, has rooms with private baths and air conditioning. Room tax and only 5% service charge added on to rates around $20–$35 US per single, $33–$42 US per double. Ask for Albert or Barbara Shaw.

The Kensington Apartments, 15/15A Kensington Crescent, 929-1153, offers non-taxed guest house accommodations in cottages or suites for rates around $25 US per single, $45–$65 per double.

Green Gables Guest House, 6 Cargill Ave., 926-6711, has some of Kingston's least expensive rooms, running around $50 JA per single, $60 JA per double.

Sandhurst, 70 Sandhurst Crescent, 927-8244, has single rooms for around $25 US, doubles $30 US, plus 10% service charge.

Sutton Place Hotel, 11 Ruthven Rd., 926-2297, charges $40 US for singles or doubles, plus room tax. Private baths, air conditioning, dining room, some suites, swimming pool. Ask for Dermot or Joan Blake.

Medallion Hall, 53 Hope Rd., 927-5721, has single rooms for about $30 US, doubles at $35 US. Only some of the rooms are air conditioned. 10% service charge and room tax added. Dining room. Good location near modern New Kingston area.

Morgan's Harbour is located in Port Royal, on the Palisadoes Rd., 924-8464. If you want to splurge, this is a decent place. Drive or take a boat to or from Kingston. This is a resort, not just a place to sleep. Contact the hotel for current rates.

Talk's Hotel is located in the village of *Stony Hill*, about half an hour drive outside Kingston, on the Stony Hill Rd. heading toward Castleton and Buff Bay. This is an amazing place, five stories of crooked, dark stairways and slightly askew rooms completely hand-built by owner Joseph Johnson, a one-time master cooper who built barrels for the Meyer's and Seagram's distilleries. It took him nine years to build his hotel on a rainy hillside, on the western edge of the Blue Mountains. He rents rooms for twelve hours at a time, for $30–$45 JA. Bar and restaurant. Wonderful painted signs outside.

MILK RIVER

Milk River Spa & Hotel, is the only hotel for many miles in a remote farming area near the south coast. This is the mineral spa with the most highly radioactive water known on earth, something you may want to think about before you check in. Of course, everyone associated with the place insists there is no danger. I am less sure, but if you want to check it out for yourself, the hotel is pretty nice—a sprawling Colonial outpost at the end of the world, but with chipped paint and cracked bath tiles that give it a run-down feeling. It feels more like a clinic than a hotel, almost like an asylum.

There is a restaurant and bar. A single room with private bath is $70 JA, $110 JA including breakfast and dinner. Singles with shared baths are $55 JA, or $95 with meals. A double with private bath is $110 JA daily, $190 JA with meals. Doubles with shared baths are $100 JA, $180 JA with meals. Air conditioners and TV can be rented for $10 JA daily, each. Government room tax of $4 US in summer, or $8 US in winter is added. The mineral baths are free to guests, limited to two baths daily for up to fifteen minutes each. Manager is Ivan Brown, 924-9544.

MANDEVILLE

Hotel Astra, 62 Ward Ave., 962-3265, is the nicest place to stay in Mandeville. Family-owned and operated, Manager Diana MacIntyre-Pike sees to it that the Astra gives you the feeling of a small country inn with personalized service. The food served in the dining room is grown in her parents' garden. Coffee is served at your door every morning. Cool and peaceful at 2,000 feet altitude, not cheap, though. Singles and doubles are \$45–\$90 US, plus room tax and 10% service fee added to credit card bills.

Diana is a knowledgeable south coast booster and a real go-getter, the source of valuable information on things to do in the area and people to see. Officially, she is the Area Chairman of the Jamaica Hotel & Tourist Association. Even if you do not stay here, she can probably answer many of your questions about the area, and also set up various tours.

Mandeville Hotel, 4 Hotel St., 962-2460, is owned by Gordon MacIntyre, Diana's brother. The hotel has a convenient downtown location, just behind the central square and within walking distance of inexpensive restaurants. Rates for singles or doubles range from \$53 US up to \$98 US for a deluxe 2–3 bedroom apartment with kitchen. Room tax is added. This used to be a dive, but has recently been purchased by the MacIntyre family, with forty years of hotel experience. They are upgrading the property and promise to finish off the hotel in genuine traditional Jamaican fretwork. They take the overflow when the Astra is booked solid.

Marshall's Pen Great House, used to have guest room accommodations. These are no longer available, but camping is sometimes permitted on the 300-acre cattle property. Talk to Robert Sutton, 962-2260. Rates are around \$5 US per person.

Caledonia Guest House, 6 Great House Dr., 962-0406. Rates on request. Looks clean and inexpensive.

CHRISTIANA

Villa Bella, is a small Jamaican-style hotel north of Mandeville. This is the closest hotel to the Cockpit country. Inexpensive rates. Phone 964-2243 for information.

Gourie Forest Reserve is located west of Christiana. There is a small cabin for rent through Kingston's Forestry Department. Rent is $28 JA daily, and camping is available for $5 JA, but only if you pay the cabin rental first. Pretty setting in a pine forest, with the source of the Black River nearby, as well as Gourie Cave, one of Jamaica's longest known caves, to explore.

TREASURE BEACH

Treasure Beach Hotel, St. Elizabeth, 965-2305, is a small secluded hotel with a fine restaurant, pool and miles of empty beaches. Sixteen rooms accommodate a maximum of twenty-eight guests. Winter rates are $50 US for single rooms, $70 US for doubles. These drop to $44 US and $54 US in winter. Judith Mitchell, Manager.

La Corner Beach Club is located half a mile east of the Treasure Beach Hotel. A moderately noisy disco at night, clean rooms rent for $50 JA nightly.

Miss Lillian, has two areas for campers, one on the beach, one a short walk inland. Camping is $5 US per person. Ask for directions in town, or at the Great Bay Co-op, a good place for stocking up on food supplies other than fresh fish, which can be purchased along the beach.

Silver Sands Cottages have half a house, with kitchen, for $50 JA daily. You can walk to the beach where you can buy fresh fish for $3 JA from local fishermen. Additionally, several villas on the beach are available for rentals. These can accommodate up to six people for $175 US nightly, including maid and cook, and can be booked through Diana MacIntyre-Pike at the Hotel Astra. Informal guest houses are also available in this area. Rates are sometimes as low as $50–$100 JA for an empty beach- or in-town house that can accommodate up to a dozen people. A little detective work is required. Ask around.

ELDERSLIE

Wondrous Cave, outside of the town of Elderslie, is on the edge of the Cockpits. A camping area is located next to a wild cave and river. Ask for Westin Thomas at Elderslie Square for directions. Camping is around $5 US nightly.

BLACK RIVER

Waterloo Guest House, High St., 965-2278, is a rambling frame structure with gingerbread trim across the street from the beach. This was the first private house in Jamaica to have electricity. The restaurant downstairs is good, and inexpensive. Rooms are $30–$35 JA, with private baths.

Bridge House is a small guest house without a listed phone, but with low rates and friendly people.

Hotel Pontio, High St., 965-2255, is a small, comfortable hotel. Comparable rates to Waterloo.

BLUEFIELD'S

Wilton on the Sea, Westmoreland, 955-2852, is an intimate guest house with four double bedrooms and a one-bedroom honeymoon cottage. The terrace overlooks the sea in this quiet town, hummingbird feeders attract the noisiest guests. Orchid garden. Serve yourself honor bar. Good food, conch chowder, homemade bread, lobster with ginger sauce. Walk to beach. Contact Joyce Gruhlke. Rates about $45 US for singles, $80 for doubles, meals included.

ROARING RIVER

Blue Hole Garden, Petersfield PO, Westmoreland, bills itself "for Lovers and Family, No Littering, No Meat." Accommodations are in one-room cottages in a gorgeous riverhead garden area. Pure Jamaican. Rustic. Idyllic. $125 JA nightly. Talk to Esau or I-Rise Kerr.

NEGRIL

Negril is loaded with places to stay—everything from tent space on the beach, to the ultra indulgence of all-inclusive Hedonism II. There are probably fifty restaurants and bars in Negril, with at least that many places to stay. The west cliffs are less crowded than the beach.

Lighthouse Park, is east of the lighthouse, a bit out of the way but very quiet and with good swimming and snorkeling. Standard cabanas accommodating one or two people are about $35 US nightly. Several more deluxe cottages are higher. Tent camping is permitted for $5–$7 US nightly, per person.

Jahbas is across the street from the cliffs. Bare rooms are $15 US nightly, camping $5 US per person.

Drumville Cove, West End, 957-4369, is a small private property on the cliffs, with ladders leading down to the sea. You can climb down and dive for a lobster to cook up in the kitchen of your individual cottage. Local cooks will help out if you like. Cold water showers. Rates are $75 nightly for two. Owned by Tony Drummond, who operates JATAL, a marketing group for medium-priced properties all over the island, in the range of $50–$80 US nightly. Bar and restaurant. Clothing optional areas.

Blue Cave Castle is a large stone structure on the cliffs. You can climb down to the Blue Cave from the cliffs or swim in from the water. Good sunset views. Sea-front bedrooms with private baths in the castle's tower are $35 US nightly in the summer, $50 US in winter. Deluxe rooms, with living/dining room are $45 US in summer, $65 in winter. A four-bedroom guest house is $25 US per room, or $90 US for the whole house in summer. It is $40 US per room, or $150 US for the whole house in winter. Nice. No phone. Send a telegram or have a travel agent make your reservations.

Rock House is an exotic cluster of thatch roof cottages on the

Rock House, Negril

cliffs. Kerosene lamps or electricity are available. Studios are $70 US for two people in summer, $80 US for two in winter. Villas, with refrigerators and hot plates are $90 US for two in summer, $110 US for two in winter. Children under 12 are not allowed. Mailing address is in the US, PO BOX 78, Park Ridge, Il 60068, phone (312) 699-1726.

Xtabi, Lighthouse Rd., 957-4336, is another exotic cliff-side resort. The name means "meeting place of the gods." Cottages with ceiling fans are set on rocky outcrops. Clothing is optional. Bar and restaurant. Pool. Rates on request.

Tigress Cottages has rooms for around $20 US nightly. Some have kitchens.

Negril Yacht Club, near where the cliffs meet the beach, is a lot less fancy than it sounds. You are more likely to bump into rastas than admirals. Bar and restaurant. Rooms are $20 US per person nightly.

Perserverance is one of the original hippie favorites from Negril's discovery by the counter-culture in the 1960's. Located across the street from the beach, accommodations are in small cabanas for \$15–\$20 US nightly. Camping is \$5 US per person.

De Buss is most famous for its delectable jerk chicken served in a retired double-decker bus, and you can camp here, on the beach, for \$5 US per person nightly.

Arthur's Golden Sunset has accommodations in small duplex cottages under shady palms, within yards of the beach. Rates per room are \$20 US nightly. Some of the rooms have shared baths, some have kitchens. Cold water outdoor showers. Camping is \$5 US nightly. Phone 957-4241 for information.

Sammy's has simple rooms for \$10 US nightly, camping for less than \$5 US per person nightly.

God's Love accommodates campers on the beach for less than \$5 US per person.

Bar-B-Barn has cottages with kitchenettes and hot water that can accommodate up to 4 people for \$75 US daily.

Roots Bamboo has thatch beach cottages with cement floors for \$15 US nightly. Camping is \$4 US per person nightly. Tent rentals are \$3 US per night.

Firefly, 957-4358, is quietly situated toward the north end of the beach. Studios and cottages have kitchens, or rooms without kitchens are available. Fruit trees and sugar cane on the property are free for the picking. Rates on request from JAVA; phone toll-free in the US (800) 221-8830. Clothing-optional resort.

T-Water Beach Hotel, 957–4270/1, has 60 rooms, 114 beds, private baths, air conditioning and a private beach. Rates are \$50–\$90 US per double, plus room tax and 10% service.

Negril Beach Club, Norman Manley Blvd., 957-4220, is a full service resort with 85 rooms. Rates range from \$50–90 US for singles, \$60–\$100 US for double rooms. Some suites are available with kitchens. \$6–\$12 US room tax is added, along with 10% service charge. Nice beach location if you are looking for an established hotel/resort.

Sundowner, 957-4225, is one of Negril's original retreats, nice, well-run, with great food, but not inexpensive. Rates are \$80–\$90 US for singles, \$120 for doubles, room tax of \$8–\$12 US added daily.

Villas Negril, 957-4250, has 60 rooms ranging from \$35–\$60 US for singles or doubles. Room tax of \$4–\$8 US added, plus 10% service charge.

Country has cozy little cottages near the north end of the beach with solar water heaters and ceiling fans. Good Ital restaurant. Rates are \$75 US daily per cottage. Sleep 3–4. Phone 957-4273 for information.

Some of the accommodation rates may be negotiable, although probably not during the winter. Beach fanatics find Negril irresistible, and because of this, the local hospitality industry sometimes leaves something to be desired. It is an interesting beach community, but Negril can be unfriendly, its residents greedy. Forewarned is forearmed.

One of the nicest places to stay in Negril is not in Negril, but several miles north of there. *Abingdon Great House* is owned by Mrs. Ivy Heath. This huge, multi-storied structure was the one-time manor house for a large sugar plantation. The remains of a brick windmill from the 1700's are next to the house. Peacocks roam the 500-acre property, which has its own beach, with a small off-shore island. Secluded off the main road, this is a little-known gem of a place to stay in one of several apartments with kitchens, or guest rooms. Rates are about \$20 US per person nightly. Camping is permitted at a negotiable rate.

The listings in this chapter merely scratch the surface of where you can stay in Jamaica. I have tried to include the best values, as well as the most interesting accommodations from a cultural standpoint.

All rates given throughout this book are at best approximations and subject to change. Wherever possible, make advance reservations, but keep in mind that you will often pay a little more for bookings made by travel agents. Once you reach Jamaica, you can always spend a night or two at one of the listed properties and poke around on your own to find something more suited to your tastes and budget.

A viable alternative in this poor country is to simply ask around for someone with a spare room in their home. You will not find a more authentic Jamaican experience and you can usually negotiate a reasonable rate. Another trick is wait for off-season bargains. The weather is good all year round, with summer being only a tad warmer. It always feels hot. Rates, however, are much cheaper between April and December. Smart times to visit, unless you enjoy crowds, are late April, November and early December, just outside the edges of high season. Fancy villas and luxury hotels may be within the reach of the budget-minded at those times.

Especially good off-season rates may be available at properties marketed under the group title Inns of Jamaica. These are generally stylish smaller properties able to offer personalized service. A number have been included in this chapter, such as Pine Grove, Morgan's Harbor, Mayfair, Astra, Richmond Hill and the Sundowner.

A Jamaica Association of Villas and Apartments (JAVA) lists a number of properties that can offer relatively good off-season rates. Phone 974-2508 in Ocho Rios, or toll free in the US (800) 221-8830.

A marketing group called *Bed & Breakfast Jamaica* can supply information on its properties. Contact Elinor Gubler, Negril Sands Beach Club, 957-4397.

A good information source for government-approved properties is the computerized Jamaica Reservation Service. Phone toll-free in the US, (800) JAMAICA. Do not expect much help from them on camping areas, private homes, small guest houses or otherwise unorthodox accommodations. For that, work from this chapter and on your own once you reach Jamaica.

"You take a look, no problem. Maybe you see somet'ing you like."—"Michie," black coral seller on the street in Montego Bay.

CHAPTER SIXTEEN

LOCAL BUSINESS

There is a catchy rhythm to the ways of small businesses in Jamaica that will grab you and spin you around if you are not careful. A black market thrives on marijuana, and to an increasingly visible extent on other drugs such as cocaine. Coincidentally, import restrictions have been eased up so that Jamaicans can bring virtually anything they want or need into the country, that is if they can afford the duty charges, which can be high. Bribes are not unheard of.

The nature of small business for the unconnected on the island is so competitive that the more aggressive people will often do anything for a sale. This includes telling you what you want to hear, then jacking up the price later. Buyer beware. The same machine-turned wooden mortar and pestle that you will pay $35 JA for in Negril is available for $20 in Kingston. Not only will the vendors in Negril expect more money for the same thing, they can become surly if you contest the point. I have seen voodoo curses hurled at haggling tourists in Negril's Crafts Market. You may not believe in it, but. . . .

The following points should be kept in mind in doing business here.

BLACK MARKET

The big black market items are drugs and American money. Years ago, when the exchange rate was closer to 3-to-1, visitors might be offered 4-to-1, or better, on the streets. Today, with the exchange rate hovering around 5.5-to-1 the offers are less intriguing. I would suggest that you skip it altogether. The 50 cents JA premium you can expect for your dollars is hardly worth the risk. Besides, you must show proof of purchase of Jamaican dollars in order to get a refund on unspent funds before you leave the island. Taking Jamaican dollars out of the country is illegal anyhow, and what would you do with them at home. Exchange your money in a bank, turn back the remainder before you head out, and forget about the petty temptation to clear a few more bucks. It is just not worth it.

Other items, such as cameras, are apparently in demand in Jamaica. Customs makes professional photographers register the serial numbers on their gear on entering the country, checks again on the way out to make sure it is all heading back. Some photographers on assignments, with the cooperation of the Tourist Board, have actually been refused permission by Customs to bring certain equipment into the country. Competing and not always cooperative bureaucracies make for a screwy system. Do not let it screw you. Go by the book and avoid hassles.

GANJA

Marijuana is major business here and you will probably be offered some as soon as you leave the airport. It is illegal, though, so be careful. Discrete use is no problem, mon. Flagrant abuse can be. Make your purchases from people you know, in private settings. Do not try to score at the airport or stupidly out in the open, say on the beach in Montego Bay or in Negril's crafts market. Avoid any furtive-looking nervous fellow who keeps looking over his shoulder. Many people rely on sales of this commodity for their only income source so the weed is more or less freely available for on island consumption.

As for taking some home, do not be foolish. This is a foreign country. Remember "Midnight Express?"

Jamaican police are notorious for random road searches. Road blocks are set-up in strategic locations around blind curves and tourists are routinely stopped and searched. License plates are color coded so rental cars are easily spotted. Police will let Jamaicans drive through a roadblock while they create havoc with a visitor's blood pressure. Pockets will be rudely turned inside-out, glove compartments emptied. If you do carry any, be imaginative as to where you keep it. The stuff is plentiful and cheap enough so that you can easily purchase more anywhere on the island, hourly if you so wish.

In the event that you are caught with your pants down, so to speak, fines are the usual penalty for possession of small quantities. I have heard that bribes are sometimes accepted by Jamaican police, but you are on your own in that area. Undercover cops are sometimes used, but the locals usually spot them quickly, so pay attention to subtle warnings that are well-meant.

Standard prices are $20 JA per quarter ounce, $40 JA per half ounce, $80 JA per ounce. Measurements are commonly vague. You usually get more than the specified weight. If you pay less you are getting a good deal, more and you are being taken. An initial offer might be as high as $75 US for an ounce. Bargain for all you are worth. Bring cigarette papers and matches from home. These are usually harder to find than pot. If you end up rolling joints in hotel stationery you will blow out your lungs fast.

SIDEWALK SALESPEOPLE

Aside from dealers of marijuana, people on the streets sell everything you can imagine. Women or men with long hair will be approached continually to have their hair braided. Some ladies have found the best way to avoid potential hassles

Straw Market

and constant interruptions is to simply give in and have it done once, soon after arrival.

Food items are usually sold for close to a standard price everywhere. Always ask the price before you buy. You will soon figure if you are being overcharged, and if you question a price you will usually find it to be negotiable.

Gift articles, crafts and the like vary in prices for the same item from spot to spot. I would recommend bypassing the crafts markets in Montego Bay and Negril. Sales pitches in those places are especially hard-edged, although you can sometimes find interesting one-of-a-kind black coral jewelry, knit tams and wood carvings. Reasonable deals can sometimes be negotiated, but it can be an unpleasant struggle. The crafts market vendors in Ocho Rios are not as high-strung, and the prices are better. Kingston's Victoria Crafts Market has the best prices of all, at least for the standard souvenir items, t-shirts, straw baskets, mass-produced wood carvings.

You usually do better finding goods at the source, although some items are surprisingly cheaper in odd places. Liquor, for example, is inexpensive at the airport. US citizens can take home one bottle of booze duty-free. I always pick one up with the last of my Jamaican money on the way out of the country. Give yourself a little extra time to catch your plane if you want to do the same thing.

Other duty-free goods are not much of a bargain. Electronics, perfumes and jewelry can be purchased for the same or less in the US.

You can bring home dried herbs, spices and coffee, but not live plants. Some items tread a fine line, such as a home-brew bottle of roots wine. Check with Customs first if you are in doubt. A lot of illegal things pass through one way or another, but the humorless inspectors can still be picky. Be smart and cautious.

LOCAL GUIDES & DRIVERS

Almost everybody is a potential guide, for a price. Get the rates straight before you start out. Children and elderly ladies are often looking for rides and will help you get where you want to go at no charge, if you help them.

A lot of people will ask for money for taking their picture, or if they answer a question for you or give you directions. How you deal with this is up to you. Some visitors ignore these requests. Others carry a roll of quarters for kids and a wad of US dollar bills to hand out on such occasions. Some leave behind articles of clothing. Others never venture outside resort compounds where a service charge is added to their bill.

Think of the occasional hand-out as a sort of informal people's tax that you pay for visiting their home.

"The bus came by and I got on, that's when it all began"—The Grateful Dead, "The Other One."

CHAPTER SEVENTEEN

TRANSPORTATION

Getting to Jamaica and getting around Jamaica are two different things. Here is the scoop.

INTERNATIONAL AIRLINES

Scheduled international airlines serving Jamaica are:

Air Jamaica has the most flights from the most cities around the world. They fly into Montego Bay and Kingston from Atlanta, Baltimore/Washington, DC, Grand Cayman, London, England, Los Angeles, Miami, New York, Philadelphia, Port-Au-Prince, Haiti, San Juan, Puerto Rico, Tampa and Toronto. They serve Jamaican food whenever possible, often play reggae over the sound system prior to take-off.

For information on schedules and rates call toll-free in the US, (800) 523-5585. In Canada call toll-free (800) 263-8137/8.

Other numbers are as follows: Kingston, 922-4661. Montego Bay, 952-4300. Ocho Rios, 974-2566. Negril, 957-4210. Cayman Islands, 92300. Haiti, 20563. Europe (London), 01-734-1782/4.

Under special agreement with British Airways, Air Jamaica runs weekly supersonic Concorde flights between New York and Jamaica. Flight time: 1 hour, 45 minutes.

Air Jamaica recommends check-in at least one and a half hours before flight time, and this is a good idea as lines tend to move slowly. In Miami, for example, you will be boarding with numerous higglers checking through bursting cardboard boxes filled with goods to sell on the island. The Air Jamaica counter at Miami International is always one of the busiest places in the airport prior to flights. Reconfirmation of all tickets is also necessary.

Air Canada flies from Toronto and Montreal. In Kingston their phone number is 924-8211. In Montego Bay call 952-5160.

American Airlines flies from New York and Boston. They have a toll-free number in the US, (800) 433-7300. In Kingston call 924-8305. In Montego Bay call 952-5950.

ALM Antillean Airlines offer flights connecting Kingston with Aruba, Curacao, Bonaire, San Juan, St. Maarten, Port-Au-Prince, Caracas, Port of Spain, Georgetown, Medellin, Panama, Santa Domingo and Bogota. Phone 924-8092 in Kingston.

Aeroflot flies to Kingston from Moscow. Reservations must be made in Russia. Air Jamaica serves as agent for them. Call 922-4661 in Kingston for information.

British Airways flies to Kingston from London, with stops in Bermuda, the Bahamas and Miami before reaching Jamaica. Phone Kingston, 922-5245, or Montego Bay, 952-3771.

British West Indian Airlines flies to Kingston from several Caribbean islands. Phone Kingston, 929-4231.

Cayman Airlines flies Caribbean routes in and out of Kingston. Phone 926-1762.

Challenge International Airlines flies from Miami to Montego Bay and Kingston, with connections to Central America. US toll-free number is (800) 343-1222. In Florida (800) 841-8879.

Cubana Airlines has flights through Kingston. Phone 922-3460.

Eastern Airlines flies in and out of Montego Bay, 952-4460, and Kingston, 924-8271. Toll-free number in the US is (800) 327-8376.

VIASA (Venezuelan International Airlines) flies between Montego Bay, 952-5531, or Kingston, 926-1762, and Caracas, with connections throughout South America and Europe.

DOMESTIC & CHARTER AIRLINES

Trans-Jamaican Airlines is the most reliable domestic carrier, with daily scheduled flights to and from Kingston, 923-8680, Montego Bay, 952-5401/3, Negril, 957-4251, Port Antonio, 993-2791, and Ocho Rios, 974-3254. They also provide domestic and overseas charters.

Express Air Ltd offers scheduled service out of Kingston's Tinson Pen Aerodrome, 923-5380, or Manley International, 924-8770, to Montego Bay, Port Antonio, Negril and Ocho Rios. They also offer domestic and overseas charters, as well as sightseeing flights over Jamaica.

Wings Jamaica Ltd. has domestic and overseas charters, rentals, leasing and sightseeing flights out of Kingston's Tinson Pen Aerodrome, 923-6573.

Airways International Ltd. offers domestic and overseas charters, as well as sightseeing trips. Call Tinson Pen, Kingston, 923-6614, or Sangster International, Montego Bay 952-5299.

Timair Ltd. flies Cessna Skyhawks from Sangster International in Montego Bay on sightseeing routes over Mo-Bay and the Cockpits for $35 US including pick-up and return to your hotel. Scenic flights to Negril or Port Antonio are $65–$120 US. Phone 952-2516 in Montego Bay for information.

CRUISE SHIPS

The following cruise lines call on Montego Bay, Ocho Rios or Port Antonio:

Carnival Cruises "Holiday" and "Jubilee." (800) 327-7373.
Chandris Line "Victoria" and "Britanis."
Commodore Cruises "Boheme." (305) 373-5502.

Costa Line "Daphne." (212) 682-3505.
CTC Lines "Fedor Shalyapin."
Cunard Line "Cunard Princess" and "Vistafjord." (212) 880-7500.
Hapag Lloyd "Europa." (312) 332-0090.
Holland America "Nieuw Amsterdam" and "Noordam." (800) 223-6655.
Home Lines "Atlantic." (800) 221-4041.
Norwegian Caribbean Line "Sunward II" and "Starward." (800) 327-7030.
Ocean Cruise Line "Ocean Princess." (305) 764-3500.
P&O Cruises "Sea Princess."
Princess Cruises "Pacific Princess."
Regency Cruises "Regent Sea." (800) 457-5566.
Royal Caribbean Line "Song of Norway" and "Sun Viking." (800) 327-6700.
Royal Viking Line "Royal Viking Sea" and "Royal Viking Sky." (800) 422-8000.
Sitmar Cruises "Fairsky" and "Fairwind." (213) 553-1666.

For cruise lines with no listed phone, or for additional information on visiting Jamaica by cruise ship contact the Jamaica Tourist Board, 21 Dominica Dr., Kingston 5, JA, 929-9200.

BUSES, MINI-BUSES AND CABS

One of the most colorful and least expensive ways to get around Jamaica is by bus. Big country buses are roomier, cheaper (60 cents US per twenty miles) and less reliable than mini-buses, which are usually jam-packed Japanese vans, but running more frequently for around $1 US per twenty miles.

The buses run practically everywhere, and a lot of the people you see standing alongside the roads, looking idle, are actually waiting for a bus. Official bus stops are about as rare as schedules. They do exist in the bigger cities and towns, but for the most part you just flag down a ride.

Mini-buses typically have a conductor who takes your money, and indeed, you can be taken if you are not careful. Going rate between Montego and Kingston is $23 JA, but you can pay more if you look like you do not know what you are doing.

As for cabs, there are licensed ones and unlicensed ones. Licensed cabs charge $2.50 JA for the first one-third-mile, 85 cents every third of a mile after that. Unlicensed cabs charge whatever they can get, which can be lower if you bargain well, or considerably higher than standard rates for trusting tourists. There are few metered cabs, so negotiate a flat rate before you get in. If you do not reach an agreement, look for another cab.

A bus costs 60 cents JA to ride from Sangster Airport into downtown Mo-Bay, another $1.80 JA to ride from Sam Sharpe Square to Sign Great House, a trip of around six miles.

In Montego Bay, mini-buses to Kingston or Ocho Rios and the north coast can be found next to the crafts market. Aggressive drivers will try to hustle you into their vehicle, working to get a full passenger load before taking off. Establish the price first and go on to the next van if you are unhappy with the rate.

Look for the mini-buses on Creek St. to Negril and the south coast.

Pick up the big country buses anywhere along Barnett St.

In Ocho Rios, pick up mini-buses at the roundabout on the west end of town, or near the clock tower in the center of town.

In Port Antonio you can get mini-buses or taxis on West St., across the street from the market and Kingsley Restaurant.

Buses and mini-buses criss-cross all over Kingston. Suburban buses stop running at 10 PM. All the buses are crowded, and understanding routes and rates can be confusing, but if you are brave and not in a hurry they afford a glimpse of Jamaican life few tourists ever see. Jamaicans actually seem to understand their bus systems, so try asking for help.

Most of the buses out of town leave from either Half Way Tree or the Parade.

In Negril, mini-buses can be found most easily near the roundabout on the south side of the bridge, beyond the crafts market.

If you plan to really use the buses to get around, be prepared for a lot of switching and waiting. The buses go virtually everywhere, and even though they do drive fast, they still take a long time.

RENTAL CARS

Renting a car can be an expensive as well as intriguing experience as you learn to negotiate Jamaica's roads. Potholes, goats, children, vendors, other vehicles and an unbelievable variety of Jamaican life and culture finds its way into the streets, and you, as a driver, must not only get where you want to go, but avoid all the obstacles. Remember: Stay to the left.

Roads are largely unmarked and the few signs may be difficult to locate or read. Still, a rental car gives you the freedom to go where you want to go, and this includes areas where buses do not run, or run infrequently. If you get lost, Jamaicans are always helpful with directions, or you can always pick up an elderly lady pedestrian or a child who will be grateful for the ride and help you along the way.

Because the roads are so bad in Jamaica it is smart to deal only with reputable car rental firms. You have to be at least 21 to rent a car, and people between 21–25 must pay additional insurance charges. You will need a valid drivers license, as well as an internationally recognized credit card, or else you will have to pay cash in advance, in Jamaican dollars, for the estimated charges. Expect to pay at least $150 JA daily, $900 JA weekly, plus 10% government tax. A $500 JA deposit is refundable on return of the undamaged car. Mileage and insurance are usually included.

Gasoline is not included in rental agreements and costs around $10.99 JA per gallon. Service stations are not that hard to find, but it may be wise to pick up a road map from each of the three oil companies doing business in Jamaica. These are Esso, Texaco and Shell. Gas stations charge around $1 US for the maps, but each one will have its company's gas stations marked. Most gas stations close by 8 PM.

Roads are often a challenge

Rent a front-wheel drive car if you plan to do any mountain driving or spend time in less developed areas. Four-wheel drive is better, but harder to find. If you plan to travel outside of the main tourist areas, it is probably not smart to try to cut corners with a cheapie rental or you could find yourself broken down far from help or even a phone.

The following are among the most reputable rental car firms:

MONTEGO BAY

Hertz, Sangster Airport, 952-4472; Casa Montego Arcade, 952-4471.

Avis, Sangster Airport, 952-4543; Ironshore, 952-4541.

National, Sangster Airport, 952-2769; Holiday Village, 953-2824.

Budget, Sangster Airport, 952-5061; Ironshore, 952-1189.

Dollar, Sangster Airport, 952-0664.

OCHO RIOS

Hertz, 974-2334 or 974-2666.

Avis, 974-2641 or 974-2057.

National, 974-2266.

Budget, 974-2178.

Dollar, 974-2594/5.

PORT ANTONIO

Avis, 993-2626.

Eastern Rent-a-Car, 993-3624.

Dollar Inter-Rent, 993-2625.

KINGSTON

Hertz, Manley Airport, 924-8028; Pegasus Hotel, 926-3690; Oxford Rd., 926-0181.

Avis, Manley Airport, 924-8013; Haining Rd., 926-5488.

National, Manley Airport, 924-8775 or 924-8344; Knutsford Blvd., 929-7204 or 929-4377.

Budget, Lower Elleston Rd., 928-4779 or 928-4911.

Dollar, Manley Airport, 924-8462; Knutsford Blvd., 926-1535.

NEGRIL

Western Car Rentals, Negril Airport, phone Montego Bay, 952-5159.

Vacation Tours Rent-A-Car, Negril Airport, phone Montego Bay, 952-0728.

There is a Jamaica U-Drive Association which officially represents the country-wide rental car industry. They put out a brochure listing thirty-three rental car firms all over the country that adhere to a standard code of ethics, as well as a standardized rate structure. Contact the association at Newlin St., Ocho Rios, Jamaica, West Indies, 974-2852.

There are many more rental car firms listed in the phone book, some of which are undoubtedly less expensive than the top-name firms or association members.

Another possibility is for you to rent a car then hire a Jamaican to drive you. Expect to pay $70–$100 JA daily for a driver, plus food and any entrance fees or accommodations charges.

Make your own deal, and make sure you pick a driver you want to spend a lot of time with, or contact tour operators to help with personalized arrangements.

MOTORBIKES

Mo-peds and motorbike rentals are available in most of the tourist areas and these can be less expensive than rental cars as well as a lot of fun if you are not going far. Remember the roads are bad, though, and you can easily wipe out if you are not careful.

MONTEGO BAY

Montego Bike Rentals, 21 Gloucester Ave., 952-4984.
Montego Honda, 21 Gloucester Ave., 952-3873.
Vacation Wheels, 29 Gloucester Ave., 952-0164.
Village Rent-A-Bike, Holiday Village, 953-2872.

OCHO RIOS

Motor Trails Ltd., Carib Ocho Rios Arcade, 974-5058.
Vacation Wheels Ltd., Carib Ocho Rios Arcade, 974-5021.
Sunnyride Rent-A-Bike, Content Garden, 974-2130.
Just-Rent-A-Bike, Main St., 974-2800.
Rent-A-Motorbike Today, 58 Main St., 974–2681.

NEGRIL

Rent-A-Motorbike, T-Water Hotel, 957-4270/1.
Tanka Motorcycle, Plaza de Negril Shopping Center.
Leonard's Bike & Bicycle Rental, West End Rd.
Island Bicycle Rental, West End Rd.

As for renting a motorbike in Kingston, it can be done but think about it first. There is a lot of traffic and the roads are bad. It just depends on how much adventure you are looking for.

TRAINS

A slow, colorful cross-country train line extends between Montego Bay and Kingston. The trains are almost always late and usually crowded. They are also inexpensive and cover a big chunk of terrain, stopping at nearly every tiny village and town along the way. There are also tourist trains that run from Montego Bay for day trips to the Appleton Rum Factory (The Governor's Coach), or to Mandeville.

First-class has padded seats, economy does not. There is no air conditioning and it is a hot and dirty ride with the windows open. The scenery is, however, memorable, as you travel from Mo-Bay through gardens and canefields, into the mountains and out again. It is noisy and the slowest motorized way to travel. Expect to spend four and a half to five and a half hours for the one-way trip cross-country—that is, if nothing goes wrong.

Vendors sell fresh fruit and cold drinks at every stop along the way. Children from the villages climb all over the slow-moving train. People come and go, carting caged chickens, or just the omnipresent bundles or bags. It seems as if everyone in Jamaica is carrying something under their arm or on top of their head.

Montego Bay to Kingston trains depart at 6:30 AM and 2:45 PM daily, arriving at 12:15 PM and 8:20 PM.

Kingston to Montego Bay trains depart daily at 6:50 AM and 3 PM, arriving at 12:30 PM and 8:35 PM.

One-way first class costs $26 JA. Economy costs $17 JA. Children under 12 are half-fare. Phone 922-6620 in Kingston for information. The station in Kingston is downtown at the west end of Barry St. The station in Montego Bay is on Lightbody Ave., 952-4842.

WALKING AND HITCH-HIKING

Everyone walks everywhere and you can too. Walking is absolutely the best way to mingle with Jamaicans, to feel the

rhythms that they live with, the ground underfoot being a good part of the basis of that.

Hitch-hiking is common throughout the island and mostly safe. Jamaican hitch-hikers wave their arms as cars go by, flapping at the drivers to stop. It looks as if they are motioning for you to go away. The only problem with hitch-hiking is that there are not all that many cars and you may have to wait a long time for a ride. A bus may show up first, while you are waiting. Or just take the time to walk and meet the people on the streets.

Adventure is all around you. Move smartly to meet it.

"You know how we work. Push, you don't get much. Take it easier, get much more."—Peter Bentley.

PART IV

DETAILS

Unless your idea of a vacation is to simply and completely vacate, say, at one of Jamaica's all-inclusive resorts, you have choices to make every step of the way while planning and accomplishing an adventurous trip. At the all-inclusives, really "summer camps" for adults, most decisions are made for you in advance by a committee.

If you want to take more personal control of your time you have to make up your own mind about what sort of trip you want, what gear to bring, and where to find any additional information you may require while on the trip. Yet, within the range of adventure, there are numerous possibilities.

Are you looking for individual or group travel?

Do you prefer to travel light from camp to camp, or do you like to adventure by day and sleep in good hotels with hot showers?

Are you perhaps shy about striking up friendships with strangers, but interested in the more formal "Meet the People" program?

The final part of this book will help you customize your trip to suit your needs and interests. By making the adventurous part of the trip your explorations into the heart of the culture and not getting through Customs at the airport, you can have the best possible time in Jamaica, with the fewest possible procedural surprises.

"It is very satisfying to discover there is a lot more you can do for yourself than you thought. . . ."—Christina Dodwell, *An Explorer's Handbook*.

CHAPTER EIGHTEEN

INDIVIDUAL OR GROUP ADVENTURES

You can find adventure on your own or with an organized group. There are advantages to both modes. On your own, you choose the itinerary, along with all the details of your trip. This takes good research and planning to take maximum advantage of the time and money you have to spend. All the responsibility for making arrangements and having fun rests with you. This is fine if you know what you are doing, or if you have plenty of time to learn as you go along.

Generally you can expect to spend a little less money on your own, unless you make costly mistakes in preparation or execution. You deal directly with the people whose services you require. There is no middleman between you and your adventure, for a minimum of cost and a maximum of flexibility, along with the uncertainties that come with freedom of choice.

With a group you generally have less input as to itineraries, where you stay or eat, and so forth. You pay someone with more experience to make certain decisions. In return for not having to think about all the details, you get to spend more time concentrating on your backstroke, or flips off rocks into river pools, or whatever it is that interests you.

You pay a premium for this freedom from care, and to many people, particularly those with healthy budgets and limited time, the sense of security is worth the cost. You have fewer adjustments to make in a foreign culture and there is undeniable security in working within a predetermined budget and time schedule. It is, however, hard to change plans if your interests change in mid-stream, and with others making decisions for you, you tend to be more insulated from the culture you are moving within. Also, unless you arrange your own group, you will be traveling with strangers, people who are supposed to have similar interests to yours. This is not always the case, though, and divergent interests or a personality conflict can spoil a trip, or at least parts of it.

A third choice is traveling alone or with friends, with a private guide. This can give you the benefits of unstructured experience in a new place, without the surprises of being forced to adhere to a group consciousness you may dislike. You can have the security of planning this sort of trip in advance, knowing loosely what you will be doing, but still being more on your own than prearranged group travel allows.

Traveling alone can be lonely. A group can give you a sense of identity in a strange place.

Traveling with a group can smother your personal interests. No one tells you what to do when you are on your own.

A private guide can give you the best of both worlds. You work out an itinerary and the guide executes your wishes. It may not be any more expensive than a group trip, although the best of the well-organized adventure tours come equipped with camping gear, inflatable boats, and other supplies you may not want to cart along on your own.

The choice is up to you. Here are the best of the adventure trip organizers in Jamaica, as well as the most up-to-date sources for help with making arrangements for an independent trip. Contact them individually and see what sort of deals you can work out.

SENSE Adventures is Peter Bentley's company. Peter goes on most of the trips he sets up and his knowledge of Jamaica can be a big help. He seems to know everyone on the island. Additionally, he has great knowledge of the flora and fauna, as well as local customs. You will pay a bit more for one of Peter's trips than you would visiting the same places on your own, but there is no way an independent first-time visitor to Jamaica would find some of the places he will show you on a short trip.

SENSE specializes in hiking, river canoeing, whitewater, backpacking, natural history and combined adventure/special interest travel. Peter will work with you to create just the itinerary you want, guided or on your own, and his island-wide contacts can make virtually any trip you dream up a reality.

In his capacity as President of JATCHA, Jamaica Alternative Tourism Camping and Hiking Association, Peter works with lively people all over the island to provide services as needed for all adventurous travelers.

He charges $15 US for a complete information packet, including a hand-marked map and reservation service. It could be money well-spent. He also gives limited free advice initially, making him a valuable resource for anyone planning to spend adventurous time here. Write SENSE ADVENTURES, Box 216, Kingston 7, Jamaica. Phone (809) 927-2657, or leave a message at 926-4291.

If you contact the Jamaica Tourist Board about adventure travel they will probably put you in touch with Peter. He is by far the best equipped person in the country to handle off-beat trips. Several other people work with JATCHA as regional reps. These are:

Pauline Stewart, Global Travel, 40 Union Sq., Kingston 5, Jamaica, 926-4291. This is a travel agency with seven offices island-wide.

Jean Gaynier, Negril Beach Club, Norman Manley Blvd., Negril, 957-4323.

Audrey Barned, Crow's Nest, Ocho Rios, 974-5188.

Parchi Parchment, PO Box 61, Montego Bay, 953-2387, or 6213 Cobb's Creek Parkway, Philadelphia, PA 19143, (215) 471-0884.

Several major adventure tour organizers offer trips to Jamaica, mostly in conjunction with Peter. You can contact these companies directly for information.

Sobek Expeditions Inc., are the people who first discovered white water in Jamaica in 1983. They run outdoor adventure trips all over the world, putting together careful adventure packages that are detailed in a yearly *Adventure Book.* An exciting book for dreamers and adventurers. Contact PO Box 333, Angels Camp, CA 95222, (209) 736-4524.

Mountain Travel has been organizing adventure trips since 1967, although they have only recently started nine-day trips to Jamaica. Approximate land cost is $890 US for each of six to nine people, $790 for each of ten to fifteen people. Dates for trips are Dec-Mar. Contact 1398 Solano Ave., Albany, CA 94706, phone (800) 227-2384, or (415) 527-8100.

There are also innumerable independent guides you can find in Jamaica, most less organized than Peter, probably not as well equipped, but also less expensive and definitely culturally authentic. You will have to hook up with most of these people after you reach the island and negotiate your deal on the spot.

If you are looking for a guide in the Blue Mountains, someone to keep you from getting lost, cook meals and help you learn the ropes, write Chris Mitchell, *Vifies Promotions—Jamaica's Mountain Hikers Association*, Jack's Hill PA, St. Andrew, Kingston 6, Jamaica. Chris is an ambitious young man who trained with Peter Bentley and knows the mountains well.

There are many other people who will help arrange adventure trips in Jamaica. The ones listed here are the best and most reliable. Even if you plan to go it completely on your own, you can check with these sources first to see how they do it and get some good ideas.

In the realm of soft adventure, Jamaica Tourist Board organizes a program called "Meet The People," which puts visitors in touch with Jamaicans with similar interests, hobbies or profession in a social setting. There is no cost to the visitor and hundreds of volunteers are registered with the program islandwide, in Kingston and the major tourism areas.

The basic deal is that visitors are entertained by Jamaicans. You might be invited to a home-cooked lunch or dinner, to a church or club, to a picnic, a day at the beach or a family trip into the mountains. You can meet Jamaicans at work, at home, or at play, in a casual setting.

To participate in this program, visitors should contact the JTB in advance of their trip, if possible, or as soon as they reach Jamaica, and list interests, age, profession, length of stay and place of residence on the island. JTB makes the arrangements for you.

Another alternative for meeting unusual Jamaicans is through a non-profit organization called *SERVAS*, 11 John St., Suite 706, New York, NY 10038, (212) 267-0252.

SERVAS is a worldwide free-hospitality clearinghouse for individuals who are interested in sharing their concerns on social and international problems. It is a co-op of hosts and travelers who pay a yearly fee of less than $50 for access to lists of hosts in more than 80 countries around the world, including Jamaica. The idea of the program is to promote peace, understanding and good will by providing opportunities for personal contacts among people of different backgrounds. Visitors are expected to share in the day-to-day activities of hosts. There is no money exchanged between visitor and host, and visitors usually stay for two to three nights, although longer visits can be arranged on an individual basis. You do not have to be a host to be a welcome traveler.

"You can't keep crow from flyin', but you can keep him from pitchin' on you head."—Jamaican aphorism.

CHAPTER NINETEEN

GEAR, CLOTHING & SPORTS EQUIPMENT

You definitely need to take care of yourself in terms of gear and clothing unless you want to spend a lot of money on what you need here. Items like film and batteries are available, but expensive. You can always pick up an inexpensive t-shirt, but you might have trouble with availability or cost of women's tampons or men's shaving gear.

The more adventurous you plan to be, the lighter you should travel.

Always carry valuables with you. Camping sites and small guest houses are mostly safe and secure but will not necessarily have a place where you can lock up your stuff.

CLOTHING

Lightweight and casual is the order in Jamaica. Jeans are too heavy. Light cotton clothing is best, or wash and wear items that will dry quickly in Jamaica's high humidity. Count on bringing the following:

Tropic weight pants, shorts, skirts or sun-dress.

Tropic weight shirts. (Lightweight button-down shirts are cooler than clingy t-shirts.)

Bathing suit or cut-offs.

Sneakers or walking shoes. Canvas is smarter than leather, as they may get wet. For the same reason, two pairs are better than one. Hiking boots are unnecessary, even in the more rugged areas.

Socks. You will need them to protect your ankles when bush walking.

Beach sandals or thongs. Jamaicans go barefoot, but you may need to acclimate to hot sand or sharp corals.

Sun hat. Wide brim is better than a baseball cap. You will want to keep the sun off the back of your neck as well as your face. You can buy inexpensive straw hats in Jamaica.

Windbreaker and/or sweater, or sweatshirt. It gets cool at higher elevations. bring something that folds up small.

Sport jacket or dress are optional, if you plan to visit the ritzier restaurants, or hotels. Even in these places, dress is mostly casual and you can usually get away without dressing up.

GEAR

Bring all your own toilet articles, including toilet paper, tampons, shaving gear (including a shaving mirror), if you plan on staying in some of the lower range accommodations or camping areas. Soap, shampoo, toothpaste and the like are expensive in Jamaica. Most important—bring insect repellent! You will be glad you did. Insect coils that burn all night are available inexpensively on the island. You may want to pick up a few. Bring any prescription drugs you may need, also aspirins. If you have a sensitive stomach you may want to bring Pepto Bismol or an antacid. Water is purified. Food is not necessarily.

Sunscreen or suntan lotion are available on the island, but cheaper if you bring it from home. The sun is strong. A quick burn can ruin your trip.

A small plastic bottle of laundry detergent is a good idea.

Jamaica is extremely photogenic. Bring your camera, with lots of film. Carry spare batteries, lens tissue, film mailers.

Carry a spare camera if you can. If you hope to photograph Jamaicans, it may be smart to carry a Polaroid. A lot of people will say no to your photo request (Do not take pictures without asking!), or may say yes if you offer them an instant photo.

A small tape player/recorder can be good to have along. You will be amazed and enchanted by Jamaican speech and music. You can buy reggae tapes all over the island, or carry blank tapes and pay a nominal charge to have albums recorded for you in a record shop. Carry spare tapes and batteries.

A flashlight is good to have along, especially if you plan to be in less developed areas. Make sure you have spare bulbs as well as batteries.

Take a small cookstove, if you plan to cook for yourself. You can buy gasoline or kerosene on the island. Carry your own utensils.

Zip-loc plastic bags are handy for food or toiletries, as well as larger plastic bags for wet clothes.

A small folding umbrella is not a bad idea, for rain showers or for walking under a strong sun.

A poncho can keep you dry and double as a ground cloth.

A moneybelt may enhance your comfort.

Notebooks, pads and pens are better brought from home. Don't count on finding them in Jamaica.

Matches are hard to find in Jamaica. Bring some or carry a lighter. Candles are good to have along. Smokers should bring cigarette papers.

SPORTS EQUIPMENT

Snorkeling, diving and fishing gear can be rented, or bring your own if you plan to stay in one spot, or are sure of your on-island transportation and have space to cart it all around.

Bring a backpack/daypack if you plan on a lot of walking.

Sleeping bag is optional. Carry only a lightweight one. If you plan to rough it, bring a foam sleeping pad.

Tents can often be rented on the island, or bring one if you prefer. If you bring your own, carry spare tent pegs, ropes, tape.

Finally, don't forget a canteen, compass, and pocket knife, with can opener, corkscrew, fishscaler, or whatever tools you may need.

Some people may require more gear, some less. Figure on what you plan to do and pack accordingly. Just remember that what you leave behind will probably be hard to find and costly on the island.

"We've got to fulfill de' book. . . ."—Bob Marley, *Redemption Song.*

CHAPTER TWENTY

GOVERNMENT REGULATIONS

There are plenty of government regulations that affect travelers. None of them are really problematical—unless you do not follow them.

IMMIGRATION & CUSTOMS

You have to fill out an immigration card before you are allowed into the country. You present the form along with identification and the address where you will be staying in Jamaica to get through the immigration desk at the airport. Save the form as you will need to present it on your way out of the country. Americans can stay up to six months.

Cruise ship passengers do not have to go through immigration. Ships get a blanket clearance.

US and Canadian citizens and legal residents of the US can use the following for identification: Passport (not expired beyond one year), residency card or certificate, naturalization certificate or card, or any *two* of the following: Drivers license with photo, voter ID, birth certificate. Married women using a birth certificate may also be asked for a marriage certificate.

You may be asked to produce a return ticket, along with ID.

Visitors from countries other than the US or Canada must show a passport, and in some cases a visa. Check first if you have any questions.

Health certificates are not required of US and Canadian visitors, nor from travelers from England or Western Europe.

Vaccination certificates are required from people coming from India and Central Africa. Visitors from elsewhere should check requirements in advance.

Customs often searches luggage of *entering* visitors. You cannot bring in guns or ammunition, illegal drugs, Jamaican currency, rum, pets, flowers, fruits, plants or uncanned meats. There may be restrictions on camera equipment, video recording gear and other electronic items with a high resale value in Jamaica. Check first with Customs if you have any questions.

You can bring in personal articles, up to 25 cigars, 200 cigarettes, one pint of liquor (but not rum), one half pound of tobacco and one quart of wine.

On the way out of the country, US citizens are allowed up to $300 US worth of duty-free purchases after a 48-hour visit. Gifts with a value of up to $10 may be mailed back to the States, with no duty imposed, although these gifts cannot be liquor, perfume, cigars or cigarettes. The gifts do not weigh against the $300 duty-free limit, but you cannot send more than one gift to the same person in a day.

Americans can take home 32 oz. of alcohol duty-free.

Canadian citizens are allowed to take $10 US worth of purchases into Canada after a 48-hour stay without paying Canadian duty. They can take up to a maximum of $50 US in any calendar quarter. Excess up to $150 US value is taxed at 25% duty. After seven days in Jamaica, a Canadian can bring home $150 US worth of products duty-free once a year.

There is a $40 JA departure tax for all visitors. This must be paid in Jamaican dollars, so be sure to have it on hand.

Only dogs and cats imported from England, Ireland or North Ireland are allowed entrance. Health certificates and a permit from the Jamaican Ministry of Agriculture are required.

CURRENCY

It is illegal to pay for anything in Jamaica using anything other than Jamaican currency, although in practice many businesses will accept payment in American dollars and give you change in Jamaican dollars. The rate of exchange fluctuates, but current rates are posted in exchange bureaus at the international airports, as well as in all banks. You can also exchange at hotels, but almost always for a lower rate.

When you purchase Jamaican dollars you will be given a receipt that must be presented if you have any funds left over to reconvert before you leave. The airport exchanges are open for all outgoing flights. Just make sure you give yourself enough time for this last transaction. It is illegal to take Jamaican money out of the country.

Travelers checks are accepted widely and usually bring a small premium in exchange rates. Sample rates might be $5.35 JA to $1 Travelers Check, $5.30 JA to $1 US cash, $5.05 JA to $1 US coins.

At the stated rates, it would cost you $5.49 JA to buy back $1 US at the end of your trip.

There are banks in all major towns and these are open from 9 AM to 2 PM Mon.-Thurs. Friday hours are 9 Am to 12 noon, and 2:30 PM to 5 PM.

TELEPHONES

The area code for all of Jamaica is 809. All the local numbers listed in this book can be reached from overseas with the code.

Phones work in Jamaica, but they are idiosyncratic. You have to connect with your party first from a pay phone before you deposit your dime. You hear the other party pick-up but they do not hear you until you deposit the money.

Dial 0 first for long distance. Dial 113 for an international operator. Directory assistance is 114.

For local calls in Ocho Rios or Kingston you dial only the last five numbers of a seven digit phone number.

For local calls in Irish Town or Red Hills, dial only the last three numbers of a seven digit number. For all other local calls dial the complete seven-digit number.

ELECTRIC CURRENT

Standard is 110 volts, 50 cycles. Some hotels use 220 and can supply transformers.

POSTAGE

Airmail postcards to North America are $.45 JA. Letters are $.55 per 1/2 oz. The mail is slow getting in and out of Jamaica. It can easily take 10 days for a first class letter to reach Jamaica from the US. An air mail package of books sent to Jamaica from the US routinely takes up to 3 months to be delivered. Surface mail is out of the question. It is a little quicker mailing from Jamaica to other points.

"One finger can't catch dog flea."—Jamaican aphorism

CHAPTER TWENTY-ONE

INFORMATION SOURCES

Everyone needs help sometime. Here are the best sources for additional information on Jamaica.

JAMAICAN TOURIST BOARD OFFICES WORLDWIDE

JAMAICA

Tourism Centre, 21 Dominica Dr., Kingston 5. Phone 929-9200.

Norman Manley Airport, Kingston. Phone 924-8024.

Cornwall Beach, PO Box 67, Montego Bay, St. James. Phone 952-4425.

Sangster International Airport, Montego Bay. Phone 952-2091.

Shop # 20, Plaza de Negril, Negril PO, Westmoreland. Phone 957-4243.

Ocean Village Shopping Center, PO Box 240, Ocho Rios, St. Ann. Phone 974-2570.

City Center Plaza, PO Box 151, Port Antonio, Portland. Phone 993-3051.

UNITED STATES

866 Second Ave., 10th Floor, New York, NY 10017. Phone (212) 688-7650.

36 S. Wabash Ave., Suite 1210, Chicago, IL 60603. Phone (312) 346-1546.

8411 Preston Rd., Suite 605 LB 31, Dallas, TX 75225. Phone (214) 361-8778.

1320 S. Dixie Highway, Suite 1100, Coral Gables, FL 33146. Phone (305) 665-0557.

3440 Wilshire Blvd., Suite 1207, Los Angeles, CA 90010. Phone (213) 384-1123.

CANADA

2221 Yonge St., Suite 507, Toronto, Ontario M4S 2B4. Phone (416) 482-7850.

110 Sherbrooke St., Mezzanine Level, West Montreal, Quebec H3A 1G9. Phone (514) 849-6387/8.

ENGLAND

Jamaica House, 50 St. James St., London SW1A 1JT, UK. Phone (011) 441-493-3647.

WEST GERMANY

Vogstrasse 50, 6000 Frankfurt 1, West Germany. Phone 069-59-75675.

JAPAN

c/o Carrington Group, Inc., Suite 404, Palai Nogizaka, Minato-Ku, Tokyo 107, Japan. Phone 03-475-4671.

FOREIGN EMBASSIES

US Embassy, Jamaica Mutual Life Centre, 2 Oxford Rd., Kingston. Phone 926-4220.

Australian High Commission, 64 Knutsford Blvd., Kingston. Phone 926-3551.

British High Commission, Trafalgar Rd., Kingston. Phone 926-9050.

Canadian High Commission, 30 Knutsford Blvd., Kingston. Phone 926-1500.

French Embassy, 13 Hillcrest Ave., Kingston. Phone 927-9811.

German Embassy, 10 Waterloo Rd., Kingston. Phone 926-6728.

Israeli Embassy, 60 Knutsford Blvd., Kingston. Phone 926-8768.

Japanese Embassy, Hampshire House, 4 Rekadom Rd., Kingston. Phone 929-7534.

GOVERNMENT DEPARTMENTS

Ministry of Agriculture, Hope Gardens, Kingston. Phone 927-9831.

Coffee Industry Board, Marcus Garvey Dr., Kingston. Phone 923-7211.

Forestry Department, 4 Hillman Rd., Kingston. 924-1997.

The Jamaica Archives, Spanish Town. Phone 984-3041.

Collector of Customs, Customs House, Kingston. Phone 922-8770.

Collector of Customs, 32 Market St., Montego Bay. Phone 952-3080.

Ministry of Health (Head Office), 10 Caledonia Ave., Kingston. Phone 926-9220.

Jamaica Information Service, 58A Half Way Tree, Kingston. Phone 926-3740.

Ministry of Mines, Hope Gardens, Kingston. Phone 927-7369.

Natural Resources & Conservation Department, 53 1/2 Molynes Rd., Kingston. Phone 923-5155.

Prime Minister's Office, Devon Road, Kingston. Phone 927-9941.

Ministry of Tourism, 85 Knutsford Blvd., Kingston. Phone 926-4220.

BOOKS

For additional information about Jamaica, the following books may be of interest:

Adams, C. Dennis. *Flowering Plants in Jamaica.* Mona: University of the West Indies, 1972.

Adams, C. Dennis. *The Blue Mahoe & Other Bush—an Introduction to Plant Life in Jamaica.* Kingston: Sangster/ Singapore: McGraw-Hill, 1971.

Avinoff, A. and N. Shoumatoff. *An Annotated List of Butterflies of Jamaica.* Pittsburgh: Carnegie Museum, 1946.

Barrett, Leonard E. *The Rastafarians: The Dreadlocks of Jamaica.* London: Heinemann, 1977.

Barrett, Leonard E. *The Sun and the Drum.* Kingston: Sangster, 1976. African influence on Jamaican culture.

Beckwith, Martha. *Jamaican Proverbs.* New York: Negro University Press, 1970.

Benghiat, Norma. *Traditional Jamaican Cookery.* England, USA, Australia, Canada, New Zealand: Penguin, 1985. History, culture and recipes.

Bennett, Louise. *Anancy and Miss Lou.* Kingston: Sangster, 1979. Folk tales written in patois.

Bennett, Louise. *Anancy Stories and Dialect Verse.* Kingston: Pioneer Press, 1950.

Black, Clinton V. *History of Jamaica*, 4th edition. London: Collins, 1976.

Black, Clinton V. *Tales of Old Jamaica.* Kingston: Sangster, 1979.

Blake, Evon. *Beautiful Jamaica*, 4th edition. Jamaica: Vista Publications, 1980. Photos.

Bond, James. *Birds of the West Indies.* London: Collins, 1960 edition.

Boot, Adrian and Michael Thomas. *Jamaica: Babylon on a Thin Wire.* New York: Schocken Books, 1976. 1970's Jamaica in B&W photos.

Brown, Aggrey. *Colour, Class and Politics in Jamaica.* New Jersey: Transaction Books, 1979.

Caldwell, David K. *Marine and Freshwater Fish of Jamaica.* Kingston: Institute of Jamaica, 1966.

Cargill, Morris editor. *Ian Fleming Introduces Jamaica.* London: Andre Deutsch, 1965.

Cassidy, Frederick G., and R.B. LePage. *Dictionary of Jamaican English*, 2nd edition. Cambridge: Cambridge University Press, 1980.

Cassidy, Frederick G. *Jamaica Talk.* London: MacMillan, 1971.

Chen, Ray. *Jamaica: The Land and the People.* Montreal: 1984. Coffee table photo book.

Davis, Stephen. *Bob Marley.* London: Panther/Granada 1983.

Davis, Stephen and Peter Simon. *Reggae Bloodlines: In Search of the Music and Culture of Jamaica.* New York: Anchor Press/Doubleday, 1977. Top-notch photography.

Davis, Stephen and Peter Simon. *Reggae International.* New York: Alfred Knopf, 1982. Worldwide reggae, photos.

Eyre, Alain. *The Botanic Gardens of Jamaica.* London: Andre Deutsch, 1966.

Faristzaddi, Millard. *Itations of Jamaica and i Rastafari.* New York: Grove Press, 1982. Poetry, patois and photos.

Forsythe, Dennis. *Rastafari: For The Healing Of The Nation.* Kingston: Ziaka Publications, 1983.

Gosse, Philip Henry. *Illustrations of the Birds of Jamaica.* London: Van Voorst, 1849.

Gosse, Philip Henry and Richard Hill. *A Naturalists Sojourn in Jamaica.* London: Van Voorst, 1851.

Green, Jonathan. *Bob Marley and the Wailers.* London: Wise Publications, 1977.

Hawkes, Alex and Brenda Sutton. *Wildflowers of Jamaica.* Kingston: Collins-Sangster, 1974.

Kaplan, Eugene. *A Field Guide to the Coral Reefs of the Caribbean and Florida.* Princeton, NJ: Peterson's Guides, 1984.

Lennox, G.W., and S.A. Seddon. *Flowers of the Caribbean.* London: MacMillan, 1985 reprint.

Lewin, Olive. *Brown Gal in de Ring: 12 Folk Songs from Jamaica.* London: Oxford University Press, 1974.

Manley, Michael Norman. *The Politics of Change: A Jamaican Testament.* London: Andre Deutsch, 1974.

Martin, Medlyn. *Jamaica Check It Out.* Kingston: Publishers Ltd., 1986. Cartoons, with patois captions.

Maxwell, Ken and Livingston McLaren. *How To Speak Jamaican?.* Kingston: Christopher Issa, 1981. Humorous look at patois in words and cartoons.

Owens, Joseph. *Dread: The Rastafarians of Jamaica.* Kingston: Sangster, 1976.

Reid, Victor Stafford. *The Leopard.* New York: Viking Press, 1958. Classic novel by master Jamaican author.

Rubin, Vera, and Lambros Comitas. *Ganja in Jamaica.* The Hague, Paris: Mouton & Co., 1975.

Seaga, Edward. *Revival Cults in Jamaica.* Kingston: Institute of Jamaica, 1982.

Seddon, S.A., and G.W. Lennox. *Trees of the Caribbean.* London: MacMillan, 1985 reprint.

Senior, Olive. *A-Z of Jamaican Heritage.* Kingston: Heinemann Educational Books, Ltd., 1983. Thumbnail encyclopedia of the culture.

Sherlock, Philip. *Anasi, The Spider Man, Jamaican Folk Tales.* New York: MacMillan, 1971.

Sibley, Inez. *Place Names of Jamaica.* Kingston: Institute of Jamaica, 1979.

Stone, Carl, and Aggrey Brown. *Essays on Power and Change in Jamaica.* Kingston: Jamaica Publishing House, 1977.

Thewell, Michael. *The Harder They Come.* New York: Grove Press, 1980. Based on the classic film.

White, Timothy. *Catch A Fire.* New York: Holt, Rhinehart and Winston, 1983. The life of Bob Marley.

Hundreds of other specialized travel guides and maps are available from Hunter Publishing. Among those that may interest you:

*THE BERMUDA HANDBOOK 228 pp. $13.95
The definitive guide, in full color.

THE OTHER PUERTO RICO 160 pp. $11.95
Away from the tourists to discover secret beaches and other attractions.

THE INSIDER'S GUIDE TO HAWAII 224 pp. $12.95
Color throughout, with large fold-out map.

Plus a selection of guides for the adventurous traveller:

WALKER'S BRITAIN 336 pp. $12.95
CYCLIST'S BRITAIN 304 pp. $12.95
BIRDWATCHER'S BRITAIN 246 pp. $12.95
WALKING THROUGH SCOTLAND 192 pp. $10.95
WALKING THROUGH WALES 172 pp. $10.95
WALKING THROUGH NORTHERN ENGLAND
208 pp. $10.95
WALKING THROUGH THE LAKE DISTRICT
224 pp. $10.95
*THE ADVENTURE GUIDE TO THE PACIFIC
NORTHWEST 224 pp. $12.95
*THE ADVENTURE GUIDE TO ITALY 288 pp. $14.95
*WALKING IN AUSTRIA 192 pp. $10.95
*WALKING IN THE ALPS 192 pp. $9.95
*WALKING IN SWITZERLAND 205 pp. $9.95
*WALKING IN NORTHERN FRANCE 192 pp. $8.95
THE MOUNTAINS OF GREECE: A WALKER'S GUIDE
176 pp. $12.95
WALKS & CLIMBS IN THE PYRENEES
206 pp. $12.95
TRAMPER'S GUIDE TO NEW ZEALAND
243 pp. $12.95